10 Steps to
Psychic
Power

CASSANDRA EASON

10 Steps to Psychic Power

PIATKUS

Visit the Piatkus website!

Piatkus publishes a wide range of bestselling fiction and non-fiction, including books on health, mind, body & spirit, sex, self-help, cookery, biography and the paranormal.

If you want to:
- read descriptions of our popular titles
- buy our books over the internet
- take advantage of our special offers
- enter our monthly competition
- learn more about your favourite Piatkus authors

VISIT OUR WEBSITE AT: **www.piatkus.co.uk**

Copyright © 2002 Cassandra Eason

First published in 2002 by
Judy Piatkus (Publishers) Limited
5 Windmill Street
London W1T 2JA
e-mail: info@piatkus.co.uk

Reprinted 2003

The moral right of the author has been asserted

A catalogue record for this book is available from the British Library

ISBN 0 7499 2293 1

Text design by Paul Saunders
Text editing by Jan Cutler
Line illustrations by Rodney Paull

This book has been printed on paper manufactured with respect for the
environment using wood from managed sustainable resources

Printed and bound in Great Britain by Mackays of Chatham Ltd

Contents

Introduction

WE WERE ALL PSYCHIC as children, because we did not know how to be otherwise. Why should we not have seen images in our mother's mind as clearly as in our own, talked to the spirits in trees or been visited by our grandmother, whether she was deceased or living across the street? It is only later that a strong sense of self-consciousness sets in, and logic and learning block the intuitive energy that flows in from all forms of life with little regard for the constraints of linear time or dimension.

However, those psychic powers are not lost but re-emerge spontaneously in adolescence when the boundaries of self are fluid once more. They appear again in parenthood and especially motherhood, when a mother's automatic radar joins her energies to those of her infant. This works even with adoptive parents, for it is a link of love, not biology.

In crises or in times of unhappiness when it seems that the material world has little to offer, our psychic and spiritual nature comes to the fore once more, to put us back on track and to give us a new perspective and sense of priorities. The same process occurs when we begin formal psychic development work and are again plugged into the universal energy field that flows through rock, plant, animal and person alike.

Psychic powers include the whole spectrum of telepathy: mind-to-mind communication, whereby a person can pick up the danger or distress of someone they love even hundreds of miles away; premonition, where a person feels that a future event will happen before it does; and out-of-body travel, whereby our spirit is able to detach itself temporarily and may occasionally be seen by relatives or friends as a living ghost.

How to Use this Book

In this book, psychic development is divided into ten graded steps, so that you can progress at your own pace. The course is not intended to be completed in a specific number of months. You can evolve psychically very rapidly if you can spare three or four hours a week. You may be interested in particular aspects rather than others, so after Step 1 the steps are designed to be worked through in any order. Step 2 may be useful to study next if you are new to psychic work. Step 3 includes psychic protection and should be read early on, as it not only helps you to shield yourself from negativity and emotional leeches in your personal and professional world, but also will protect your personal psychic space when you are exploring different energies.

There are a number of exercises and rituals in each section that are entirely optional but may help to clarify the material and enable you to find your own pathways. As you progress over the weeks and months you will evolve your own ways of working from the basic template and range of methods I suggest and as a result will become more focused, more intuitive and also more inspired in your everyday world at work and in your relationships.

From quite early on in your work, you will discover specific innate psychic gifts evolving quite spontaneously. You may become an expert healer, a medium or a clairvoyant, or startlingly accurate in dream interpretation in a matter of months. You will, however, find that the more you learn generally, the more enhanced your specific psychic talents will become. In every field of psychic expertise, you actually draw on a number of related spiritual gifts, for the world of the spirit is an interconnected web of wisdom.

Beginning Work

This book is your book, a true workbook in which you can try any exercises or rituals I suggest, as well as the tools and methods given in each section, and then adapt them to your own lifestyle and what seems to work well for you.

Although you will acquire increasing expertise as you master each step, your progress will be more like a spiral dance than an uphill climb. At each stage you can refer back to previous sections and apply the information you have found in the later steps to enrich the earlier exercises and explorations. Similarly, the later steps incorporate and build upon the ways of working that you discovered earlier.

There are many paths to psychic awareness that are equally valid, so I have provided a wide variety of techniques and ways of exploring them. As well as enhancing your daily life, each technique will lead you on to a road where you can communicate with nature spirits and move easily in the world of dreams and nature essences. You will be able to travel beyond the physical body and material realms, and by the tenth step you will be able to receive wise advice from spirit guardians and angels, and experience momentary visions of the Divine power behind the universe, if you choose to do so.

Some steps may seem unusual as part of psychic evolution, for example magic and spellcasting, but they are in fact integral tools for utilising our natural repository of mind-power. We can use such age-old natural sources of strength to enhance visualisation as we transfer energy from one realm to another. By using herbs, crystals or repetitive words and actions, for example, we can create a state of mind in which daily limitations no longer apply.

We can also use traditional elemental substances and forces of the Earth and the Sun or the different phases of the Moon to enhance meditation, visualisation or divination. Alternatively, their symbolic strengths can be absorbed through ritual, and they can automatically connect us to a deep universal source of the wisdom of power created by the accumulation of human experiences over thousands of years

Finding the Right Path

Just as there are many methods of psychic development so too there are myriad goals, depending not only on the place where you begin but also on how you see the purpose of your work. You may wish to reawaken your sleeping childhood psyche, and as an adult you can direct those powers both for spiritual development and to aid decision-making in your professional and personal life. On the other hand, you might want to become a professional clairvoyant; some people actually develop these gifts in later life.

If you are already experienced in certain aspects of spiritual work, you can read my suggestions and see if they cast a new perspective on what may be a well-trodden path. If you have specialised in a particular field you may want to extend your knowledge in other related areas and use your expertise in a wider context.

If you have a friend or family member, or indeed even a group who would like to work through this book with you, each person may develop areas of expertise that can be shared with the others. Many of the exercises in this book can be adapted for group work.

Living the Psychic Way

The process of developing your psychic powers may initially seem strange. Like exercising muscles you have not used for years, performing rituals will reopen your chakras or psychic energy centres and make them flow freely again.

For me the most important aspect, and one I emphasise again and again, is that all psychic and spiritual experience is interconnected, and that the most important lesson is to let your psychic powers emerge naturally. The power is within you and, like paths radiating from the centre of a circle, it will lead you to unfold and express your abilities in the world.

I would suggest that where possible whenever you are at home you try to spend a few minutes each day in the special place you create for psychic work. If you are stressed, light an incense stick, an essential oil burner or candle, and sit holding a crystal that will fill you with harmony, and help you to connect with your spiritual centre.

Allowing for the constraints of smoke alarms, I have many times set up a mini-altar in a hotel bedroom for restoring my equilibrium after a difficult journey or a period of intense work. You can meditate in a crowded train or at your office desk; you can cast psychic protection around you by visualisation if you are waiting on a deserted station platform at night. I always carry with me my mini-bag of tools, crystal pendulum and a few herbs in a tiny purse to give me the strengths I need. A favourite crystal is always with me to help me sleep in a strange place – at 53 I still get homesick for my family – and I collect special shells or buy small artefacts on holidays or happy days to add to my symbolic repository of power. My bag often takes some explaining at customs. In the following sections I will share with you everything I have learned and taught over a number of years. I wrote my last major psychic development book five years ago. The present one reflects my own learning since that time and has involved some major reassessments and, I hope, a deeper understanding, for psychic development is a living, growing river. It is a journey of pleasure with a few rapids and the odd waterfall to navigate, but also sections of deep stillness and tranquillity. As you join your own talents to the living river, so you will help create as well as navigate the ocean of psychic power.

Preparation for Psychic Development

PERHAPS THE MOST important step in your psychic journey is the way you prepare yourself. When we begin to build a piece of furniture, create a garden, a sculpture or a painting, or follow a complicated recipe, we gather the components or ingredients together in advance, read any instructions and make sure we have all the basic skills necessary to carry out the more complex aspects of the task. With psychic work, each step of preparation is in itself a way of marking out a special place and time apart from the world. In doing so you may recall from childhood ways you then spontaneously accessed the psychic self we all possess within. So enjoy these preliminary stages and take your time for, as you know with any creative work, it is the foundations that ultimately assure the success of the venture.

Making a Sacred Space

The first stage is to prepare a special space where you can practise the methods that will be discussed later in the section to enable your psychic channels to open.

Remember the special places you created in childhood? One of mine was under the living room table that was covered by a thick, dark-green velvet cloth. There I played for hours with the button jar that held pearl buttons, sequins, rhinestone beads and all manner of broken necklaces. My outdoor place in the city-centre terrace in Birmingham, where I grew up, was the swing attached to a tree that stood in the backyard in a circle of earth that was covered with yellow flowers in summer. As I swayed backwards and forwards, my sturdy little legs pumping like pistons, I wove my fantasies, flying over the smoking chimney tops to the green hills where bluebells grew wild.

In adulthood our special place can be surrendered to the pressures of communal working and living. The special place is one that we need to recreate inside ourselves as well as an actual physical location. It is worthwhile spending time recapturing that stillness, sitting in a clump of bushes in the garden or making a screen of plants on the balcony so that you can get used to that wonderful feeling of being invisible to the everyday world once more.

An Outdoor Sanctuary

You can set up a temporary altar in a grove of trees, create a circle of small stones on a beach or riverbank or draw a circle within which to work in sand or soil. However, even on a small garden patio or balcony you can set up a more permanent magical sanctuary that can be illuminated with garden torches, perhaps positioned at the four main compass points. Even in a small garden, you can create a circle of stones for meditation and ritual.

You can create your magical outdoor place with a circle of fragrant herbs and perhaps a water feature in the centre, which is my own particular favourite, for outdoor rituals. You may also wish to leave stone or treated-wood statues there, perhaps representing a creature that suggests to you the power of each of the four cardinal directions, for example an eagle in the east. On pages 135–42, I have suggested creatures that are associated with the four main elements, earth, air, fire and water, which are linked respectively with north, east, south and west. Native North Americans believe we each have affinities with particular creatures, so choose ones that are right for you.

An Indoor Sanctuary

If you share your home, it can be quite difficult to create a place of your own, but this in itself is a first valuable step in reclaiming your psychic as well as your physical personal space, especially if you have children. You can dedicate your space to nature, to your personal god/dess form or as a personal shrine where the positive energies of special treasures and your private rituals can accumulate. It will offer a sanctuary from the world and a repository of power and protection. You can use an attic, basement, summerhouse, conservatory or even a garden shed, or a curtained-off area of your bedroom, or adapt part of a home office or study. For the latter, turn off and cover all computers, and temporarily disconnect phones and faxes while you are preparing for this psychic time.

Cleansing your indoor space

Traditionally, witches would sweep out an area intended for magical work, having first sprinkled it with lavender. Modern witches have continued this practice. In the modern world, where there is so much noise and pollution, it is especially important to clear and cleanse the space where you will set up your altar and to keep it regularly physically and psychically cleansed.

✦ First clear out any clutter and find a box or cupboard in which you can store any items not on display on your altar but which you will use in your psychic work. This would include everything from tarot cards to pots of dried herbs.

✦ Cleanse any dust from your indoor space as close to dawn as possible so that the new light floods in as you work.

✦ Open the windows and door of the room.

✦ If the floor is carpeted, scatter dried lavender or chamomile flowers (the kind used to make tea) or salt, a traditional cleanser that from time immemorial has symbolised life and has symbolically offered psychic protection in many cultures. Lavender and chamomile are also gentle cleansers of negativity. You can also use fresh pine needles or chopped sage.

✦ Feel free to use a vacuum cleaner, the modern equivalent of the broom, to clean up the flowers, if they are small enough to be sucked up without clogging the machine. Make nine anticlockwise circular movements and recite over and over:

One for joy, two for gladness,
Three and four to banish sadness,
Five and six away with anger,
Seven, eight, nine linger no longer.

✦ Alternatively, use a broom and sweep the flowers out of the door with nine anticlockwise movements and reciting the chant.

Cleansing by smudging

Smudging, wafting smoke from a stick of bound herbs, a bowl of lighted dried herbs or an incense stick as a form of cleansing, has been central to magic and spirituality from ancient times. Herb smudging and smoke rituals have been used traditionally, especially by Native North Americans, for centuries and are increasingly becoming part of Westernised cleansing rituals. Herbs, both in their natural state and as incenses (mixed with a resin to create a rich, long-lasting stream of smoke) are a powerful method to cleanse homes and people's auras or psychic energy fields, as well as to make offerings to the deities.

You can use smudging effectively to cleanse your indoor place, but if you do so you should ensure that the room is well ventilated, and you should avoid using it in the presence of young children, pregnant women and anyone with respiratory problems. Smudging is especially potent outdoors. Smudge sticks made from cedar or sage are easily obtainable and very easy to use. You simply light the top, allow the flame to die down and then blow gently on the glowing herbs to create a steady stream of smoke.

✦ Work as the Sun is rising.

✦ Walk around the area you plan to use, whether temporary or permanent, in a large circle, noting any natural boundaries such as bushes and trees that can form a shield just outside the circumference. (If performing the ritual indoors, then the walls would form the enclosure.)

✦ Place a white candle on a broad metal tray in the centre of the visualised circle, and use it to light a sage smudge stick, made from sagebrush. This is the most popular form of sage grown in mountain and desert regions of America, Canada and Australia and is very effective for smudging, since it lights easily and gives a constant steady stream of smoke. Sagebrush can be bought from New Age stores, health shops or by mail order. It is available both in stick form and as broad leaves to burn in a flat ceramic dish. Culinary sage is not so satisfactory for smudge work. If it is windy, position the candle in a sheltered, safe place so that you can easily relight the smudge if it goes out. Remember never to leave a lighted candle unattended.

✦ Alternatively use a firm, broad pine or mint incense stick with a handle you can hold. Special outdoor versions are available.

✦ Beginning in the east, the direction of the rising Sun, make a waist-high clockwise circle of smoke until you have created a complete circle. As you smudge, chant:

Darkness flee, blessed be.
Keep light always within.

✦ You can also say this when you begin and end work in your permanent outdoor space.

If you are pregnant or suffer from a respiratory complaint or other chronic illness, you may prefer not to use smudging even outdoors. Create your circles with a small bowl of spring water to which three pinches of sea salt have been added and stirred clockwise with a silver paper knife or crystal quartz. (See page 141 for making sacred water, pages 74–75 for herbs you should not use in pregnancy. If in doubt consult a doctor or pharmacist.)

Equipping your indoor space

There are just a few basic items that you will need to make your sacred space.

Table

This will form the focus of your sacred area, where you will keep your special treasures. The table can be round or square as both can easily be divided into quadrants with invisible markers at the four cardinal points: north, east, south and west. These points represent the four ancient elements: earth, air, fire and water (see pages 135–42). You can use a variety of altar cloths, and if you are skilled with a needle you could create a different one for each of the seasons. However, sarongs and large scarves from ethnic craft outlets also make good altar cloths. You may like to have large cushions, a comfortable chair or a low futon in front of your altar so that you can sit or kneel comfortably. If you do not have a suitable table, you can create a sacred space on the floor with a cloth. How you adorn your altar is your personal choice, and you may like to change your altar artefacts according to the work or season. I have also seen very small, portable altars that are simply a piece of slate or wood no more than 60 centimetres (2 feet) square, which can be placed on a larger table if space is at a premium and put away when not in use. However, it is obviously better to have a permanent display.

I find the following items are a good focus for energy work of all kinds and for rituals.

Seasonal fruits, nuts, flowers and branches
These provide an excellent source of the life-force or universal energy force. Many cultures around the world have a word for this life-force: in India it is prana, in China it is called ch'i or qi and in Japan it is called ki, in Polynesia mana, in Ancient Greece pneuma and in Hebrew Ruah.

Use living plants and herbs in pots. You can choose herbs that have particular significance for your current work (see pages 76–81), for example chamomile for healing children and lavender for bringing reconciliation and kindness in love. You can also have differently coloured flowers and fruits so that you can absorb the colour energies by breathing in their psychic light (see pages 95–102 for colour meanings).

Candles
You may wish to have a single central candle to represent the unity of life and the source of Divinity. This is traditionally white and is best made from beeswax, which has been used in rituals for thousands of years, signifying the Mother Goddess in early cultures and later the Virgin Mary in Christianity. You could alternatively have two candles, one on the left in white or gold, for divine masculine energies, and one on the right in white or silver, for the goddess forces. If you are tired or stressed, sit in their light for a few minutes and perhaps add a third candle for the qualities you need, for example orange to restore self-esteem that has been battered by the day's events or overcritical people.

Statues or power animals

You may like to have a special god/dess form as a focus on your altar. Some women work with the Virgin Mary or the Black Madonna even if they are not practising Christians. The Black Madonna is a dark-coloured, usually wooden Madonna whose form predates Christianity. Black Madonnas have been linked to earlier Middle Eastern mother goddesses, such as the ancient Egyptian goddess Isis, who is often portrayed with her infant on her knee. Others use a symbol, for example a large spiral shell for the goddess and a horn for the god.

You can also use pictures of the lovely Orthodox Christian icons from the Eastern European tradition, and the Far East offers powerful foci, for example statues of Buddha, or one of the Hindu Goddesses, or Ganesha – the elephant-headed God of wisdom. Spend time looking at statues belonging to different cultures and generally you will find one or two that seem especially beautiful and significant. The different archangels (see pages 66 and 225–28) can also be adopted for different purposes, but some practitioners prefer to have the candles by themselves.

Psychic Tools – Crystals

You can work entirely by visualising symbols. However, if you use psychic tools, for example crystals, you are strengthening your innate powers by adding natural forms of positive energy to them.

Capable of transmitting their own energies and also those of the earth and cosmos, crystals can amplify personal psychic energies or heal a sick or distressed person or animal. Places too can become polluted or spoiled by insensitive development, and it is quite possible to direct healing power through crystals or by sending visualised healing light. An energy field was discovered by the Russian scientist, Semyon Kirlian, who found that both crystals and fossilised living materials, such as jet and amber, were surrounded by a radiating energy field that could be captured by special photographic techniques.

Crystals will form an important part of your psychic development work. You will need a variety in large and small sizes for meditation, to absorb the life-force, or prana, of which they are an especially pure source, for creating crystalline waters for energy, for psychic protection work and for divination. There are three kinds that are central to almost every kind of work: clear crystal quartz, as a sphere if possible, citrine and amethyst. They are often arranged in a triangular formation on the altar. All crystals have specific properties, but I have found that these three kinds provide the balance of energising and harmonising power that will serve most of your needs in both psychic development and healing work.

Your first psychic explorations can involve sitting by the light of your altar candles, holding each crystal between your hands in turn and identifying the different energies and feelings they invoke. Hold the amethyst first, then the citrine and lastly the clear crystal and you will in turn be harmonised, filled with self-love and finally with power and vitality. This can form a regular way of retuning your personal energies after a frantic day.

A clear crystal sphere

If there could be only one healing and energising stone, it would be clear crystal quartz, recognised in all times and cultures as a powerful transmitter of physical and psychic energies, and regarded by peoples as far apart as the Australian Aborigines, the Chinese and Native Americans as a manifestation of the living creative spirit. Easily charged and cleansed, clear crystal quartz will amplify the energies of the user, drawing out negative energies and sending positive ones in their place, triggering the body's own healing system to resist infection and negativity.

The crystal ball, traditionally associated with seeing into the future, is perhaps the most useful of all crystals as it will transmit and amplify sunlight and moonlight and the energies contained in coloured candles, as well as releasing its natural store of the life-force that is amplified by its shape. It is also a powerful healing tool, triggering the body's immune system and innate regenerative powers. These are especially potent if you carefully direct sunlight or full moonlight through the sphere on to a painful part of the body. The sphere need not be large, but should be of pure crystal and not glass. I find that one with inclusions or imperfections inside is the most powerful and best for scrying, that is seeing images that are reflected within. A crystal sphere is also good for unblocking stagnant energies and for infusing energy, light and positive feelings, and is potent for meditation and divination (see page 91).

You do not have to use a crystal sphere, although I have seen tiny ones that are no more expensive than any other crystal. You can use an ordinary clear quartz crystal if you wish.

Citrine

A pure, sparkling yellow Sun crystal, citrine is naturally warming and is gentler than the crystal quartz. Melting away pain and tension, it encourages the gentle flow of warming energies that will create a sense of well-being and rebalance the body. It enhances self-esteem and confidence and is sometimes called the wish crystal, as it can be used to focus thoughts and bring them into the material world (see also pages 52–56).

If you find relaxation and meditation difficult, hold this crystal or wear one as a pendant to break down barriers and melt psychic as well as physical rigidity. Citrine helps channelling work, where you direct healing energies and messages from angels, evolved nature spirits or spirit guides via the power of the crystal into your mind. It will also help to control emotions, increasing self-knowledge and focusing mental power, and to strengthen relationships.

Amethyst

Varying in colour from a pale, transparent lilac to a deep, translucent purple, amethyst is a gentle all-healer, restoring harmony and encouraging inner stillness and rest. Soothing for adults and children alike, amethyst will melt away emotional as well as physical pain, replacing it with calm and the slow infusion of healing energies. Amethyst is good for past-life work, and for increasing clairvoyance.

A crystal quartz pendulum

In this book you will find that I use the crystal pendulum in almost every section. This does not mean that you should not adopt meditation, visualisation or any other method to use as well. But in twelve years of work I have found the pendulum to be the single most effective tool for psychic work, and the more you use it the more powerful it will become.

The crystal quartz pendulum is one of the most valuable healing, cleansing and empowering tools, and it is well worth making the initial purchase. Pendulums are not at all expensive if you buy a small one, but choose crystal quartz. The pendulum has many properties: it will identify energy channels; unblock stagnant energies and chakras, the psychic energy centres within our bodies (see page 114–20); identify ley energies, the psychic power lines within the earth; and help to dispel places of negative energy at home and work. It will also aid decision-making (see page 29). It is a tool that is worth carrying with you at all times. I use mine two or three times a day for decision making, to unblocked knotted energies and even as I travel around to identify a ghost path instantly. (A number of other crystals are also helpful and I have referred to these in the relevant sections.)

A Psychic Journal

This will be one of your most valuable tools and can be used as a means of recording your spiritual development over the months and years to come. You may find it useful to buy a loose-leaf folder – some have attractive ornate covers – so that you can add to your work and rearrange it.

You can arrange alphabetically your records of the symbols you have discovered and their meanings both in dreams and through scrying. Combinations of herbs, oils and incenses that work well can also be included, as can a list of crystals used for healing lore.

You may decide to keep a special section listing people you know who are ill or unhappy who need healing and any healing rituals you carry out. You can perhaps have a special night of the week when you light a white candle, read through the list and perhaps offer a prayer for them.

Also record divinatory readings for yourself and others, rituals you devise, special days working by the sea or in the countryside, visits to sacred places and seasonal celebrations. Channelling from devas (higher nature spirits), angels and spirit guides, dreams and out-of-body experiences, past-life recall and prophesies should all be included.

You may wish to share some of your insights with others; perhaps you might even publish them in print or on your website. In any case, your book will some day be a wonderful gift for a special child, whether your own or a younger person who is very spiritual, to pass on your wisdom and discovery.

Self-preparation

When you have time, you can prepare yourself for psychic work. If you are new to it, I would suggest that you make time once a week for a ritual bath. You should then follow this by relaxation and some gentle breathing by candlelight or in sunlight or moonlight, holding one of your special crystals and flowing with the feelings and the images.

Ritual Baths

For thousands of years purification baths have been used in many traditions as a prelude to spiritual work. If you are outdoors, this could be a dip in the sea, a river or lake, perhaps using a herbal infusion (see pages 72–3) to pour over yourself as a way of connecting with the powers of nature that will amplify your own positive energies. The most magical baths I have ever encountered are the open-air hot springs at Alhambra de Granada in Andalucia, where people still come to bathe in the fountain and pass from hot pool to hot pool and then to the cold river. But your home bathtub or even a shower will symbolically cleanse you of stress and negativity. Warm rather than hot water is best.

✦ Unless sunlight or moonlight is flooding through the window, light some pink or purple candles where they will cast pools of light into the water. In a shower they should cast light on to the glass cubicle.

✦ Add a few drops of lavender, rose or ylang-ylang essential oil to the filled bath. If you prefer, place dried rose petals, lavender or chamomile flower-heads in a muslin net (or knotted tights), and either hang it from the hot tap as you fill the bath or let it float in the water for ten minutes. Alternatively, you can make an infusion using four teaspoons of the dried herb to two cups of boiling water, leave for five minutes, strain and add the liquid to the bathwater. This can be made in advance. You can also use a herbal gel in the shower.

✦ Swirl the pools of light around you and feel it being absorbed through every pore.

✦ When you are ready, get out and towel yourself dry, then pull out the plug, saying:

Sorrow, sadness flow from me,
From the rivers to the sea,
Leaving only harmony.

✦ Put on something loose and comfortable made from a natural fibre that you keep for your psychic work.

Relaxation

You may feel so relaxed after your bath that you will need no other formal method of relaxation. However, a number of practitioners do carry out relaxation and breathing exercises, especially as a prelude to meditation or visualisation work. There are a vast number of relaxation techniques and if you practise yoga, t'ai chi, Zen or Reiki, for example, you will already have your own way of relaxing and breathing.

The principle behind relaxation is to tense the muscles and then relax them. You can do this, simply starting with your toes and moving up the various areas of the body. The following method works for me, using simple visualisation (see page 22), although sometimes I go straight to stilling the mind (see page 25) and find that the muscles follow. This also works wonders before an important meeting and you can practice relaxation indoors or outdoors.

✦ Sit or lie comfortably in your special place.

✦ Close your eyes and breathe in very gently and slowly through your nose and out again so that one breath follows another in an unbroken stream.

✦ Visualise two beautiful butterflies that are resting on each foot. Hold your feet as still as you can as you gently inhale and then, as the butterflies move upwards, relax and exhale.

✦ Next, see the butterflies land on your knees and, again as you inhale, hold your knees motionless so as not to disturb them.

✦ Exhale gently and slowly as they take to the air again.

✦ Continue as they land together on your navel, then separately on to your hands, separately on each breast, together on the throat, separately on each shoulder, together at the top of the spine and finally the crown of your head.

✦ Allow them to move down again stage by stage to the feet and finally to fly off.

✦ This is a lovely exercise with your toes digging into the sand and a gentle breeze all around your body.

Breathing Techniques

There is a great deal of confusion about the correct way to breathe: the correct number of counts; whether you should count up or down numerically for a set number of breaths; whether you should regard each breath as a self-contained unit or whether you should be creating an unbroken stream of inhalation and exhalation. If you are already studying yoga, Buddhism, Reiki or another form of directing your spiritual energies in a specific way, your own discipline will have its suggested methods.

I have listed a few ways that work for me and other people I have taught, but as long as you remember to keep your spine straight, your muscles relaxed and your chin slightly downwards, then the only other factor is to breathe deeply from your abdomen. Put a hand just below your navel to check, as in modern society we tend to breathe far too shallowly and quickly. Incorrect breathing at its extreme can cause poor circulation of the life-force around the body, hyperventilation and panic attacks.

Slow, gentle breathing is a very good way of stilling the mind. If you visualise the breath of life as golden or pure light circulating through your whole body with each breath, this can also help you to avoid too rapid a breath pattern. Zen Buddhism and some yogic schools centre the breath around the hara, a psychic point which is about 5 centimetres (2 inches) lower than the navel. They visualise the breath descending through the crown of the head and ascending through the feet to meet at the hara.

Where does the breath come from? Each person draws primarily from one source at different times and in different places, from the golden-red light of the earth or the brilliant light from the cosmos. If you are sitting by your window in a high-rise building, the most instantly accessible source would be the sky. While sitting on the ground in a shady forest, you would breathe from the earth rising through your feet and legs and your perineum. Experiment in different settings. You are your breath and your breath is you, so find a rhythm that is right, and as you work it will become automatic.

In acting classes I was taught to breathe in slowly and deeply through the nose, and out equally slowly and deeply through the mouth. This goes counter to Eastern methods, which mainly practise nasal breathing whereby both the in and out breath are through the nose. However, I find it useful when reciting a mantra or word on the out-breath and for movements such as dancing in ritual. I also use it for pranic or life-force breathing (see below), where you absorb light or colour from natural sources and exhale darkness or negativity. In my method I sigh darkness away.

Some people sit cross-legged or in the lotus position while practising breath techniques, while others use the Egyptian position: sitting on a cushion on a chair with the buttocks on the front third of the cushion. This will ensure a straight posture. The chin is held slightly down. Close or lower your eyes and gaze 60 to 90 centimetres (2 to 3 feet) ahead, or use a focus, for example a lighted candle (see meditation, pages 48–49). There are a variety of hand positions that you can take: palms downwards or upwards held on your thighs or knees, or resting in the lap, palm uppermost. Alternatively, you can hold your hands cupped one on top of the other, with your writing hand underneath. Experiment. If you are not comfortable, even after repeated practice, the point of the exercise is lost. If you have back problems, you may need firm back support. Here is a breathing exercise:

✦ Breathe in through your nose, counting in your mind one and two and three and four.

✦ Hold the breath, again counting in your mind one and two.

✦ Breathe out through the nose one and two and three and four.

✦ Finally, pause for one and two before repeating the cycle.

✦ Repeat the cycle up to ten times, slowing the count even more, if you wish.

Another popular method is to breathe in for seven, hold for one, out for seven and rest for one. Many yogic traditions suggest lengthening the out-breath, using one of the counting sequences above.

Counting down

In a number of healing traditions, counting breaths in cycles is considered beneficial in creating the necessary stillness for meditation and channelling. It also creates a rhythm that can help if you tend to have natural irregular breathing patterns. Some Reiki schools, for example, count down from ten to one in cycles of ten separate breaths, each unit within the cycle consisting of inhaling, holding that breath and exhaling it.

The first cycle is called ten. This is followed by a pause, and then the next inhalation begins. This next holding and exhalation unit is called nine. You continue until you have completed the exhaled breath of the tenth cycle, then the next sequence of ten units begins. On the other hand, some Zen Buddhist schools count the other way, with the first unit being called one and the last ten. The breathing pattern is the same. This method of working in cycles of ten-breath units works best if you inhale and exhale through the nose.

✦ Count from ten to one or one to ten initially for three cycles.

✦ Concentrate on breathing deeply from the abdomen, keeping the shoulders still and circulating the breath around the body for three cycles or more if you wish.

✦ Slow the breath gradually. Experts can manage three breaths a minute, but in practice most people need more.

✦ If you lose track or become distracted by irrelevant thoughts, you can return to ten or one to begin again.

✦ If you can continue for twenty minutes, you will find that your psychic awareness expands quite spontaneously as well as giving you a greater sense of well-being and harmony.

Counting is also a good way to begin your meditation or visualisation work.

Pranic breathing

Prana is the Sanskrit word for the life-force. It involves drawing in the vital essence from natural sources, the earth, the air, water and the Sun, and eventually through meditation. So working outdoors, especially in the sunshine, sitting on the grass or the sand near the sea or even by an open window, surrounded by fruit, nuts, seeds and growing flowers, will allow you to absorb prana through every pore of your body.

True pranic breathing is defined as drawing the life-force through the spirit or inner body primarily by opening the crown chakra at the top of the head, which is the psychic energy centre, to receive the power. This is visualised as light. However, I have found in my years of teaching and researching psychic development that you can also absorb this force through every pore, using a technique very similar to the one you have already learned. You can use the technique for cleansing, healing and strengthening the aura – the psychic energy field we have around us all (see page 110) – the chakras, or psychic energy centres in the body, and for sending healing to others (see page 121) as well as for increasing energy and power within yourself.

+ Inhale slowly though your nose, drawing in breath to fill your lower abdomen.

+ Continue to breathe until the diaphragm/chest is also full of breath.

+ You may visualise this breath as golden or pure light or the colour of the flowers or fruit you are using as a focus (see colour breathing on pages 107–8).

+ Sense every pore absorbing the life-force, permeating not only your physical body, but also the spirit or etheric body within (see page 27).

+ Exhale slowly from the chest. Any impurities will be transformed by the earth and cosmos from the chest out through the nose. You may see this as a dark mist. I personally exhale through the mouth, but traditionalists say otherwise (see page 19).

+ Pause before continuing with the next inhalation. As with earlier methods, each inhalation, hold and exhalation sequence count as a self-contained cycle. Aim for about ten cycles initially.

+ Some practitioners recommend a specific counting cycle of inhaling for six, holding for three, exhaling for six and then resting between breaths for three.

Visualisation

Another way to open the psychic channels and fill your physical body and spirit with energy is to create a body of light within yourself. Visualisation is no different from the imagination of childhood, except that it is more focused and deliberate. The idea is that if you create light in thought-form through picturing it and even feeling its warmth, you can manifest that light as actual energy in the outer world. This is achieved through transference that is willing it into being by focusing entirely on the inner image of light and endowing it with your power.

◆ Sit in sunlight, or any natural light, however dull the day, so that your feet are touching the floor, either in a chair or on the floor with your palms uppermost.

◆ Visualise white light pouring into your body through your aural field from all around, but focus on your feet. Feel as well as see the light rising from the soles of your feet like warm liquid, pure gold from the earth.

◆ Focus next on your ankles and allow them to fill with light. Be aware of the gentle pressure as the light moves upwards through your ankles and to the perineum so that your root or base chakra, or psychic energy centre, is not red but golden.

◆ Now move your attention to the crown of your head and be aware of pure white light entering through the fontanelle – the area at the top of your head that was soft when you were an infant and so more open to spirit – and spreading through the skull down through the ears and eyes.

◆ Turn your attention back to the light ascending slowly from below, visualise it continuing to rise and becoming paler as the white light from above descends.

◆ Each time light from below or above reaches one of your psychic energy points, or chakras, you will experience a lovely, warm swirling sensation, and the streams moving closer, extending out to your arms and hands via the heart chakra. The heart chakra or psychic energy centre controls the minor chakras in the palms of the hands and so is naturally channelled via the arms.

✦ Once the light gains impetus, relax and enjoy the sensations as the light entering each chakra simultaneously adds to the upwards and downwards flow, ending as a glorious waterfall somewhere between the throat and heart chakras.

✦ Sit quietly and let the light flow within you and around you.

✦ You can carry out this ritual daily or whenever you feel depleted and out of touch with your psyche.

The energies will disperse naturally throughout your physical body and the layers of your etheric or inner-spirit body during the day. If you look in the mirror you may see with your inner eye, or even your physical eye, a luminous glow around you. This is created by the newly energised psychic energy field that surrounds your physical body.

Grounding, Centring and Stilling

The three psychic stages of grounding, centring and stilling the mind can be used separately or in sequence.

Grounding

The act of linking with the earth energies is known as grounding. It can be done either by visualising yourself as a tree and directing energies upwards or by visualising a tube of white light or a red thread going downwards through all the layers of the earth. This tube or thread passes from the head through the body and into the earth. It then connects with the earth's core. This is useful for drawing strength and earth energies into your body and spirit.

It also provides stability if you feel insecure, anxious or angry, or it can be used after psychic work of any kind, channelling higher energies or healing work to root yourself in the real world again. If you think of yourself as having a line running down your centre, this forms the central column of the visu-alised tree.

✦ Stand with your hands loosely by your sides, fingers pointing down, legs slightly apart, back straight, muscles relaxed and chin slightly lowered.

✦ Raise your hands slowly above your head while breathing in to a count of four, then, fingers extended upwards and arms in a curved position inwards, hold the position and breath for a count of two.

✦ Slowly lower your arms downwards towards the earth while breathing out for a count of four, so they are by your sides with the fingers pointing to the earth.

✦ Pause for two and complete the cycle twice more. You can also try counting seven-one/seven-one – that is breathing in to a count of seven, then pausing for one, out for seven and pausing for one – or when you are very practised, eight-four/eight-four.

✦ After the third cycle, press your feet hard down on the ground as you inhale slowly.

✦ Release any darkness through your feet into the ground, exhaling the negativity which flows into the soil, where it will be recycled into positivity.

✦ If you still feel afraid or angry, end the ritual by stamping your feet, saying: 'It is gone, it is done, peace come.'

✦ A faster method of grounding is to sit on the ground and raise your arms, then press down with your hands, your feet and perineum.

Centring

This is the logical progression that follows on from grounding, to exclude irrelevant thoughts and focus all your energies on your spiritual work. This is a good exercise if you find meditation difficult, and it will, over a period of time, enable you to select what needs attention both in the everyday world and in decision-making as well as spiritually.

✦ Hold your arms by your side and point your fingers downwards.

✦ Stand on soil, sand or grass if possible to make a direct connection with nature.

✦ Visualise all the energies that are not yours, such as the demands of others or emotional pressures, or those that are not connected with your spiritual work or current need. Imagine them leaving your body, flowing downwards and out through the fingers into the earth where they will be transformed into a new and separate life.

✦ Make an arc of light all around you with your hands holding your fingertips extended. See the energies of spiritual power and healing pouring into your fingers. Alternatively, you can rotate your arms together in opposing directions as if you were a windmill whose sails catch the sunlight. This, however, will take some practice. In this way you are defining your personal psychic space and focusing your psychic powers for your work.

✦ If this is difficult, you can centre yourself by inhaling slowly and saying a word, such as peace, love or harmony, silently on your in-breath so that you extend every syllable, and then exhale the word out loud, again pausing on every syllable. Repeat this ten times and you will be centred.

Stilling the mind

You may wish to begin by grounding and centring yourself. Stilling the mind enables you to switch from your everyday mode to a higher state of consciousness. It can also be used as a form of psychic protection.

✦ Still your body by going to your special outdoor or indoor space, preferably in sunlight or moonlight. If you are not able to do this, use the radiance of a tall beeswax candle.

✦ Do nothing except listen to your breathing – do not try to control, count or change the rhythm.

✦ If thoughts intrude, gently push them away as though launching a toy boat on a pond and watching it sail off. Visualise your problems tied to a helium balloon and floating away, or set them on a fluffy cloud in a clear blue sky.

✦ Picture a sky full of stars and watch them going out one by one until you are enclosed within a velvety blackness.

✦ Or visualise a jug of clear water you are pouring into a stream drop by drop until it is gone and only the rhythm of the stream remains.

✦ Another method is to picture yourself on an empty train that slows down and suddenly stops in the middle of the countryside, where all sound and motion gradually ceases. My own favourite is to visualise myself on a half-empty plane looking out on bank upon bank of white clouds, and then floating through the window and being cocooned by them in warm sunlight.

Closing down your energies

After psychic work or whenever you feel afraid or enervated, close down your energies by visualising a gentle velvet darkness descending from the crown of your head all the way down to your feet, like snuggling into a warm blanket in that very special safe place you loved in childhood. Now spend a little time having a meal or a warm drink, doing a few basic chores or tending plants to root you back in everyday life.

The Next Step

When you have worked through this section and are sitting quietly, you may begin to see images either externally or in your mind's vision, and you may hear voices from other dimensions. You may also become aware of the forms of nature spirits in the trees, close to flowers or in piles of leaves, or of pictures in water and in the clouds. Or you may be aware of information about the past that has not come from conscious sources of knowledge when you visit ancient sites.

As you continue with the next step, you will see how the symbols and images that come to you when you sit quietly by candlelight or look into one of your special crystals hold information about your best course of action. All these are the natural results of opening your psychic channels once more. Enjoy these early steps and move on only when you are ready.

As you evolve psychically, this preparation/breathing/visualisation work will remain an essential part of your repertoire. It is always best to still and to centre yourself before any concentrated psychic work. Meanwhile your spontaneous psychic senses, such as intuition, can be constantly tuned by learning to trust them and to practice using them in your everyday life.

Working with the Psychic Senses

MANY RESEARCHERS INTO spiritual and religious studies believe that we possess a spirit or etheric body in addition to our physical body. This is sometimes seen by others as a living ghost or doppelgänger while we are sleeping or when we are travelling beyond our physical body in a light trance while we are awake. This astral body may be the part of us that survives death (see page 116).

It would also seem that as well as the five physical senses we also have psychic senses. Just as our spirit and physical bodies are connected, so these psychic senses operate through the same channels as our physical senses – taste, touch, sight, smell and hearing – but they are not restricted by the physical sensory mechanisms or the limitations of linear time.

Intuition

The power of understanding something without conscious thought is usually the result of several psychic senses combined, and is known as intuition. It is perhaps closest to clairsentience or clear-sensing that embraces taste, smell, physical sensations and the transmission of emotions, sometimes from past events at ancient sites or haunted houses. Indeed, intuition can often appear as a physical sensation: a buzzing in the head, the restlessness akin to drinking too much coffee, butterflies fluttering in the tummy; or like a kick in the guts from a mule if it is a particularly strong warning.

Also included in intuition is clairvoyance – seeing into the future or to distant places with the mind's eye or in dreams – and clairaudience, when the inner voice or an external one from an unseen source gives advice or a warning that is subsequently proved to be correct. Psychometry, the psychic power of touch, also comes into play when we shake hands with a stranger or acquaintance and instantly know in spite of their smile and eye contact that they are not to be trusted with our heart or finances.

Trusting Intuition

Intuition is a power we ignore at our peril. For example, in July 2000, I felt unusually anxious about a journey I was to make to the Midlands with my youngest son Bill. He had been offered an interview at a school that he very much wanted to attend as a fortnightly boarder, about a hundred miles away. Though I am an experienced driver and the trip was to be combined with a mini-holiday, I was so uneasy that I nearly cancelled. But as this was the only interview date on offer, logic won the day. I still felt on edge as we booked into the motel near to the school for the night. The next morning Bill, Miranda, my younger daughter, and I checked out of the motel and were loading the car when another car hurtled across the car park towards us totally out of control. I pushed Bill out of the way and seconds later the car smashed over the case he had dropped on the spot where he had been standing.

We were not injured, but Bill was very shocked and anxious about travelling for some time afterwards. I had not experienced a true premonition, in that I had not experienced a dream or a vision of the future disaster, but I had had a real sense that the journey was a mistake and this manifested itself as queasiness, irritability, shivering and increasing disorientation prior to the incident.

Intuition and Decision-making

The majority of intuitive insights are not about crises, but are guides to the best actions at work as well as in our personal lives. Should we trust a new acquaintance, use one firm rather than another, or take a new job or wait for opportunities to develop in the current workplace? Even areas for which facts are available – holiday destinations, new cars, homes, money-spinning schemes or days out with the children – may benefit from an intuitive decision to supplement information that is imprecise or conflicting.

'Does it feel right?' is a sound criterion when deciding which house to buy, whether to move in with a lover, or if we should call a doctor to a sick child or wait to see how the child seems after a night's sleep.

Learning to trust your intuition using a pendulum

In situations where you have a decision to make and there are conflicting options or no clear pointers, you can use a pendulum as an external guide to your inner voice. This may be heard as an actual voice that is our own but distinct from our everyday tone, sometimes described as the clear voice we last used in childhood. It transmits information from the psychic senses. You can note down in your psychic journal each time the pendulum helped you to make a decision and then if and when it was proved right; sometimes an intuitive decision may take months to be verified and it is easy to forget.

The pendulum is guided by unconscious muscular responses from a form of psychokinesis – the ability of mind to move matter – in the same way that your hand selects the most relevant tarot card from a face-down pack to answer a question (see page 56).

✦ When you have a decision to make, pause and, if possible, step away from the situation for a few moments.

✦ Hold your pendulum in your power hand – the one you write with – with the chain between your thumb and middle finger and at a length that feels right. Now ask the question in your mind or out loud.

✦ If there is a number of options, draw a circle and divide it into sections according to the number of choices you have, or make a grid formation of square boxes. If there is an uneven number of choices, you can blank out spare sections with a pen. Write the options briefly in the sections.

✦ Hold your pendulum slowly over each section in turn so that it is a few centimetres above the paper. See if it pulls towards one option as though magnetically attracted.

✦ There may be two equally weighted options or it may not be attracted to any, so trust the pendulum. Two options indicate a compromise, but if no option is indicated this means that you may need to explore other avenues.

✦ If you do not have the opportunity to use your pendulum, wear a pendulum-type pendant around your neck or keep one in a pocket and hold it as you state each of the options in turn. You will feel a distinctive vibration at the correct one.

This is a method that you can teach to friends and family or use in a professional consultation, perhaps after using tarot cards or another form of divination. In time intuition will become part of your everyday life: listening to your inner voice, choosing a tarot card from a shuffled pack and allowing the picture to suggest ideas, stilling your mind and posing a question like dropping a pebble into a pool and letting ripples form. The answer may come instantly as images in your mind, or later as you are travelling home on the train, or even in your dreams that night.

Clairsentience

Like intuition, clairsentience is a psychic sense that many people already possess, although they may not trust it. For as with other psychic senses, it may not accord with the external evidence or with information we have been given or which may seem logical. You may go into an unfamiliar house or ancient site and know instantly that something bad happened there, and if you carry out research you will usually discover you were right.

In the everyday world this knowing, based on what you feel, can guide you through a social or business minefield and bring you safely to the other side. It may manifest itself as a sensation of jaggedness like a mild electric shock when someone who is smiling but is potentially malicious collides with your aura, or it may give a sense of harmony and trust, even when you meet a perfect stranger.

How is clairsentience manifested? It might be through a sudden apparently unrelated taste in your mouth, the smell of smoke on the site of a bad fire that occurred years before, or as a sudden wafting of the perfume of a deceased relative on the anniversary of their death or birthday. Or it might be a sensation of hairs standing up on the back of your neck, a sense of unease or sudden total happiness (more of this on page 184 when I discuss encountering ghosts). While on the site of a battlefield, you might feel great sadness and fear, or a sense of peace may prevail when you are in the garden of an abbey where nuns or monks had lived over centuries in an unbroken tradition of tranquillity. You might find yourself tapping into the sensations of that world or time as though you were sharing the moment – and you might also be flooded with images and sounds, as clairvoyance and clairaudience are simultaneously triggered by the strong well of emotion you have uncovered.

Working with Fragrances

Of all the aspects of psychic sensing it is fragrance that seems to offer the easiest route to developing clairsentient powers. In the initial stages, certain fragrances that possess a long tradition in different ages and cultures offer almost instant access to the collective folk memory in which they have strong roots. The more sensitised you become to different fragrances, the more information your psyche can acquire via this sensory channel. Even if you are experienced psychically, you may find the following method helpful.

Buy a variety of herbs, fruits or flowers from the following list, or visit a garden where they may be growing. If they do not grow in your region, substitute fragrant or strong-smelling ones that are indigenous to the region. Alternatively, burn fragrant candles, incenses or oils in small burners.

Initially, choose three or four from the following:

Basil (*Ocimum basilcum*)

Bay leaves (*Laurus nobilis*)

Eau de Cologne mint (*Mentha/piperata f. citrata*)

Eucalyptus (*Eucalyptus*)

Honeysuckle (*Lonicera*)

Jasmine (*Jasminum*)

Lavender (*Lavandula*)

Lemon (*Citrus lemon*)

Lemon verbena (*Aloysia triphylla*)

Lime (*Tilia*)

Mint (*Mentha*)

Mimosa (*Acacia dealbata*)

Pine (*Pinus sylvestris*)

Rose (*Rosa*)

Sage (*Salvia officinalis*)

Thyme (*Thymus*)

✦ Sniff each separately, closing your eyes and concentrating not so much on what you see and hear, but what you feel. It might be peace, joy or sudden knowledge about a place or time where the fragrance had significance.

✦ Work next with other strong smells: spices such as cinnamon, garlic or ginger, baking bread, old-fashioned soap and furniture polish, oil, tar and wood smoke. Some of these you may find in natural settings. You may also discover that the lesser but equally valuable taste-buds evoke feelings and sensations. Visit the ocean or a salt lake or marsh, close your eyes and taste the tang of the sea. Note the strong emotions and perhaps also the scenes it evokes.

Clairsentience and old places

Use clairsentience to discover details about the past in old buildings and locations.

✦ Choose a location where many events have occurred over at least the past one hundred years but with which you are unfamiliar. You can choose a much older location if you wish. Such a place will have acquired many impressions of the different periods, and of the people who lived and worked there.

✦ Go to an old house, a church or cathedral garden, a ruined abbey, castle or old botanical gardens early in the morning or in the evening, when it is quiet.

✦ Sit near a scented plant such as a rose bush, an orange tree or a bed of lavender and, closing your eyes, allow the scent to carry you across the years. If the scented plants are not flowering when you visit, you can carry a selection of aromatic oils to sniff instead.

✦ You may feel that some of the features of the building or garden have changed, for example a current entrance may seem to be wrongly sited, or a grove of trees may once have grown in a particular spot.

✦ Open your eyes and write down what you sense in a notebook. Include any other details, such as names. Dates can be perceived as impressions and these experiences can be quite detailed. Jot down a sketch map if there seem to be any inconsistencies.

✦ Now go inside the building and find a place where you can close your eyes and allow impressions and emotions to fill you.

✦ Initially, you may wish to sit near to a bowl of dried lavender in a room or close to a log fire in the grate, to kick-start your psychic senses. Some old buildings have special days when they cook banquets or bread in the original kitchens and such smells can be very evocative for the psychic detective.

✦ Merge with the place so that you are not a visitor or even a separate entity but part of the fabric.

When you have finished jotting down notes, buy a guidebook or take a tour. You can check your feelings against the information you gain from these more mundane sources. Books of local folklore and legends, often reproduced from old archives and on sale in local shops, may offer clues. But do not feel you need to prove all your clairsentient discoveries for them to have meaning. Many of the feelings you experience would not be recorded or be able to be tested.

Widen your venues to industrial museums, reconstructed pioneer towns, and parts of towns with exotic street names such as Spice Alley, Coriander Street and Silk Wharf. Other areas may recall fertile creeks, camel trails, olive groves or nomadic watering places. As you walk, allow your psyche to tune in. The names are clues to the activities that once took place at those locations and they will be steeped in the emotions of those who lived, loved, laughed and cried there over the centuries.

Clairsentience and Decision-making

Just as dogs will growl at some strangers but not others, and a normally confident child will instinctively back away from a friendly smile and outstretched hand if it senses danger, so adults can use their clairsentient powers as part of decision-making. Stop and ask, 'What do I feel about this person, place or situation?' Allow instinctive impressions and feelings to have an equal part alongside logic and expert advice in making decisions. Invariably, a feeling of strong unease will alert you to important factors not available to the conscious mind; the more you take note of your feelings and initial impressions, the more refined and accurate your clairsentient powers become in the everyday world.

Psychometry

The art of psychic touch, psychometry is an extension of clairsentience, and is the ability to detect information about people, places and events, past or present, by holding an artefact connected with that person, place or event. Spontaneous psychometric ability is common among ordinary people and forms a valuable channel for the other psychic senses.

I, like many other researchers, believe that artefacts and places do have a psychic energy field around them and that thoughts and impressions become imprinted on them, especially those where strong emotion is involved. For example, a tea set that has been used by a family for generations will contain the family history, not only of momentous events but of quiet times while sitting around the teapot talking, laughing and sometimes crying. Experienced mediums will sometimes ask for a small treasure belonging to a deceased person in order to establish a clear line of contact.

An object that is associated with one person can also act as a transmitter for the energy field of the owner and his or her unique qualities and history. With practice, you will be able to hold a personal treasure and then access the owner's aural field. Through this you can learn not only about their past and present but also the potential opportunities and obstacles in the immediate future. These will have entered the outer layers of the aura but are not yet manifest in the everyday world. With this knowledge these opportunities or obstacles can be maximised or avoided.

Psychometry of the Place

This is the easiest form of psychometry for a beginner and links in very closely to clairsentience. Indeed, by visiting old sites and touching stones or artefacts you can almost instantly gain access to knowledge of those who lived there through the generations, and also receive clairvoyant images and voices from the past. We have minor but very sensitive chakra or psychic energy points in the palm of each hand that link with the major heart chakra. Therefore our hands can detect energy fields by touch. Before you leave to visit the place, you may like to spend a little time grounding yourself, perhaps by performing a tree visualisation, so that you do not become overwhelmed by psychic impressions.

✦ Revisit the places where you practised clairsentience, this time making hand contact, perhaps with a very old wall at a castle or ruined abbey, or any artefacts you are allowed to hold, or an old chimney breast where people sat and talked over the centuries (see also pages 184–86 for establishing ghost paths in ancient places).

✦ Sit in pews or the choir stalls in old churches or cathedrals, visit reconstructed rooms in industrial museums where the furniture and artefacts are typical of the period. Run your hands along the wood, press your feet against old tiled or wooden floors and sink into a deep sofa, or press your spine against the leather of a stagecoach seat. Though psychometry works primarily through the chakras – the psychic energy points in the palms of your hands – you can also receive psychic information through the soles of your feet, your root or base chakra at your perineum and your back.

✦ Go to museums where there is a hands-on policy, and handle pottery from different periods. Museums are increasingly making areas where people can handle some of the less priceless and more robust items and may also have children's corners where, for example, broken Roman pottery can be pieced together, bone tools handled and fossils held. One of the best museums I have visited is the Museum de Cluny on the left bank of Paris, built on the site of an ancient abbey and Roman baths. There you can touch stone columns from Celtic times, Roman statues and medieval Black Madonnas, although more delicate artefacts are behind glass.

+ In each case close your eyes and, if possible, touch or cradle the artefact in both hands. Breathe very gently and slowly in and out through your nose, feeling your own boundaries melting and those of the artefact or building expanding so that you merge temporarily and enter the aura of the place or artefact.

+ Information may be channelled as impressions, emotions, and physical sensations, or through sounds and images.

+ To disconnect from the source, slowly push away from it. As you concentrate once more on slow, gentle breathing, become aware of your own boundaries re-establishing.

Object psychometry

Though it is often easier to verify the impressions from objects belonging to friends or family, I have found that performing for people you know can cause your natural abilities to freeze. So leave this stage until you feel confident.

+ Begin by holding artefacts at antique fairs or car boot sales and afterwards writing down the history of the objects and perhaps details of particular owners.

+ Then you can try items belonging to friends and acquaintances that have been in their families for generations.

+ You may be able to pick up current issues, especially if there is a family crisis or strong emotion. If you trust your instinct, with practice you will learn to discriminate between the two.

Predictive personal psychometry

Just as you tuned into places and past times, so you can use an object that has personal significance for the owner, to tune into his or her aural field. This method can be used to help them solve a problem or make a decision about the future, by tapping into information not available to the conscious mind. You can then gain information about the past, which may bear relevance to situations in the present, current issues and possibilities. If the item, for example a ring, watch, necklace or a key ring, is carried or worn regularly by the person seeking the reading it will be endowed with their unique blueprint and with emotion that will amplify its psychic energies.

✦ I have found that closing your eyes to attune yourself, or seeking energies from higher forces, works less well with psychometry than attuning to your subject, standing as it were in their shoes and merging with their vibrations. You can begin this process by asking the owner to hold the object and to touch it yourself at the same time, to open the psychic channels. Rest it on a table if it is quite heavy while you both talk about the purpose of the reading and any problems or opportunities that require a decision to be made. It is the object itself that serves as the channel for the psychometrist's intuitive powers and so, like the pendulum, this is a particularly effective method to use initially until you are able to trust your abilities.

✦ When your subject has finished talking, take the object and run your fingertips and palms over it – frequently the item becomes warm as the psychic energies build up.

✦ Early impressions often relate to the questioner's childhood. You may then gradually connect with events from the recent past, forming a timeline. If allowed to flow uninterrupted, this timeline will reveal potential pathways from the questioner's aural radar to the object, which you can then identify.

✦ If you see images, sense impressions or hear voices, share these in an ongoing dialogue with the subject, who may want to add personal feelings, perhaps about an unacknowledged area of his or her life.

✦ Do not stop to check if you are correct. If the questioner cannot place a piece of information, it can cast doubts in your mind that will block your natural intuitions.

✦ Make a tape recording of the reading and tell your subject you can discuss the reading in detail afterwards.

✦ Remember that in psychometry, pure clairvoyance and mediumship, the messages are often in symbols that have meaning to the questioner rather than the channeller, so ask about any that seem especially vivid.

✦ Sometimes an event can only be verified after checking with older family members or after looking through old photographs, so do not be disappointed if the reading is not instantly clear.

✦ The most important part concerns present and future paths, so if you seem to be receiving information that is mainly about the present and future, the influence of the past may not be as strong as current factors for the situation under consideration. Go with the flow.

Clairvoyance

Also called clear-seeing or second sight, clairvoyance is the ability to see into the future or to know things that cannot be discovered through the normal senses. Like intuition, it is believed by some researchers to reside in the third eye, which is the seat of the brow chakra, the psychic energy centre that is linked to all forms of spiritual and psychic functioning. The third eye is situated just above and between the eyes.

The process has been described as seeing images in your mind as though on a video screen, or even seeing energy forms externally, projected from your inner vision. They may be scenes, people known or unknown, or symbols, such as those you might see when looking into a candle flame or reading tea leaves.

Even if you are a total beginner to psychic development, I would be very surprised if you had reached this stage in the exercises and not seen images in your mind either of the ancient places visited and the people who lived there or symbols connected with a subject's destiny.

I believe that clairvoyance – seeing both into the distance far beyond the range of even the most keen-sighted person, and into the future – originated among early hunter-gatherers. We can understand a great deal about early people as well as the rituals before the hunt from Palaeolithic cave paintings of figures wearing antlers and imitating the successful culmination of the hunt in dance.

From the few societies where hunter-gathering is still a way of life, such as those of the north of America and Canada, we also know that hunters do not rush about waving spears or weapons when they are out stalking the creatures. They wait silently, first visualising where the hunt will be and then the movements of the individual animal and how it will react. When stalking, the hunters project themselves into the mind of the animal moments or even minutes ahead, to anticipate if it will run and if so in which direction, and if it will attack or wait.

This may also be the origin of out-of-body travel (see pages 170–71) which is similar to remote viewing: perceiving beyond physical eye range (see page 42). Hunters or at least their shamans, the priest-magicians of the tribe, travelled in their mind's vision or perhaps their detached spirit bodies over miles to discover where the animals were hiding.

Seeing the Future

We know from proven cases that people can see into the future. Most commonly, these images are seen as spontaneous flashes or premonitions that warn of danger to self or loved ones, and often occur in dreams (see page 161). So why cannot even very practised clairvoyants predict the lottery numbers every week? I am convinced that it is because we do not need to win the lottery, and, according to the laws of magic, we can attract by psychic means enough for our needs and a little more only. However, even lottery wins can be predicted, and occasionally in dreams we can be given a push to enter at a particular time, even though we will not be given the winning numbers.

Take the example of Deanna Sampson. Her late and much-loved brother Glynn, who had severe learning difficulties, had died in his sleep in June 1996. He had given his sister an old toffee tin in which he kept his prized possessions, and Deanna, 34, who lived in Stradbroke in Sheffield, used it to draw out numbers to use in the National Lottery each week. She had won nothing and eventually lost faith in the system. However, three days before the draw on 5 October 1996, she dreamed that Glynn told her to use the tin again. Three hours before the draw she pulled six numbers from the tin – and won £5,439,681. At the time, Deanna's husband was working in Germany, as he could not find a job in England. He missed their children desperately and Deanna believes that her brother wanted the family to be back together.

Developing Clairvoyance for Future Events

Elsewhere I describe clairvoyant scrying techniques in which you gaze into a reflective surface such as water or a crystal sphere (see pages 89 and 91). In this section, I will concentrate on methods you can use in your everyday world. Visual images in the mind are the most usual and powerful form of clairvoyant communication from deep within your psyche. Some people believe these images are retrieved from the outer layers of our aura that have access to the non-material planes where linear time does not operate.

Practising clairvoyance – the example of travel

Trains, buses, planes and traffic queues can be unpredictable – even under normal weather conditions. As they are usually invested with a certain amount of emotion – we *need* to get somewhere on time – they are good subjects on which to practise clairvoyance. Indeed, it can be incredibly useful to know when to leave an extra half an hour early for work, or to wait an extra half an hour before making the homeward journey to avoid an unexpected traffic snarl-up. Similarly, clairvoyance can suggest when to change the route of the school run, or to a holiday destination, or just to go to the shops. You can also decide to take a different metro line, change routes or train hop at intermediate stations to keep ahead of any problems.

Drivers who regularly cover a large number of miles have a keen instinct for potential hazards. On the regular 450-mile round trip to Manchester I was doing at one stage of my life, the Granada television drivers, Rick and John, would often avoid traffic delays before they appeared on the mini-computer hazard screens they had in the car.

The following are some suggestions; you can create your own exercises around your personal routine.

✦ On the day of travelling, get up a little earlier and spend five minutes sitting either before a blue candle for travel (see meditation on page 48) or in the open air.

✦ Create a bubble of stillness in your mind by breathing deeply and rhythmically, inhaling and exhaling gently through your nose.

✦ Place within that bubble of stillness an image of you leaving home. Unlike creative visualisation when you draw a desired result towards you (moving a gridlocked motorway system is beyond even experienced practitioners), allow a video clip to unfold before your eyes.

✦ Bring any direction boards into sharp focus and, as the film continues to run, note any unexpected snarl-ups or diversions.

✦ Leave in plenty of time. If you are driving, keep your eyes and conscious mind on the road so that you can receive further psychic updates en route to changes caused by individual destinies crashing into the back of others through inattention.

✦ While you are practising clairvoyance, do not use radio travel updates. Often they will advise you of a jam when you are sitting in it!

✦ If travelling by public transport, use your quiet pre-travel time to give you an overall travel time and an image of the best route for that day, which may not be the shortest in miles.

✦ While standing at a bus stop, allow a picture to form of which bus will turn up first and where yours is in the system. You can do a similar exercise on the railway platform, so that you can anticipate delays and allow your inner radar to alert you to advantageous changes en route.

✦ While at an airport, to anticipate your flight gate and the precise time it will be indicated, use the flight board to concentrate on the flights that are scheduled to leave at the same time as your own. Allow an image to form in your mind of the destination of the first plane that will be called on the indicator board. Now focus on the flight gates for your own plane and the others departing at the same time.

Some of the above travel predictions you can verify, others you cannot. As mentioned earlier, verification is good in that it helps us to trust our clairvoyant vision. Sometimes, however, you cannot find out if you have avoided a snarl-up or even a potential accident, for by your decision to change your normal routine you have subtly altered the kaleidoscope pattern of destiny.

In time you will find that you no longer need to deliberately tune in, but that the images will form spontaneously when needed, and you will find yourself getting off the train or bus a stop earlier, thus avoiding the effects of a train breakdown higher up the line or a traffic snarl-up.

Remote Viewing

This is a clairvoyant technique where a viewer can detect an unknown object, person or scene in another place, beyond the range of the physical eye, whether this is in another room, another building or a hundred or more miles away. Children can routinely see around corners and through walls with their clairvoyant eye, but it is an ability adults lose, although mothers spontaneously regain it when they have a child to care for. A mother may have a sudden vision in her mind that her child is in danger seconds or even minutes before the incident occurs and is able to avert potential disaster.

However, there is no way of knowing whether remote viewing involves actual out-of-body travel or whether the mind can project itself to see over great distances and across dimensions.

✦ The night before you visit an unfamiliar town, building or even an acquaintance's home, close your eyes and walk through the town or building in your mind, noting which way you turn from the station or the car park and any unusual buildings. If visiting a large building, note specific rooms and distinctive décor as you mentally walk through.

✦ Visualise yourself as in a picture framed next to a distinctive artefact or archway in the town. You may see a street or square name. Now expand the frame and you may see shops or other distinctive features.

✦ Jot down your impressions, this time as a sketch map. And follow it on your actual visit.

✦ You can also practise weather guessing. The international pages of a weather service on the Internet are the most effective as they include current information, but you can also use newspapers that provide temperatures and conditions for a number of locations throughout the world.

✦ Choose a place you know and visualise yourself at your favourite café or by the sea.

✦ Now focus on the weather. Is it raining? Foggy? What is the temperature? Even exotic places can have bad days or unpredictable weather, so do not try to rationalise if what you have pictured seems unlikely.

✦ Look up the place on a weather chart. Continue to focus on the same location for about five minutes each day for the next week. You will find that even your temperature predictions will become more accurate.

✦ As you gain confidence in your remote viewing abilities, you can check out potential holiday hotels, venues for days out, even which café in a crowded shopping centre has spare tables or where there are parking spaces. Psychic abilities are meant to improve your everyday world as well as being used for more exalted purposes.

Clairaudience

The ability to hear words or sounds that are not part of the material world and to hear channelled wisdom from wise guides, nature essences or angels (see pages 168 and 180) is known as clairaudience. Usually these messages are transmitted within the mind. A discarnate voice, whether internal or external, may be that of a deceased relative, a warning voice from another dimension, perhaps of a guardian angel, or our own inner voice that can instinctively guide us on to the right path.

The concept of guidance by disembodied voices can seem worrying, especially as certain mental illnesses are characterised by voices suggesting bizarre or dangerous actions. However, those instances of intrusive or unpleasant voices are very rare and when they do occur they are generally due to stress or illness.

If a voice seems frightening or intrudes uninvited, use your grounding exercises, avoid psychic work for a while, and concentrate on healthy outdoor or physical activities. If you have any worries about your daily life or unresolved anger, talk to a friend and make sure you have plenty of positive company and activities, in order to counter any negativity you may have suppressed that can occasionally cause negative experiences.

Developing Your Psychic Ear

Earlier, when you practised clairsentience you sensitised yourself with different fragrances. You can develop your psychic ear in a similar way. Sounds that occur in certain places will be similar to the sounds from times past, so that by tuning into these sounds we can gain insight into the past.

Through the ages and across different cultures, sound in its more harmonious forms has been regarded as central to spiritual development. Chants and song are ways of attuning the chanter, musician or listener to sounds that pass beyond the everyday world and lift the spirit. Some people believe that when we are attuned to perfect forms of human song, we can hear psychically angelic choirs and the harmonious music that fills the cosmos. Silence is considered the most perfect form of sound. Practise listening to silence, and in time it will break into wonderful musical notes in your mind, sometimes called the music of silence (for working with mantras, see page 189).

The following sounds can be used to expand psychic awareness. It is best to hear them in a natural setting, but if you cannot, there are a variety of CDs of the sounds of rainforests, oceans and birdsong that you can listen to in your special place.

✦ Gregorian chants are a single-line melody, also known as plainsong. They are still used in monasteries, but have also entered the wider musical field as a consciousness-raising tool.

✦ Birdsong, if possible in natural surroundings, both during the day and as birds swoop around in the evening. The call of seagulls can be especially evocative.

✦ Water from a river running over stones, especially a fast-flowing watercourse.

✦ The sea.

✦ Wind rustling through leaves in a forest or grove.

✦ Children playing.

✦ The calls of animals and birds in the countryside or at an animal conservation park.

✦ Markets with street vendors. Old-fashioned fairgrounds with steam organs and carousels – now enjoying a revival.

✦ Church or temple bells.

✦ Ships and tugs at a port, fishing boats, and vendors on the beach.

When you have found your source of sound, do the following:

✦ While sitting in a comfortable place where you will not be disturbed, focus on that particular sound, allowing others to gradually fade as though you were tuning in a radio to a specific frequency. By now your other psychic senses may be so finely tuned that it will be difficult to receive impressions only through the auditory channel, but this is to be welcomed as a sign of progress.

✦ The sounds may trigger images, fragrances, tastes, impressions or whole scenes of other times and places when birds sang and bells called people to church for a wedding or a Sunday service.

You will find that the scenes you experience during these psychic exercises have particular significance for you and will recur in the everyday world – often in unexpected contexts – as core symbols in dreams, during scrying and as you explore other dimensions.

Divination with the Voices of the Natural World

Some societies, for example the Maoris of New Zealand and the Celtic nations of Western Europe, have long known that the natural world has many voices, carrying wisdom on the wind, in the flowing rivers and in the call of the birds and animals. Indeed, wise animals and birds are said to speak directly to the minds of individuals who withdraw into the solitude of the countryside or to a remote seashore, imparting wisdom and sometimes healing powers at times when the material world or conventional sources of wisdom fail to offer solutions.

✦ Begin by standing in a circle of trees when it is windy, whether in your garden, a park or a forest, and allow your mind to become attuned to the rhythm of the rustle followed by a lull.

✦ When you are ready, ask a question in your mind or recall an area of your life in which there is uncertainty.

✦ Listen to the leaves and the wind as they intermingle, as though a person was speaking to you. The message will sometimes be in verse or in a single phrase, followed by a lull.

✦ Jot down any words and images or impressions that come into your mind.

✦ Do not ask any more questions, but if you sit quietly you may gain other words or impressions.

✦ In the evening, sit quietly by candlelight and, as you transfer the material to your journal, recreate in your mind the actual sounds. While you do this insight will come.

Alternatively, fill a small crystal bowl with spring water and drop five or six small crystals into it one at a time. If you stand above the bowl and gently drop the crystals into it, each will give a single word or phrase as it falls. This method works well with a single question or by focusing on an area of concern. Allow a pause in between each so that psychic ripples can spread through your mind, casting images and impressions as well as words.

A tune played by church bells, or a choir singing in Latin or an unfamiliar language, can also channel wisdom. In this case, do not ask a specific question. Record the music or work from a CD so that you can listen first and write down any impressions afterwards.

Clairaudience and Higher Realms of Consciousness

As you practise your clairaudient abilities, you may become aware of discarnate voices. These may be like an out-of-tune radio or perhaps heard in other languages you do not recognise. This is quite natural and nothing to fear. In time you will find that you can channel voices from angels, from wise ancestors and, if you develop mediumship abilities, from spirit guides as well.

Do not force this higher clairaudient ability, but note down any words or phrases, perhaps passages from the Bible or I Ching you may recognise. Much of the material comes from a cosmic source of wisdom that you can interpret with your clairaudient ear. Some people do not like this aspect of clairaudience. If you do not, close down your energy by snuggling into your psychic blanket or ground yourself – there are many other ways of communicating with higher forces.

The Next Step

Developing the psychic senses is an area that needs to take seed. You will find that these abilities will help in many aspects of your psychic work and that they will evolve quite naturally in parallel with other skills. In the next step you will channel these psychic senses into using your mind-power to enrich your life. It will protect you from negative influences and feelings received from others and from living in a polluted world.

STEP 3

Psychic Empowerment and Protection

THE MIND IS LIKE AN iceberg and the powers we use are merely the tip of it. Increasingly, however, we are learning that the mind is able to operate on many levels. It can transmit information to other minds over great distances without words, and it can affect and even move matter. For the first part of this section I concentrate on different ways of developing these powers, and in the second part I describe the all-important psychic protection that you should use while working regularly with psychic powers and when counselling or healing others. It is also a way of creating harmony and preventing negativity from adversely affecting your home and work environment.

Meditation

You met the early stages of meditation in Step 1 in the form of relaxation and breath control. It is one of the most important ways of learning to control your mind and directing it towards specific targets. It is also a way of raising your consciousness to higher levels where you can absorb power and healing into both your everyday world and psychic explorations.

Meditation at its most simple is a way of focusing the mind on one thought, therefore improving concentration, which will lead ultimately to more effective decision-making. Because meditation stills all external noise, it can also act as an oasis of calm, and if practised over a period of months will result in a less stressed and more focused way of living. Meditation also acts as a pathway to higher levels of awareness, enabling an openness of spirit sufficient to channel wisdom from angelic and spirit guides. If practised over a long period of time, it leads to an enhanced awareness of the beauty and sanctity of nature, and lessens the externally caused swings of emotion by strengthening the inner still centre we all possess. In this section I describe various forms and stages of meditation.

If you have ever sat by a fountain and been filled with a sense of peace or watched a beautiful sunset, gazed into a crystal or a deep pool or daydreamed of a beautiful place and felt part of a magical world, you have already experienced meditative states. Watch a child totally absorbed by a butterfly or while colouring an intricate design, or humming as she sits in the sunshine, and you will witness advanced techniques of meditation.

Meditation is not a chore, but a joy and wonder. If you find, as I used to, that formal instructions and techniques hinder rather than help you, then begin meditation work by sitting in a place of natural beauty or powerful earth energies. An old standing stone or a spot known for its magic, such as the top of Glastonbury Tor in Somerset, is an ideal location.

By shutting out the daily world and clearing inner mental chatter, you can open the channels of the mind through which you can tune into the higher energies of nature and the universe, the wisdom of devas, angels and spirit guides (see pages 168 and 180).

Through merging with a point of focus, be it a crystal, candle or word in your mind, you can lose a sense of separateness and in time you will learn to concentrate wholly on the focus while remaining aware that you are meditating. This is an important psychic technique, and can be used, for example, in lucid dreaming – the state when you are aware you are asleep and therefore can change the dream while you are in it (see pages 164–66). Of course, you will not achieve all these the first time you meditate. Different meditations may bring to the fore different powers depending on the purpose of the meditation and, to some extent, the focus. Finally, meditation creates a space and stillness in which your spiritual development can take place.

Beginning Meditation

In the early stages of meditation, a single tangible focus is very helpful, whether a fragrant flower, a crystal, a candle or a sacred pattern, such as a mandala or labyrinth (see pages 193 and 196). You may also use a stimulus that involves sound – for example a fountain or water feature where you could work with the patterns of the flowing water or just the sound. As you become experienced, you can work with more abstract stimuli: a point of light, an image in your mind, a mantra, or a single word or phrase spoken first on each exhaled breath, then in the same rhythm silently in your mind.

◆ Work by your own rhythm and not by the clock. When you feel the outer world returning, do not fight it. You will quite spontaneously increase your meditation times the more you practise, but the length of the meditation is not in direct proportion to the quality.

◆ Sit in your special place, either by the light of a lavender, rose or sandalwood fragranced candle, or in natural daylight or moonlight. Dawn and sunset are especially magical; in the Indian ayurvedic healing tradition meditation in the morning and evening forms an essential part of the maintenance of health and well-being. Set in front of you your focus, whether visual, such as a candle, or both visual and auditory, like a water feature. You should be able to look at this without straining your neck or back. Sit for just a moment or two with your eyes half-closed, tuning into the stimulus before beginning meditation.

◆ Start by relaxing using the technique on page 17 or your own favourite method.

◆ Then carry out one of the breathing methods on pages 18–20 or devise one of your own, while looking at the object through half-closed eyes and allowing your own boundaries to soften so that you become one with the focus.

◆ Gradually your breathing will become automatic as your full attention is centred on the focus. If troublesome thoughts emerge, allow each to form like a huge raindrop and then disperse.

◆ Sometimes non-intrusive background music or the sounds of nature can help to blot out the distractions of the world. You might find the sounds of a rainforest or the sea helpful and there are many such CDs available. Alternatively, pan pipes, a combination of Celtic music or even a gentle, flowing classical piece, such as Grieg's *Morning Song,* may help you to flow with the natural rhythms, especially if meditation is an unfamiliar technique.

✦ Some people sway slightly at the beginning to establish fluidity, and certainly you should not feel you cannot move a muscle or blink. You may find it helpful to use the breathing position of chin tucked in and eyes slightly lowered, so that the object is in soft focus. Let the body take care of itself.

✦ After a few minutes, you may want to close your eyes and visualise the focus all around enclosing and protecting you.

✦ You may fall asleep. While this is not the object of meditation, you have not failed – relaxation is a beneficial by-product of this work – and as long as you are in a safe place then the sleep may bring meaningful images or dreams.

✦ Contemplate the object of your focus. Feel its energy, look at its light and then merge with the focus so that you are the flowing water or the crystal that has formed in volcanic fire on windy mountains, washed by millennia of rain seeping into the rock.

✦ When you are ready and can feel the external world returning, move away from the focus and concentrate once more on your gentle, regular breathing and then open your eyes, if you closed them, and sit still for as long as you wish.

✦ Finish by stretching like a cat after sleep and, if possible, go into the open air or open all the windows.

After a few weeks of practising meditation you will spontaneously hold the focus, but be aware of yourself immersed in the focus. You will find you can split your mind momentarily, as though sitting above yourself on a cloud looking down on yourself. This may sound strange, but it will happen spontaneously.

This is a useful tool for later work on lucid dreaming, or during out-of-body travel, where you realise that your spirit is free to move about without physical constraints. Initially, you will manage this awareness for only a second or two without losing the concentration on the focus.

Try meditating on the seashore, in a forest, in the centre of a labyrinth or stone circle, on a mountain, in a quiet garden or in a church, and also for brief minutes at your desk during breaks. If you are in a public space, leave your valuables in a safe place.

If you see images or hear voices, accept them but do not analyse them during the meditation. In the time afterwards you can write down any insights. A number of people say that they first hear or see their guardian angel or a deva during meditation, and on pages 168 and 180 I describe how you can use mediation in this way.

Creative Visualisation

Next to meditation, visualisation is the most important method of exploring and developing the hidden and untapped potential of your mind. It is an art in its own right and can be used for everything from psyching yourself up to succeed in a job interview – by imagining a successful outcome – to manifesting a need on the thought plane into the everyday world. By this I mean you can visualise something you want or need so vividly that it appears in the physical world shortly afterwards. This technique is central to spellcasting and to positive thinking. For example, you might think yourself into promotion, making it a reality by giving off the vibes of success from your imagination to your bosses.

Visualisation is a means of focusing mind-power on a specific symbol in order to either transmit that image from one mind to another in telepathy, or to move matter. This is achieved by merging your mind with an object so that it can be moved into your life from the thought plane to the actual, and is known as psychokinesis. Like meditation visualisation can be used for relaxing body and mind, balancing energies, opening and closing psychic energy points and, indeed, any psychic work involving imagery.

As mentioned in the previous section, when talking about clairvoyance and the other psychic senses, children naturally think in images. Furthermore, the ability to translate psychic insights into imagery is central to all the major forms of scrying and divination. Dion Fortune, the 20th-century occultist, believed that an image or symbol that has been common to a number of different cultures and ages holds within it the combined power of all the people who had used the image over the centuries.

As you meditate less on an external focus and more on internal images, so the power of visualisation becomes central. This occurs whether you are meditating on a colour, a flower, or an angel, or on nothingness, which is as active a process as creating a vivid scene.

Creative visualisation involves four main stages:

1. A Need

✦ Creative visualisation is always fuelled by a need, a hope or even a fear to be banished, for like all mind/spirit arts, it operates most powerfully in the sphere of human emotions and real desires, rather than a vague dream or hope.

✦ Realism makes the visualisation easier to translate from desire to action. Wanting a million pounds is a less realisable focus than wanting five hundred pounds that is urgently needed to keep the car on the road.

✦ It may help to write or draw a summary of the purpose of the visualisation.

2. A Focus

✦ A tangible focus can make visualisation easier in the earlier stages. The focus could be a postcard of a resort or country you want to visit, a photo of someone you love from whom you are estranged, a brochure of a car or house you desire. Be as specific as possible, describing the colour and make of car, kind of dwelling and location, and so on.

✦ Look at or hold the symbol for a few minutes before beginning your actual visualisation and place it where you can easily see it, as you did with the object for meditation.

3. The Visualisation

At first you may need to set aside a specific time for visualisation, but with practice you can use the technique anywhere, by allowing the image of the desired result to build up in your mind.

✦ Begin with simple relaxation and gentle breathing while focusing on the image, if you have one, or creating it in your mind.

✦ Now close your eyes and bring the desired item or situation closer and closer until you can visualise yourself with it, such as inside the new home or touching the new car.

✦ If it is a car, for example, visualise the exact model in a showroom, a used car lot or in someone's drive, if it is for sale privately.

✦ Go through every detailed negotiation with the owner or salesperson: opening the doors, looking at the engine and feeling the upholstery.

✦ Concentrate on small details, the number plate, the colour, etc.

✦ Go through every step, including sitting in the driving seat, starting it up and going for a test drive. Finally, visualise paying for the car and then driving home.

✦ Invoke every sense, the smell of leather on the seats and the sound of the traffic.

✦ Most of all, savour the emotions: the anxiety that you might not find the right car at the right price, the mounting excitement when you see a vehicle you like, and the initial tension as you feel for the gears or put it into 'drive' and ease away. Link into the emotions associated with the fulfilment of your need, as well as fragrances, sounds, touch, and even taste, to make the visualised aim as three-dimensional as possible.

✦ Just before you shut the garage door at your home, note the number plate – you may be surprised when you finally get your new car by the similarities to those in your visualisation.

✦ When you are ready, allow the vision to recede slowly, and sit quietly while normal sounds and sights return.

You may find that during your visualisation a deeper level takes over and you see your car, new house or lover in an unexpected location – you may see clues that will be of help in the outside world. For example, if visualising a new house, you might spontaneously see a particular house down an unfamiliar lane. Then, days later, you might get lost on the way to view another house and take the wrong turning and end up in the lane; there is the visualised house, or a similar one, for sale. I have encountered a number of such cases. My explanation for this is that during the powerful psychic process of visualisation our automatic radar comes into action and shows us an image of what would make us happy and then diverts us to the location.

You can build into any visualisation a shortcut back to the feelings of happiness or assurance of success, by saying a phrase such as: 'When I touch the centre of my brow or squeeze my arm gently, I will recall the joy, calm or assurance of success that I am now feeling.' This can be of immense help as you start a new job or take an examination, so that you instantly experience the rush of confidence to make a good impression or recall all the answers.

4. The Action

In many ways, the action is the most important stage of all, although it is often one that is forgotten.

✦ It can be something as simple as re-reading or repeating your intention, creating a mantra, a word or a single image to summarise your wish and encapsulate the visualisation. It can then be repeated at regular intervals, perhaps while on an early morning walk, or while digging the garden, kneading bread, making pastry, vacuum cleaning or some other rhythmic task.

✦ If you had a focus, it will be empowered with your intentions and will, if you touch or hold it, fill you with instant confidence.

✦ Then your visualised desire has to be helped from the plane of thought to the plane of actuality, whether it be applying for a job, meeting new people, learning new skills or practising your interview techniques. Make sure you are clued up on the relevant information, or join clubs or classes or go to places where you can meet like-minded people.

✦ Repeat the visualisation at regular intervals, especially before a major stage in your plan.

Psychokinesis

For visualisation to be effective and bring a desire into actuality, the mind has to focus its power to moving an image of the required object into the actual world. This is an innate power, called psychokinesis, that we all possess, and it can be used in all kinds of ways to will events to occur and even to draw good luck towards us.

The term psychokinesis is derived from the Greek words *psyche,* meaning breath, life or soul, and *kinein,* meaning to move. Psychokinesis, the power of the mind to affect matter, is popularly associated with spoon-bending feats and poltergeist activity, whereby a stressed person, often a teenage girl, unconsciously causes objects to fly through the air. However, such occurrences are rare and psychokinesis most usually manifests itself every time we turn over a tarot card or ask a pendulum a question. We unconsciously influence the selection so that the most appropriate symbol invariably appears.

Coincidences and Psychometry

Sceptics attach no significance to coincidence – the striking occurrence of events happening together or in sequence. But the psychologist Carl Gustav Jung believed in what he called synchronicity – significant coincidences – considering them to be part of a deeper pattern of connection. Scientists, too, are increasingly acknowledging that even the fluttering of a butterfly wing affects the movement of the universe. But the most remarkable examples of psychokinesis in the everyday world are how we may be drawn to a faraway place we have not visited before and will then meet someone we went to school with, at a time when neither of us intended to be there (at least not consciously). Often you will have thought of that person immediately prior to meeting them, and it may have been for the first time in years.

About four years ago Susanne, who lived in Dublin, had written to me with an experience for a book I was writing on maternal instinct and she had sent me a lucky shamrock. Unfortunately, I mislaid her address.

In November 2000 I was booked into a hotel in Dublin, my first visit to Ireland. Because of an international rugby match, the hotel was the tenth one I had contacted for a booking. On the morning before I left, I noticed the small hotel shop was open, but since I always buy my children's gifts at the airport to save carrying them too far, I walked past the shop. However, I turned back, as I felt drawn to go inside.

On entering the shop I saw a statue of the Irish saint St Bridget, whose legendary life had fascinated me. I went over to the lady behind the counter to ask if she knew about a particular legend connected with St Bridget. In the conversation I mentioned that I wrote about New Age topics. She asked: 'Are you Cassandra?' I replied quite spontaneously: 'You are Susanne?' And she was. Usually, Susanne only worked weekends in the shop but was working that day to cover for someone's holiday. Out of more than a million people in the city our paths had crossed. She had not known I was coming to Ireland.

Such events are spontaneous, but I believe it is quite possible to learn to control and direct psychokinetic power. You could, for example, find a parking space or by chance meet someone who wants to sell a fax machine cheaply at the time yours has broken down. In the same way, you can come across people who have the job contacts you need or with whom you could form a friendship – a sort of psychic Internet that avoids the hazards of on-line dealings. This is possible by tapping into the cosmic melting pot and drawing to you what or whom you need.

Of course, with so many energies battering you may not hit instant success, but practise does improve your chances. However, you should not specify the latest model of car or a film star as your bride or groom. What is more you have to be open to giving what you no longer want, or to passing on information, in order for the system to operate efficiently.

Psychokinesis in Practice

As psychokinesis works best in cases of real need, you should practise in real situations. For example, if you need a sum of money urgently, be specific, and in your mind draw it towards you visually whether in the form of a cheque or actual cash. In psychokinesis you are not moving something from the thought plane to actuality, but you are moving an existing commodity in the real world from where it is not needed to where it is needed. You can also use the power for the positive good of others by focusing on aid arriving for people or places in need.

✦ For an urgent need, centre and still your mind to banish anxiety, which would divert psychic resources, and focus on the amount or item needed. Be specific as well as realistic and work for three or four minutes, first thing in the morning when you wake, at around midday, at dusk and before you go to bed.

✦ Make a positive affirmation as you begin, for example: 'Two thousand pounds is winging its way towards me to replace the family car.'

✦ Using visualisation, pull the money or object towards you as though using a magnet, but let the drawing be effortless, as if on wheels or castors, and flow with it.

✦ Focus on the object alone, not its background or source.

✦ The money or artefact may come from an unexpected source and may have strings attached, for example a relative who is no longer able to drive thought you might like her car, or money towards one, in return for taking her on regular shopping trips. It is amazing how the sum of money asked for and the sum received are usually identical to the penny.

Telepathy

The word telepathy comes from the Greek *tele* (distant) and *pathe* (occurrence or feeling). There are countless examples of this mind-to-mind communication that can span oceans instantly. It usually occurs between close relatives and friends at a time when one of them is experiencing strong emotions, whether love or distress. The communication may be seen as images, heard as words or experienced as feelings. They may be inexplicable to the recipient but nevertheless cause him or her to change their normal pattern of behaviour in response to the telepathic message. Sometimes the telepathic channels can be used to send psychokinetic energy as strength or protection to a relative who is in danger.

Daphne, who lives in Scotland, described this phenomenon, which was manifested by hearing her son's voice, although he was miles away:

My teenage son Alistair was out driving in March 1982 when an unexpected blizzard hit. I was standing by the dining room window watching enormous snowflakes fall, when I suddenly heard his voice, call, 'Mum, help me'. I said to my husband, John, 'There's something wrong with Ali.' John said that it was just the snow making me nervous.

About an hour later Ali appeared in a terrible state covered in snow. 'I've rolled the car, but I've got it home,' he said. The car had crashed through a hedge and down a bank into a field. But Alistair had managed to right the heavy car, get it back on to the road and drive it home.

When we saw where the car had gone through the hedge and where it finally stopped we could hardly believe he had managed to right it. Had I sent him the extra strength he needed? I asked him later what he was thinking. He replied: 'I think I said: "Mum, help!" Or something like that.'

On an everyday level many people routinely pick up the telephone to contact their mother or a close friend to find the phone is engaged and the other person is dialling their number at the same time. This happens even when there are no specific call times, for example when a sailor has to rely on irregular satellite contact to phone his home. Thinking of a person you have not seen for years prior to receiving a letter or telephone call is also so common that it usually occurs unremarked.

Developing Your Telepathic Powers

It is quite possible to strengthen telepathic links with loved ones and friends, although ironically with the use of mobile phones and pagers, the art is declining.

✦ Make a section in your psychic journal for spontaneous telepathic experiences and note incidents that occur over several weeks. See if a pattern emerges with certain people and at times when you are especially receptive. Note what you were doing and your mood before and after the experience.

✦ You might, for example, record how many times you knew the phone was going to ring before it happened and who the caller would be. There is, of course, an overlap with intuition and clairvoyance since all these powers are closely entwined.

✦ Before you pick up your mail, see if any people come into your mind, especially those with whom you have not had contact for a while. Do the same before checking if you have any emails.

✦ Anticipate the questions friends or family will ask when you meet, and mentally finish their sentences. Though some topics are predictable, many may not be, especially those relating to unusual happenings during the day.

Transmitting Your Thoughts

When you have the opportunity, stop using your mobile phone, email and other forms of technological communication for a few days, except when they are essential. This can be a good exercise to learn how to transmit your thoughts when you are at home for three or four days.

✦ Where possible, reduce the external noise of stereos, televisions and other electrical appliances in order to clear the psychic channels of clutter.

✦ Work with people you know from your journal monitoring are receptive and who will be happy to assist you, or use children and animals, who are psychically open.

✦ If you have young children or can borrow friends' and relatives' offspring, ask them a question silently or ask them to fetch something for you without speaking.

✦ Children in crèches have also been known to wander over to the phone if it rings during the day when their mother is calling. If you have a pet, ask a friend to sit with it when you go out and then change your normal time of returning. Animals invariably sit by the door or on an outside wall five minutes before you return.

✦ At a pre-arranged time when someone can monitor your pet while you are away from home, start to talk in your mind to your pet and mentally stroke it. Ask the sitter to note any unusual reaction.

✦ With a co-operative partner, spouse, parent or best friend, focus on the person at a time of day when you do not normally have contact. Do not warn them in advance of your intention. Mentally send a message of love and ask him or her to phone or email you. If this does not work, don't give up. It may be that the other person is preoccupied.

✦ When you and your partner or friend are quiet together, mentally ask a question or request they make you a drink. Make sure that it is at a different time from usual. If you do not get a response, persist at five-minute intervals, gradually turning up the psychic volume of your inner voice.

✦ If you want a person to get in touch, you may find that using a photograph of them or holding one of their possessions will open telepathic channels. This, of course, is partly psychometry.

✦ Alternatively, speak out loud to the person; this will bring fairly rapid communication – because positive vibes travel faster than negative ones.

✦ Go to an unfamiliar shopping precinct or town with a friend or family member and take it in turns every half hour to transmit a rendezvous at a distinctive landmark. Focus on each other for about five minutes before the meeting but otherwise avoid thinking of the other person.

Psychic Protection

As you develop your mind to receive and transmit psychic energies from other people and from different planes of existence, so inevitably you will be receptive to negative as well as positive forces. What is more, if you carry out healing or psychic counselling, negativity shed by the subject can become attached to your aura, leaving you feeling drained and even unwell. To avoid this you need to create a shield around yourself before working (see pages 62–65 for some ways of shielding yourself from harm).

In the everyday world, an office can accumulate bad vibes if it is not regularly cleansed of the inevitable tensions and frantic pace and noise of modern technology. Once you are home, the stresses of the day can result in irritability, an inability to relax or even quarrels caused by free-floating negativity from the outside world. You can also suffer from the effects of a psychological or psychic attack that may not be deliberate but the result of negative thoughts communicated by another. Perhaps this is someone who lies awake at night fuming about your talents, your success, your partner or your children. This unconscious malevolence can give you headaches or leave you jittery and unable to relax.

Personal, domestic and workplace protection is very easily achieved by amplifying the innate protective powers of the mind with naturally defensive substances, such as herbs and crystals.

Useful Protection Techniques

On pages 8–10 I described how you could cleanse and empower your sacred space using herbs, water, salt and smudging with burning herbs or incense. I also explained that this was a good idea before and after psychic work. Sweep, scrub and smudge those areas, as well as rooms where there have been quarrels or tension and the boundaries of your home, to keep out bad vibes and intruders. You and others will notice how light the rooms are and how bright your home and garden is, even in winter.

Below I describe some specific methods of protection for various situations.

Creating a triple circle of protection

The triple circle is one of the most ancient and powerful forms of psychic protection. You can create it around yourself, your home or workspace. You can also create it around items, for example a bag or mobile phone to keep them safe while away from home. The triple circle can be cast with salt, water and smoke or even by drawing three circles around an image of yourself, your loved ones, your home or workplace. The drawing can be made by hand or on the computer.

You can carry out this ritual, or any of the protective rituals below, while holding or wearing a protective crystal (see pages 105–6) so that it becomes empowered. It will then activate the protection of the original ritual when it is touched or worn. The following circle uses salt for earth, water for its own element and smoke for air, which are the three main elements in the Celtic druidic tradition, representing respectively earth, sea and sky.

✦ Create your first circle clockwise with sea salt around any person, artefact or place you wish to protect. You can, if you wish, use empowered salt (see page 72). Beginning in the north, say: 'May the circle that is cast remain unbroken. Blessings be as I invoke the protection of the earth.'

✦ Then make a second circle clockwise with pure mineral water or sacred water (see page 141) if you prefer, just beyond the first, beginning once again in the north. As you do so, say: 'May the circle that is cast remain unbroken. Blessings be as I invoke the protection of water and the seas.'

✦ Finally create a third circle using a smudge or incense stick of sage, cedar or pine outside the circle of water, saying: 'May the circle that is cast remain unbroken. Blessings be as I invoke the protection of the air and the sky.'

✦ Alternatively, if you want to include the fourth element, fire – which was believed in the Celtic world to be the generative principle of the cosmos – sprinkle a few grains of salt into the water, stir it clockwise with a clear quartz crystal and use that for the first circle, adapting the chant to invoke all four elements: 'May the circle that is cast remain unbroken. Blessings be as I invoke earth, fire, air and sea.'

✦ The second circle then becomes smoke/air and the third fire/the Sun that you can create by passing a candle around the perimeter of the visualised circle to create the third layer of protection.

✦ You can visualise this circle around you when you are under attack.

Creating a shield of invisibility with smudging

In the previous ritual, you created a circle around yourself that could be activated whenever you need protection. However, there are situations or places where you are vulnerable, and at those times you need to be less visible. Most ancient invisibility spells relied not on making the physical body disappear, but on lowering a person's profile so that he or she could walk unnoticed in places of potential danger. If you know in advance, you can carry out the ritual the evening or morning before to assume a psychic cloak of greyness. But it is also possible to store up this power so that you can rapidly create the aura of invisibility at any time. You do this by carrying out the ritual monthly; then, when you need the shield of invisibility, you simply visualise the smoke shield you created in the ritual.

The process can be adapted to calm you if you are stressed and unable to sleep or after psychic work when you feel the energies buzzing around in your head (see also grounding on page 23). Sit in a comfortable position, out of doors in a sheltered spot, if the weather is suitable, or indoors in the centre of a room.

✦ Light a sage smudge stick or some large firm leaves of grey or white sage of the sagebrush variety. Grey sage, the Mother Goddess herb, is especially effective. Small, squat smudge sticks burn especially well and give out a steady but subtle stream of smoke. You can substitute broad incense sticks in pine or juniper, if you prefer.

✦ Swirl your stick in front of you, visualising the rainbow colours of psychic energy around your head and body growing fainter.

✦ You can hold feathers or a fan in the other hand to spread the smoke if you wish.

✦ Fan or swirl the smoke upwards from your feet over your whole body and around your head so that gradually a gentle grey mist seems to enfold your whole being and the aural field around you. You will then no longer be giving out signals to the external world.

✦ Place your smudge stick in a deep container so that the flow of smoke slows.

✦ Sit quietly as you did when you were a child in your favourite hiding place when you did not want to be found, and savour the enfolding darkness.

✦ When you are ready, extinguish the smudge stick by tapping it against a ceramic container.

✦ Shake yourself like a puppy in a shower of rain and your aura will be bright again, but now you will have the greyness in reserve.

When you are entering a difficult or potentially dangerous situation, visualise the smoke shielding you. It may help to carry a few of the unburned herbs in a tiny purse and sniff them to recall the fragrance.

Visualising protection

You can equally well use a single circle of white candles or a circle of protective crystals, such as haematite, jet, obsidian, agate, amber or jade, to create a single powerful circle of protection. However, many people, myself included, find it easier to visualise a single protective circle of light rather than actually creating circles. You can visualise yourself within a silver bubble, a sphere of light or pink cotton wool. You can also draw circles in the palm of your hand – we all have our favourite methods.

Invoking protection from higher powers

Throughout history, people have asked for protection from God, the Mother Goddess or the archangels when faced with danger or undertaking any form of psychic work. However, you may see this higher energy as something different altogether: an undifferentiated benign light, cosmic bliss, life-force in its most perfect form, or your own divine spark – what Quakers call the God or Good within.

Invoking the source of light and goodness under whatever name you prefer to use is an important part of spiritual work, not only as a prelude to psychic exploration, meditation or divination, but also when you are alone and feeling vulnerable. You might, for example, find yourself alone in a deserted or dark place and feel the need to invoke those higher powers.

The most effective method to do this that I have developed involves using four tall, white candles to represent the four main archangels. If you prefer, you could see the candlelight as four deities, or as more abstract pillars of benign or divine light. The following four angels are traditionally used in Kabbalistic and Western magical traditions. In Westernised magic they are assigned cardinal directions, colours and attributes; however these associations may vary according to the teachings of different practitioners; for example, Raphael is sometimes seen as green. As there is no absolute right, if an association feels wrong, go with your intuition.

Uriel

The name Uriel means Fire of God. He is associated with earthquakes, storms and volcanoes, is the archangel of salvation, and is sometimes linked with the courage of the planet Mars. Uriel warned Noah of the impending flood and was credited with giving alchemy to humankind and the wisdom of the Kabbalah to Hebrew mystics. He therefore stands as wise protector and keeper of the sacred mysteries and magical wisdom. Uriel's power is manifest in his control over storms, earthquakes and other natural phenomena. Uriel stands in the north and his colour is the deep blue or purple of midnight.

Raphael

The angel Raphael is the healer and travellers' guide and is often associated with the planet Mercury. As the messenger of dawn he is the angel who offers healing to the planet and mankind. Raphael is also guardian of the young. He is depicted with a pilgrim's stick, a wallet and a fish, showing the way and offering sustenance to all who ask. Raphael stands in the east and his colour is yellow.

Michael

Archangel of the Sun and light, Michael is the warrior angel. As commander of the heavenly hosts, Michael, who is often pictured holding a flaming sword, drove Satan and his fallen angels out of the celestial realms. As Angel of Judgement, he also carries a scale weighing the souls of the dead. Michael offers the power to overcome obstacles. He also brings inspiration and illumination and shows the direction of the right path. Michael is the archangel who combats fear. He stands in the south and his colour is gold.

Gabriel

Archangel of the Moon, the messenger archangel and the heavenly awakener, Gabriel appears many times in the Bible, visiting the Virgin Mary and her cousin Elizabeth, mother of John the Baptist, to tell them that they were to bear sons who would lead mankind to salvation. To the followers of Islam, Gabriel is the Spirit of Truth who dictated the Koran to Mohammed. Gabriel stands in the west, bringing wise words of truth and compassion and the acceptance of the weaknesses of self as well as others. His colour is silver.

An archangel candle ritual for protection

You can use candles as a focus for the energies of these four archangels or indeed substitute any of your own favourite angels. By visualising and invoking them you create a powerful circle of light around yourself that you can recall in your mind whenever you feel alone or afraid.

✦ Stand in the centre of your visualised circle of light with a candle at the four main compass points.

✦ You can hold a crystal – for example celestite or rutilated quartz, which are said to contain angelic energies – and this will become charged with the protection and can thereafter be used as an amulet.

✦ Sit in the centre at a safe distance from the candles (be careful if you have trailing sleeves).

✦ Light first the candle in the north. Inhale the light of Uriel, exhaling any fears concerning material security or safety to be absorbed by the candle. Visualise him controlling the storms and the earthquakes, and repeat: 'Archangel of courage, drive away the dangers of the day and the dark fears of the night. This I ask and give thanks for your protection.'

✦ Face east and light the candle of the east, inhaling the light of Raphael and exhaling any fears concerning illness, old sorrows or guilt to be absorbed by the candle. Visualise Raphael healing people, animals and the land, and say: 'Archangel of peace, drive away the fears of the day and the sorrows of the night. This I ask and I give thanks for your protection.'

✦ Turn next to the south and light the third candle. Inhale the light of Michael, exhaling any fears of seemingly insurmountable obstacles or people who stand in the way of your happiness and success. Visualise Michael defending you against all that would harm both earthly and paranormal spectres and say: 'Archangel of the Sun drive away the oppressors of the day and the spectres of the night. This I ask and I give thanks for your protection.'

✦ Finally, face the west and light the fourth candle. Inhale the light of Gabriel, exhaling any negative feelings whether anger, pain or grief, and doubts about your self-worth. Visualise Gabriel enfolding you in his compassion-ate, loving wings and say: 'Archangel of the Moon, drive away all the doubts of the day and the loneliness of the night.'

✦ Sit in the candlelight facing north again. Visualise the light rays entering the sphere of psychic energy all around your body, forming a golden shield and penetrating every aspect of your being.

✦ Create a psychic short-cut so that you can recreate the golden sphere of light whenever you feel vulnerable, for example in a lonely place or at work when you need to guard yourself against spite, gossip or unfair pressure.

✦ One method is to touch your head, then heart, navel, womb and genitals, naming the four archangels at each point: 'Uriel, Raphael, Michael, Gabriel, archangels all, protect me when I call.'

✦ You can recite the mantra in your mind when you need protection at work or while travelling.

✦ Allow the candles to burn through. You can, if you wish, remain within the circle of protection as it enfolds your body and penetrates every level of your being.

✦ For any rituals where candles are used, buy ones that last only an hour or so and make sure they are placed in a safe place. Remember: never leave a burning candle unattended.

Other protection techniques

One of the easiest methods of protecting your home or yourself is to light a sage smudge stick, and to fan yourself or the room with a feather to waft the smoke. You can smudge around a drawing of your office to avoid setting off smoke alarms. Another way to protect yourself, your home or workplace is to sprinkle sacred salt and water around the area. You can also visualise spheres of light or create boundaries of light around them, plant protective herbs (see pages 76–81) or sprinkle herbal infusions over artefacts and places. Protection could be provided for a species of plant or creature by either smudging or sprinkling specific herbs of protection over the animal or plant or over a picture of it. As your psyche develops you will develop certain methods that work well for you in almost every situation.

The Next Step

Now you have developed your psychic senses and channelled your mind-power, you are more than ready to swim out of the learner pool and into the sea of wisdom. People have practised healing and psychic development over millennia. They have amassed a body of knowledge relating to the powers of natural substances and forces that can amplify our own powers and give depth and richness to our work. The next sections introduce the theories and symbol systems that underpin all forms of psychic and spiritual work. Sometimes the emphasis will be on external magical ritual or using tools for healing rather than purely inner powers alone. As our ancestors knew, our personal psychic development is linked with the interconnected web of natural and cosmic power.

Working with Magical Tools and Ritual

Y OU COULD CARRY OUT psychic work and healing using purely your mind and psychic senses, relying on visualisation and psychokinesis to create a focus and bring thoughts into actuality. However, by using nature's gifts – her plants, trees and crystals – you can tap into the earth mother's storehouse of power and protection, rather like connecting your portable computer to the mains lead to charge the battery.

Although visualisation is a very powerful method of bringing desires into actuality, magic is even more dynamic because it amplifies your own psychokinetic powers, by harnessing the energies that exist within the natural world in such forms as herbs and crystals.

In addition, because positive magic has been used for thousands of years by following age-old steps and using materials associated with natural energies, you can tap into the magical heritage of your ancestors. I believe that the ability to weave magic is a natural innate psychic power, transmitted in our genes and so easily accessible by following the form of folk rituals.

The Wisdom of Folk Memory

Sadly, the knowledge to use this magic, once handed down through the generations by the women, has reduced in the past hundred years, because with increased urbanisation many of us have lost regular connection with the countryside where these energies are easily tapped. However, once reconnected with the natural world, the buried knowledge rapidly returns. Many people say that when they use herbs, flowers or trees for spellcasting, they know instinctively what to do and what to say.

Because folk magic based on the natural world is common to every land and age, there is a great deal of ritual knowledge that has attached itself to particular plants and trees. So simply by touching or holding them, this wisdom becomes instantly accessible, like opening a zip file on a computer. In ritual we unite the inner world we experience during meditation with the outer world by the actions we perform, the words we say and the materials we use. The oak tree and rosemary, for example, hold the cumulative energies of the men and women from different lands and ages who have danced around oak groves or made rosemary sachets to attract new love.

Each plant has its own symbolism that can be used to galvanise and direct our natural psychokinetic energies to bring love, abundance, success, health and harmony into our lives and to places and people in need.

Herbs

Dried herbs can be placed in small purses or sachets made by tying or sewing up a rectangle of cloth. The herbs can be empowered to amplify their specific powers. One way that this is done is to crush them in a mortar and pestle, or by using a ceramic bowl and wooden or toughened glass/Pyrex spoon, while chanting with increasing speed and intensity the purpose for which the herbs will be used, such as: 'Rosemary, rosemary bring me a faithful lover.' When the herbs lose their fragrance they can be scattered to the four winds or buried. More herbs can be empowered in a ritual as before, so that you have fresh ones to add to the sachet or purse, if you need to carry the sachet for a number of months for an ongoing need. Below are some other ideas for using herbs:

✦ You can use fresh or dried culinary herbs in food or as teas. In this way you will absorb the magic in an age-old tradition.

✦ Empower pots or bunches of fresh herbs by placing them on a table in front of a lighted candle of the appropriate colour (see pages 95–102) until it has burned down. They will protect your home and attract love, luck, good health and money. One age-old spell involves surrounding a pot of basil with coins and allowing the wax from a lighted green candle to drip on to them. The coins are then buried in the compost surrounding the plant. As the plant grows, the spellcaster visualises the coins growing into large quantities of money.

✦ Strained infusions and decoctions (see below) can be added to hot water for use as protective floor washes. You can then marry your inner powers by *seeing* the darkness of sorrow, quarrels and disappointments being collected in the bucket and then tipped away. The infusions can also be sprinkled around the home, possessions or workplace, or even over people to bring protection, attract good luck, success, health or healing, according to the properties of the herb used to make the infusion.

✦ Strained infusions can also be added to a bath to give confidence, increase inner radiance, bring personal harmony or give courage, depending on the herb used. We already possess these qualities as part of our psychological/psychic make-up, but they may never have developed or may have become depleted by events in life or negative people or situations. An essential part of psychic development is to strengthen our minds and spirits so that our natural positive qualities can shine through and be amplified at times when they are needed.

✦ You can bind firm herbs in bunches or around a circle of wire, then hang them to dry from the ceiling or over doors. They can then be made into amulets tied with protective red thread. Replace the herbs when they crumble. Dried seed-heads of dill hung over doorways and above cradles, or scattered around the boundaries of the home, offer protection from malevolence and envy.

Preparing infusions

Delicate leaves and blossoms are best infused to prevent their healing powers being destroyed. It is important to chant over them as you stir, as previously described for sachets. You can use herbal teas or tea bags; if at the workplace, stir your tea while chanting its magical purpose in your mind. This applies at home or in a café if you need instant protection from an intrusive or critical visitor or a sudden boost of confidence, clarity of thought and communication, an injection of good luck or whatever is the sudden or urgent need.

You can make an infusion to focus specific energies in a cup, a tea pot or a jug according to the amount of liquid you will need, whether to add to a bath, sprinkle around a whole house, wash a floor or drink at your morning break. Whether you are making a few drops or a whole jug full you chant over it in exactly the same way and for the same time.

✦ To make an infusion place one teaspoon of dried herbs or three teaspoon-fuls of fresh herbs in a cup and pour on boiling water. Cover with a saucer and allow to stand for five to ten minutes without stirring, then strain.

✦ For enough to add to water to wash a floor for example, use 30 grams (1 ounce) of the plant substance to 600 millilitres (1 pint) of water. By experimenting and reducing the quantities proportionately, you can create infusions for any magical need.

✦ Stir the infusion, chanting to empower the herbs.

✦ Let the solution stand for five to ten minutes, stirring occasionally.

✦ After this time has elapsed, strain the infusion and use the liquid. Bury the herbs, or if this is not possible, put them in a biodegradable bag with a sprinkling of salt to psychically purify them, and dispose of them with your domestic rubbish.

Preparing decoctions

A decoction is a method of extracting healing and magical agents, usually from roots and bark. These are the stuff of witch's brews, as they need constant stirring.

✦ The roots or bark should be powdered. You can buy ready-crushed or pow-dered roots and bark or crush them yourself using a mortar and pestle. This is also wonderful for reducing frustration. Add 30 grams (1 ounce) of the prepared roots or bark to 600 millilitres (1 pint) of cold water. Leave to stand overnight before brewing.

✦ Simmer the mixture until the water is reduced by half.

✦ Strain before using and squeeze the herb to remove all the liquid. Discard the used herbs as for an infusion.

Herb safety

The following are some of the herbs that should be avoided during pregnancy; this does not represent a comprehensive list. Check with a herbalist or pharmacist before using any substance when pregnant, especially in the early months.

Aloe vera (*Aloe vera*)

Angelica (*Angelica archangelica*)

Autumn crocus (*Colchicum*)

Barberry (*Berberis*)

Basil (*Ocimum basilicum*)

Caraway (*Carum cavi*)

Cayenne (*Capiscum frutescena*)

Cedarwood (*Cedrus*)

Clary sage (*Salvia argentia*)

Fennel (*Foeniculum vulgare*)

Fern (*Pteris Aquilina*)

Feverfew (*Tanacetum parthenium*)

Golden seal (*Hydrastis canadisis*)

Hyssop (*Hyssopus officinalis*)

Juniper (*Juniperus*)

Mandrake (*Mandragora*)

Marjoram (*Origanum* sp.)

Myrrh (*Commiphora myrrha*)

Parsley (*Petrosilinum*)

Pennyroyal (*Mentha pulegium*)

Pokeroot (*Phytolacca americana*)

Rosemary (*Rosmarinus*)

Rue (*Rutus*)

Sage (*Salvia*)

Southernwood (*Artemesia abrotanum*)

Tansy (*Tanacetum vulgare*)

Tarragon (*Artemesia dracunculus*)

Thuja (*Thuja occidentalis*)

Thyme (*Thymus*)

Wintergreen (*Gaultheria procumbens*)

Wormwood (*Artemesia*)

Yarrow (*Achillea*)

Do not take any herb in large quantities or for prolonged periods.

Herbs and spices and their psychic properties

The magical properties of herbs and spices can be accessed in several ways: in a bath, drunk as an infusion, hung outside the home or sealed in a sachet. Flowers, berries or leaves can be made into an infusion; use the bark or roots as a decoction.

Some uses of herbs follow with suggestions where the herb can be taken as a decoction or infusion. Those listed in this way can be drunk as a tea or added to a bath but do check with a herbalist or pharmacist or refer to a detailed herb book if you have any chronic medical conditions, are breastfeeding or before giving them to children or the elderly. You need only drink or add to your bath a very small quantity of infusion or decoction to absorb a magical effect and should monitor yourself for any signs of skin irritation or stomach problems.

Agrimony (*Agrimonia eupatoria*)

Good for psychic protection, it will return negative energies to the sender. Use it in a herbal protection purse or sachet and as an ingredient in a sleep sachet underneath your pillow for pleasant dreams. Can be used as an infusion. Ruled by Jupiter.

Allspice (*Pimenta dioica*)

A herb for healing all aspects of life, allspice can be burned as incense or sprinkled in a candle flame to attract good luck and money. Use also in cooking or to fill tiny love purses or sachets to attract passion; they can be carried or placed under a pillow. Can also be taken as an infusion. Ruled by Mars.

Aloe vera (*Aloe vera*)

Protective; keep as a house or office plant to bring luck, success and prosperity and to guard the home and tools used for work against malevolence of all kinds. Ruled by the Moon.

Angelica (*Angelica archangelica*)

Bringing energy, health and long life, angelica offers protection especially for children, when worn or carried as an amulet, in a purse or woven and tied around a small ring. Grow in the garden or a window box to defend the boundaries of the home. It can also be eaten in the form of a cake decoration, or use the leaves in salad, or as an infusion or decoction. Ruled by the Sun.

Anise/Aniseed (*Pimpinellla anisum*)

Offers protection against all negative influences. Keep pots of the plant or dried anise in the kitchen to deter intruders. A sachet or potpourri of anise in the bedroom prevents bad dreams. Use with bay leaves (see page 16) in ritual baths; can also be taken as an infusion. Ruled by Jupiter.

Basil (*Ocimum basilicum*)

This is a herb of love and fidelity. It can be scattered around a lover's possessions, or a few grains can be hidden in their case if they are going away. In a pot it will attract abundance and prosperity to the home and success to the workplace. Carry a basil leaf with your money or credit cards to attract wealth. It can be used as an infusion as well as in cooking. Hung or grown in the home or outside, it protects against intruders from the winged-insect variety to human predators. Ruled by Mars.

Bistort (*Polygonum bistorta*)

As a herb of fertility, the empowered root of bistort can be made into a talisman for women who want to have a baby, or for anyone who is seeking to bring an idea or project to fruition. An infusion of bistort sprinkled near the doorway of a house will deter those who come with malice in their hearts. Burned as an incense with frankincense, bistort increases psychic awareness and divinatory powers. Use as a decoction. Ruled by Saturn.

Borage (*Borago officinalis*)

This is the herb of courage and protection. The flowers can be worn or dried for potpourri or empowered sachets. Borage guards against the dangers of the external world, especially on potentially hazardous journeys or in lonely places, so carry a tiny purse of borage with you at such times. As an infusion, it increases psychic awareness. Ruled by Mars.

Burdock (*Arctium*)

The herb burdock repels negativity and heals the wounds of betrayal or loss if gathered or empowered during the waning Moon; when picked or empowered on the waxing Moon it enhances passion and sexuality. Use as an infusion. Ruled by the Moon.

Caraway (*Carum cavi*)

The seeds of caraway are effective as protection against theft and vandalism. A tiny empowered sachet hidden with valuable items is a traditional way of protecting them. The sachet can also be glued to security tags attached to the item to be protected. The seeds are an aphrodisiac and so can kindle or rekindle passion. Eat the empowered seeds: use on bread, in cooking and as infusions. Ruled by Mercury.

Catnip (*Nepeta cataria*)

This herb is especially healing for children and cats. Combined with rose petals, catnip makes a potent love sachet or potpourri. Place the dried leaves in your psychic journal to increase spiritual awareness, and float one or two on water used for scrying (see page 88). Grown around or near a home, catnip attracts good fortune and joy to the home and all within. It will also repel negativity. Use as an infusion. Ruled by Venus.

Chamomile (*Chamaemelum nobile*)

The most gentle and soothing of herbs, chamomile added to a bath will induce a meditative state, and will enhance self-love after betrayal and attract gentle love. It is good added to potpourri, and used in pots or dried around the home, or as a chamomile lawn for bringing abundance and family happiness. Chamomile is also protective and deters those who would do harm. Use as infusions, even for the young. Ruled by the Sun.

Fennel (*Foeniculum vulgare*)

From Roman times fennel has been the herb of courage and stamina. Eat the seeds for enhancing courage and mental clarity. Fennel hung in the home or grown outside in a protective border also brings protection from unwanted visitors of all kinds and from malevolence. It is especially protective for babies and young children. Use as an infusion. Ruled by Mercury.

Fenugreek (*Trigonella foenumgraecum*)

This herb is associated with prosperity. Place a few seeds of fenugreek in an open jar on a kitchen shelf or in your hearth on the day of a new Moon. Add a few seeds each day until the jar is full. Plant the seeds in the garden or a window box to ensure your money supply will continue to grow, and then begin a new jar of seeds. Ruled by Saturn.

Garlic (*Allium sativum*)

Hung in the kitchen on strings or ropes, garlic bulbs keep away hostile influences, natural and supernatural. A clove of garlic placed on the sill of an open window at Hallowe'en traditionally ensures only family ghosts will return to the home on this day of the ancestors. Use in food for protection against gossip and spite. Wild garlic makes a good protective boundary. Ruled by Mars.

Hyssop (*Hyssopus officinalis*)

The biblical herb hyssop is one of purification; sprinkle the infusion to improve the atmosphere in rooms after quarrels or sorrow and also to cleanse artefacts acquired from others or used in psychic work. Ruled by Jupiter.

Lavender (*Lavandula*)

Sweet-smelling lavender can be added to any sachet or potpourri, for it has calming and restorative properties and promises a gradual and gentle improvement in health and happiness. Use dried empowered lavender heads in bowls around the home to encourage a calm, non-confrontational atmosphere. A tiny bowl at work serves the same purpose. Lavender in sachets or in the bath attracts gentle lovers. Burn a lavender-fragranced candle and make a wish, dropping a single flower-head in the flame for each wish. Use as an infusion. Ruled by Mercury.

Parsley (*Petrosilinum*)

A divinatory herb, parsley is said to encourage fertility, love and passion (for scrying with parsley, see page 88). Use it in cooking or eat raw for prophetic powers and sweet breath. In traditional magic, dolls were filled with parsley and kept in the home or workplace to deter or return malice and spite. It is also useful planted in a protective boundary. Use as an infusion. Ruled by Mercury.

Peppermint (*Mentha – piperata*)

This is a good herb for anyone who needs to travel by any form of transport and should be added to car sachets for children. It is good for preventing road-rage attacks and accidents. Burned as incense, used as an infusion on floors or sprinkled around the home, it will clean away negativity and drive away illness. Ruled by Venus.

Rose (*Rosa*)

Like lavender, rose is an essential ingredient in healing and stress-reducing sachets or purses or in potpourri, relieving exhaustion and calming hyperactivity in adults and children. Roses are used in love rituals. To attract new love, scatter tiny roses across a map showing your home to cover as wide an area as you wish. While you do this, chant: 'Love come, come to me, if it is right to be.' Use rose petals as an infusion, rose hips for a decoction. Ruled by Venus.

Rosemary (*Rosmarinus*)

This is another divinatory herb that is effective for scrying. Sprigs of rosemary, a small handful of chopped herbs in a bag or a strained rosemary infusion are traditionally added to a bath to increase clarity of thought and improve memory. Circle a book whose contents you need to memorise, or your computer, with three clockwise circles of rosemary, chanting: 'Rosemary, rosemary, thus I turn, rosemary, rosemary so I learn.'

Tiny cloth dolls without features were once stuffed with dried empowered rosemary and tied together with red twine to attract a lover or make one remain faithful. Add to cooking for increased passion. Ruled by the Sun.

Sage (*Salvia officinalis*)

A popular culinary herb, sage is the herb of long life and good health whether grown in pots, in the garden, used in cooking or made into an infusion. Like rosemary, sage improves concentration, so it is ideal in sachets for people under pressure from examinations or at work; its powers are heightened when mixed with rosemary.

As a divinatory herb, sage can be used in scrying or burned as incense to increase psychic awareness and allow glimpses of past and future. Ruled by Jupiter.

Sagebrush: California white sage (*Salvia alpiana*), Western grey sage (*Artemisia tridentata*)

Western grey and California white sage are two species of sagebrush that have larger leaves than culinary sage. They are traditional smudge materials – cleansing, healing, protective and empowering – and can be used in any kind of ritual. They can be burned as smudge sticks, or as leaves in a flat ceramic bowl. Sagebrush is ruled by the Sun, although some people use the grey sages for female rituals, in which instances they become linked with the Moon.

Sweetgrass (*Hierochloe odorata*)

Another traditional Native North American smudge and Mother Goddess herb, this is usually burned as a braid or as strands in a ceramic bowl, bringing healing, gentle empowerment, beauty, harmony and abundance in all its forms. The braids are also hung unburned over doorways for protection. However, grey sage is an easier Mother Goddess herb to burn. Ruled by the Moon.

Thyme (*Thymus*)

A divinatory herb used in scrying, thyme is also burned as incense, creating a powerful pathway to the past (see page 176) and also towards the future. Use in cooking or as an infusion for courage and improved mental acuity. Occasionally you can buy broad-leaved thyme that can be used for smudging lit in a ceramic bowl. Ruled by Venus.

Yarrow (*Achillea*)

The herb of marriage and fidelity, yarrow is traditionally kept in a sachet or purse from the wedding day for seven years and replaced just before the seventh year is over. Thereafter every seven years throughout married life a new sachet is prepared and kept. Burn as a smudge stick to banish fear, or use as an infusion sprinkled around the home to deter all forms of negativity, especially jealousy. Ruled by Venus.

Magical Ritual and Spellcasting

Mind-power that is focused and strengthened through ritual uses magic to bring a particular wish or intention into the material world. It involves the use of a variety of tools and substances, both natural and man-made, as foci for the energies. These rituals are sometimes called spellcasting, making the all-important link to the mind of the caster as the primary force behind magic.

A spell can be as simple as writing down a desire or intention on a piece of paper, reading it aloud or creating a chant from it and then burning the paper in a candle flame to release the powers into the cosmos. When joined with cosmic energy, our own released power can form the impetus to achieve the desired result.

There are a number of kinds of magic that are common to all ages and cultures, although in modern magic we no longer summon spirits to do our bidding. Nor do we use dark powers to obtain what we desire or to curse others, even those who have done great wrong. We prefer to allow natural justice to take its course. For magic, like all psychic work, operates under the principle that you should harm no one and that every action or thought returns threefold to the sender. So magic must only be used with positive intent and for a real personal need, or for the good of others or the ecosystem.

When using magic, you should always end requests by stating that whatever you do should be for the highest good, whether you call this power Divinity, the god/dess or light. Remember, of course, that you can carry out any or all of the following stages using visualisation and psychokinetic powers (see pages 52 and 56).

Some people find the idea of spellcasting strange. If this is the case for you, you will find that the process is similar to the stages of visualisation except that you manipulate the energies to increase the power, giving it a kind of catapult effect to bring thought into actuality. You sometimes see small children muttering a phrase over and over again with great concentration, willing their wishes to come true.

My own problem with using only visualisation and not using actual tools, words or actions is that the amount of energy expended by inner work alone is very great and you may tire yourself and actually deplete your psychic stores.

Sympathetic Magic

This involves performing a ritual that acts out what you want to bring into the real world, endowing your thought form with structure and energy generated by the ritual. So if you want a baby, you might create a tiny cradle, place a doll inside and keep it by your bed when making love. You might also use a fertility symbol, such as an egg, and prick it gently with a needle before making love at the time of a full Moon. This cycle of the Moon is the period of peak fertility (see page 145), and the use of the egg is to emulate the sperm and ovum coming together in sexual intercourse.

Contagious Magic

In contagious magic, power is transferred and absorbed directly from an animal, bird, crystal, metal, the wax of an empowered candle or the earth. This principle is central to the potency of talismans and amulets. Traditionally, hunters might wear the pelt of a lion to bring them the beast's courage and ferocity. You might, less dramatically, soak a clear crystal quartz in water for eight hours and then drink or bath in the water that contains the psychic energy and health-bringing properties of the crystal.

Attracting magic

When both sympathetic and contagious magic are combined to bring you something you desire, this is known as attracting magic. You might tip a small quantity of salt, which is the symbol of healing, into flowing water to imitate the flow of better health into your life. You could write a wish on your computer screen and increase the size of the words or image until they fill the whole screen, saying: 'Grow and increase ever be, wish fulfilled come now to me.'

Banishing magic

Driving away negative feelings, fears, bad habits and influences by casting away or burying a focus of the negativity is called banishing magic. One way this can be done is to etch an image or word that represents what you want to lose on to a stone, then to bury it. You could also cast a dying flower on to the ebbing tide or leave a chalk drawing out in the rain to dissolve.

Binding magic

If you were binding another to you in fidelity or preventing someone from harming children or animals, or from destroying a place of beauty, you would use binding magic. This is a more complex ritual although the mechanics themselves are easy enough. Take the fidelity issue. You could, for example, join two small dolls together with three knots of red twine while chanting such words as: 'Three times the lover's knot secure. Firm be the knot, firm the love endure,' and keep them in a circle of rose petals. I would, however, want to allow for free will by adding something like: 'Come my love and stay with me, if it is right to be.'

When binding magic is used against someone who is doing harm, however, all you can do under the threefold return of energies is to create a featureless clay image (no pins or melting black wax) and gently wrap it in pink silk, then rest it in a drawer, saying: 'Naught harm thee, peace calm thee, rest in peace, anger cease.' You are thus binding the oppressor with love and kindness, and by the threefold law of receiving what you send out, he or she should stop being spiteful and send out more peaceful vibes in your direction or that of the victim in future. You are also neutralising the unhappiness that may be causing the attacker to be unkind.

The Four Stages of Magic

Both informal spells and more formal magical practices tend to follow four stages, although you may combine one or more of them. They mirror those of visualisation, but magic is more active and so can be used for a very urgent need or a major project that will need lots of energy to manifest it as actuality.

1. The focus

This defines the purpose of the ritual or spell and is generally represented either by a symbol or symbols, or a declaration of intent. The symbol could be a candle etched with an image of the need, the name of the person the candle represents, or a zodiacal Sun-sign glyph to indicate the connection with the person. Alternatively, you might use a silver key charm or an actual door key in a spell to find a new home, a picture of a projected ideal holiday location, a pot of herbs or a crystal for improving health or for the protection of a particular person. After the spell is complete you can give the herbs or crystal to the person on whose behalf the spell was cast.

At the beginning of the ritual, visualise a circle of light around yourself and anyone else present, or draw one clockwise using a lighted incense or smudge stick, beginning in the north. Hold the symbol and name aloud the intention of the ritual, defining it quite clearly. If you are working in a group, the symbol can be passed from person to person, while each adds a personal slant to the spell.

2. The action

This is the stage where you use actions to endow the symbol/s with magical energies and to intensify the focus. This is part of the continuous process of translating your magical thoughts and words from the first stage of planning in your mind to manifestation. For since both thought and matter are energy, when you stir the energies you make the translation between the two easier.

For example, you could increase the power of the symbol by adding to it the power of the four elements to create the fifth element in which magic can take place (for explanation of the elements, see pages 134–42). So, you might sprinkle the focus with salt to represent the practical manifestation of the desire through the energy of the earth joined to your own practical efforts. You would then encircle it with the smoke of an incense stick – for air – for the power of the mind through psychokinesis, to move the desired result either from one place to another or from thought towards actuality. Then you would pass it through a candle flame, or circle a candle flame around it, to give the focus clarity and the spark to create the necessary energy for fulfilment of the ritual through fire. Finally, you would sprinkle it with water for the water element, to enable the energies on the thought plane to flow into actuality.

An alternative way to get the energies circulating is by chanting or singing words that express the wish. This can be combined with a slow spiral dance around the circle or symbol. A drum or rattle could also be used to add a rhythmic pattern that will help you to relax to a slower mindset and so allow the psychic part of your mind to take charge. If you are working with a group, holding hands in a circle enables you to pass the power clockwise from one to the other so that it gains in intensity.

3. Raising the power

This is the most powerful part of the spell, as the magical energies are amplified. You may find that the power of the ritual carries you along and that the energies all around become fluid. At this stage you could repeat the chant, dance faster or drum with greater intensity. While doing this you could also visualise a cone of spiralling coloured light rising and increasing in size and intensity over the centre of the circle, enclosing the focus, which glows bright and reveals pulsating cells of light.

Extend your hands vertically as high as possible to absorb power from the cosmos. If you have been linking hands in a group, when the power increases to a great intensity loosen them. Allow the sparks of energy to leap from one hand to the other as the cone becomes higher and encloses the spellcaster/s and fills with coloured stars, whirling faster and faster at its point.

4. Releasing the power

When you release the power in the final stage, you may see the cone exploding and cascading as coloured stars or light beams, surging away into the cosmos and breaking into brilliant rainbow colours. The release may also take the form of a final shout or a leap, or perhaps you suddenly extinguish a central candle or candles that represent the person or people for whom the spell is cast – ensure a background candle remains alight if working by night.

Grounding the power

Sit or lie on the ground, allowing excess energy to flow into the earth. If working with friends, enjoy a simple meal while still in the circle. Uncast the circle by walking anticlockwise from the north, visualising the light fading, and saying: 'Though the circle is uncast, let it remain unbroken in our hearts and in our lives.' Then clear and wash any tools and sit quietly, making plans for bringing the aim to fruition by earthly efforts.

Scrying

The interpretation of images or symbols in a reflective medium is known as scrying. The medium can be a crystal ball, mirror or a naturally moving source of inspiration, such as fire, water or clouds. Scrying has been practised in every age and culture.

You have already worked at developing the psychic senses that will come into play when scrying. The main psychic sense is, of course, clairvoyance – seeing images that connect with some inner need in your life, either in your mind's vision or externally in the reflective surface. However, you may also hear words – either externally or with your inner ear – experience sensations and smell fragrances. These multi-sensory experiences are especially common if you are touching a crystal as you scry.

Candles can be lit when scrying. However, although they are potent, the best methods of scrying in my own experience are those that use mediums that are endowed with the life-force, especially herbs and crystals. With all forms of scrying, if you are giving a divinatory reading for someone else, ask for their interpretation of the images as you work so that they can contribute to the psychic picture. This will then link to their own inner symbol system, as symbols have unique significance for each person.

You can prepare for scrying in a number of ways: by taking a ritual bath, or by lighting incense in a room and sitting in it by candlelight or natural light and stilling your mind. Some people begin with a prayer when they ask for the protection of the benign forces of light, and state that their work will be for the highest good. Others, however, believe that if this intent is in our heart then no words are necessary.

Creating a Personal Symbol System

In all the following methods, you will see images that will spontaneously suggest relevance to the question you asked. A symbol system is never fixed, but most people's systems have common factors, based on what Jung called archetypes – meanings that have held true in many times and places. Examples are butterflies as symbols of happiness and regeneration; falling leaves as symbols of the end of an era; huge mountains to be climbed for obstacles to be overcome; a fluttering moth that does not hold still as a permanence you crave but which may not be right at this stage of your life. Symbols may appear in dreams as well as through scrying, and we all have a core set of personal symbols that recur throughout stages of our lives in both dreams and actuality (see pages 162–63).

I have not given a comprehensive list of symbol meanings as I think it is important to have the confidence to create your own.

✦ Start an alphabetical list in the loose-leaf part of your folder or use a word processor so that the entries can be updated.

✦ Each time you carry out a divination, write down or draw the symbol and what it meant in the context of the reading.

✦ Note with stars or marks any symbols that turn up regularly.

✦ When you have time, sit in your special place, relax and still your mind, and then select a symbol at random from your list and write down all the things you associate with it – positive as well as negative. Some may merit a page or more, others a few lines.

+ Buy representations of key symbols, use pictures, or visualise your symbol and use it as a focus for meditation.

+ If any symbols seem especially significant, research the mythology and folklore behind them.

+ Use clay, paint, write poetry or create songs or dances to explore the image.

+ With animals or birds, a recurring symbol may indicate this is your personal power or totem creature whose qualities and strengths reflect and can strengthen your own. In all indigenous societies totem animals are an important source of wisdom for each individual and also act as a guardian in out-of-body travel and in dreams.

Herb Scrying

This is similar to tea-leaf and coffee-ground reading, but is much older and more versatile. Given the revival in popularity of herbal brews it is likely to become the new method of scrying with leaves. You can use any herbs that do not stain the water too darkly and you should use the dried leaves or flowers. Parsley, sage, rosemary and thyme are the traditional divinatory herbs, but you can also work with lavender and chamomile flowers, basil and tarragon. Experiment and you may find herbs that work well for you. Strained mugwort infusion is traditionally used for staining the water for scrying by candlelight.

+ For the best effect, add boiling water to a teaspoonful of dried herbs in a white or clear glass heatproof cup. The latter has the advantage that you can study the images from above and the side. Ask a question or state an area of concern.

+ Almost immediately, some herbs will form an image on the surface. Close your eyes, open them, blink and say out loud what the image is. You have only a few seconds before the rational mind interferes. This first image defines the true issue or question, which may be very different from the one you thought you were asking. Do not analyse the image.

+ While the water is still fairly clear, you will see a second image in the bottom of the cup. Again, close your eyes, then open them. Blink and name the image.

✦ This will tell you what the best action is, or alternatively, if inaction is better.

✦ Now stir and either drink the tea unstrained, allowing your mind to work on the images without any conscious input or analysis and leaving a small amount of liquid in the bottom; or if you prefer, drain away the tea with a saucer on top, leaving only a tiny amount of liquid.

✦ Either way, swirl the remaining liquid three times clockwise, then invert the cup on the saucer and turn it three times anticlockwise.

✦ You should now have a number of leaf images on the sides and bottom of the cup.

✦ Holding the handle towards you, read the images clockwise starting with those nearest the bottom and working around the cup segment by segment. These images will tell you the likely outcome of any action or inaction and may form a story or timeline from where you are now.

✦ You can read tea leaves and coffee grounds in the same way, starting with the swirling of the cup, as the liquid is too dark to read in the earlier stages. Again, use the blinking method to get clear instant answers.

If you give the images free rein, they will interpret themselves in the context of your current needs and situation.

Scrying in Water

Water is one of the oldest forms of scrying, and because of its fluidity is especially good for obtaining a series of images or for capturing less tangible emotions, albeit fleetingly and in symbolic form.

Using inks

This is a very popular method that originated in the Middle East. It is one of the most exciting forms of scrying since it relies on moving images that can change during the reading, therefore giving a series of meanings.

✦ Add water to a clear glass or a wide, deep white bowl and squeeze either calligraphy or permanent ink cartridges directly into the water drop by drop. Alternatively, a brush or dropper can be used to add the inks, one or two drops at a time. The key to success is to use the ink sparingly, so if you are carrying out readings for others, practise beforehand. You can use different coloured inks, but in practice black or dark blue is best.

✦ Ask a question or allow your mind to go blank as you drip the ink, a drop at a time, on to the surface. You should get two or three images before the water becomes coloured, and these will form a sequence that represents either three steps on your life path or three salient factors you need to note.

✦ Afterwards draw the shapes in your journal, along with any impressions they created, whether as images in words or feelings.

✦ You may dream of your symbols or see them in your everyday life, perhaps in an unusual setting. This, according to the psychologist, Jung, demonstrates the interconnectedness of different levels of existence and the importance of paying attention to symbols in dreams and divination as a way of understanding the meaning of our lives (see also page 38).

Using water and candlelight

A common method of using candlelight and water is by staining the water dark, either with mugwort or black ink, and placing a horseshoe of pure white or beeswax candles behind the bowl so the light shines on to the water.

✦ If you work near an open window or on a sheltered balcony or patio, the breeze will create patterns on the water. The ancients scryed in lakes with either moonlight or sunlight shining on the water and trees overhanging it to create patterns. If you can do this then you will find that the images are very vivid.

✦ If scrying with a bowl and candles, stir the water with a clear quartz crystal wand or a twig from one of the magical trees, such as elder, rowan or willow, each time before reading an image on the water.

✦ If you find it difficult to discern images, look through half-closed eyes and concentrate on the patterns of light, seeing what feelings or ideas they evoke. Continue until no more images can be discerned.

Using water and wax

This is my own favourite form of scrying, and if you find using light and water hard, try this and then return to light and water scrying at a later time.

✦ Use a glass bowl of clear water and position a horseshoe of four candles in strong colours, for example bright red, blue, orange and green, behind the bowl. For the best effect, use candles where the colour penetrates right through to the wick.

✦ Light the candles, naming your question/s for each, and then focus on the candlelit water but without trying to discern any images.

✦ Allow your mind to go blank and merge with the water.

✦ Taking the first candle in your receptive hand and the second in your power hand, shake a few drops of the wax from each simultaneously on to the surface of the water.

✦ Rapidly take the third and fourth candles and add their wax to the water. You will need to be very fast in order to read an image before the wax sets.

✦ At first you may find it easier to read two separate images as you add the two sets of wax. These often refer to the aspects of the current situation that are changing or new opportunities opening.

✦ When the wax sets, you will obtain a second more permanent image referring to several months ahead. Some people are able to interpret a whole scene in the hardened wax.

✦ You can add fresh wax at any time as the first is hardening to create an interim image of potentially fruitful avenues.

Using Crystal Spheres

When scrying with crystal spheres the process is much slower and involves stilling the mind and allowing images to form almost unbidden in the quietness. Breathe in gently, drawing the crystalline energies of the sphere around you and visualising the walls of crystal enclosing you. Sense your own boundaries melting so that you merge with the crystal's energies and feel as though you are within it, cool and gently vibrating with its slow, rhythmic pulse.

Clear crystal quartz spheres are good for scrying, but choose one with inclusions, as this will be more evocative for visions. You can also use deep blue beryl, known as the stone of the seer – the oldest form of scrying crystal – pale amethyst or pale rose quartz, again with inclusions. While you are scrying, you may hear snatches of songs or poetry, phrases or just a single word in your mind's ear through clairaudience, for the psychic senses are closely related.

✦ Light a candle or work in natural sunlight or moonlight so the light is reflected in the sphere.

✦ Sit for a minute or two holding the sphere with your eyes closed while you connect, and if you are reading for someone else ask him or her to hold the sphere at the same time to establish connection.

✦ Talk gently either aloud to yourself or ask the subject about his or her feelings. Let the power flow between you both or from the ball to yourself and back again, if you are reading for yourself.

✦ You may receive a number of impressions through your fingertips and inner ear. Recently I have moved away from my original method of obtaining three images to an ongoing stream of images and feelings.

✦ Open your eyes and, while the person and yourself are still making contact, start to talk. Make a tape recording of the session if working alone and if desired by your subject when reading for another.

✦ Whether you believe you are receiving insights from an angelic or higher guide (see pages 229–30) or by the connection between yourself and the crystal in its most evolved and perfect shape, you will be amazed by the fluency and accuracy of your words, even with a perfect stranger.

✦ If you empty your mind of conscious thought and allow the images, sounds, fragrances and feelings to flow, the words will be quite spontaneous and can be inspiringly prophetic.

✦ The reading is usually couched in symbols, animals, birds, butterflies, mountains and seas, and you may both experience sounds and fragrances, as these psychic creations are multi-sensory.

✦ If reading for someone else, he or she may also contribute images or interpret what you have seen.

The Next Step

There is no limit to the media with which you can scry: clouds, mirrors or flickering flames. Once you begin scrying the whole world becomes a source of magical images. Psychic development moves between inner and outer worlds, although the two move closer as you evolve. In the next chapter we will work with the energies within and beyond us, with colour and crystals and our own personal energy systems. This energy is fuelled and enhanced by contact with the energies of both Mother Earth and her rich store and the powers flowing from the cosmic life-force. You might like to pause before going on to reflect how your own energies are affected by other stimuli. People, the weather, what you eat and drink, colours, noise and any pollutants that are unavoidable in your current environment can all affect your energy. Similarly, there will be times when your energies have seemed to flow freely and others when you have felt blocked, knotted inside, or sluggish, and psychically as well as physically bloated.

Working with Energy

WE LIVE IN A VAST OCEAN of energy, sometimes called the universal energy field or life-force. It is made up of cosmic and earth energies, from planets and weather systems, and the energies of people, plants and trees, rocks, crystals, insects, birds and animals. Each of these has a personal microcosmic or mini-universal energy field. Science confirms what indigenous peoples have always known, not only that everything consists of energies rather than solid matter but also that these energies flow between people, animals, plants, rocks and crystals, the earth and cosmos in a continuous interchange.

There are many ways in which these energies can be categorised and channelled. One that links the powers of nature with personal energy systems is colour, so this is perhaps the best entry point into the whole field.

Colour

One of the most instantly recognisable and readily available sources of energy comes to us through colour. When we absorb the energies of a specific colour, it strengthens or endows us with a particular quality that we need. For example, yellow gives us the clear focus and concentration necessary to complete a project.

Colour magic and healing has a long history. The Babylonians called the healing power of light the medicine of the gods. Healing colours, especially those manifested in crystals, were used in Ancient Egypt and have been used for thousands of years in China and in the ayurvedic medicine of India.

What is Colour?

White light contains all the colours of the rainbow. This was proved by Sir Isaac Newton in 1665 when he beamed sunlight through a prism and saw that it split into seven colours: red, orange, yellow, green, blue, indigo, and violet. Each beam of coloured light has its own wavelength and is absorbed by the body through the skin and the optic nerves. This triggers complex biochemical changes. People who spend prolonged periods in darkness suffer from vitamin deficiencies, hormonal disorders and disturbances of the normal body cycles, including irregular sleep patterns, metabolic imbalances and depression. Seasonal affective disorder, or SAD, is caused by a lack of sunlight, and can trigger depression and lethargy during long, grey winter months.

Each of the seven primary wavelengths or vibrations of light visible to the human eye focuses on different parts of the body, evoking in them both a physiological and a psychological response. Red has the longest wavelength of visible colour and violet the shortest. The colours that we can see make up only a very small segment of the electromagnetic spectrum and lie between the infrared and ultra-violet rays. Black, the absence of colour, is associated with negativity, while white, the combination of all seven colours, was first associated with the godhead and purity by the Pythagoreans. The physical body is usually associated with red, the mind with yellow and the spirit with blue.

Colour Meanings in Magic and Healing

White

Magic and psychic development
White is the synthesis of the colours of the rainbow. It is associated with higher energies, increasing spiritual awareness, enhancing meditation and creating channels of light for contact with spirit guides, angels, Divinity and the

higher consciousness. White increases the flow of the life-force especially from cosmic sources and so is helpful where a new beginning, inspiration or a sudden burst of energy is needed.

Healing

White promotes healing of body, mind and spirit at all levels: white light is a natural pain reliever, increasing and maintaining energy levels and relieving depression and inertia. It also helps bone and tooth maintenance and dispels negativity from the body's energy field.

Gems and crystals

Calcite, diamond, clear fluorite, clear crystal quartz, zircon.

Red

Magic and psychic development

Red represents action, power, determination, physical energy and health, sexual passion and potency, survival and the impetus for positive change. It also offers courage to stand against injustice and inertia.

Healing

Red stimulates the entire system, instantly boosting energy levels and kick-starting a sluggish immune system. Red light is linked to reproduction and fertility and relieves menstrual problems and sexual dysfunction, especially impotence.

Gems and crystals

Blood agate, bloodstone, garnet, jasper, ruby.

Orange

Magic and psychic development

Orange enhances self-esteem and confidence, strengthening identity and creativity and establishing personal boundaries. Orange is the colour of joy and brings about the successful integration of all aspects of the personality into a harmonious whole.

Healing

A gentle energiser, orange warms aching limbs, boosting a weak pulse rate, relieving gall bladder and kidney problems, menstrual and muscle cramps and allergies. It also lifts exhaustion and is used to strengthen the immune system.

Gems and crystals

Amber, beryl, cornelian, jasper, sunstone.

Yellow

Magic and psychic development

Yellow sharpens logic, focus, and all aspects of conscious mind-power, including memory, learning, mental acuity and concentration; it strengthens willpower and enhances clear communication. Yellow will also aid any involvement with technology, job changes and overcoming money problems.

Healing

Yellow stimulates the nervous system, calms the digestive system and eases eczema and skin problems. It also promotes a healthy metabolism, and reduces anxiety and stress-related ailments that may adversely affect the digestive system. It balances emotions and strengthens an over-sensitive person.

Gems and crystals

Calcite, citrine, jasper, rutilated quartz, topaz.

Green

Magic and psychic development

Green increases the flow of love, empathy and compassion. It is also potent for working with the energies of nature, for healing the planet and especially the forests and the land. Because of its association with growth, green can be used for the gradual increase of all energies, especially wealth and resources, as well as good luck.

Healing

One of the most effective healing colours, green strengthens the heart, lungs and respiratory system and helps to fight infections and viruses. It also counters panic attacks and addictions. Green stimulates general body regeneration and is the colour for healing the planet, especially the earth and forests.

Gems and crystals

Aventurine, emerald, fluorite, jade, malachite, moss agate, tourmaline. (Safety note: malachite can be poisonous if taken internally so use another stone for small children and animals and do not add to water.)

Blue

Magic and psychic development

Blue brings an increase of existing opportunities, such as promotion in your current career or area of learning, expansion of business or social opportunities or a financial improvement based on past efforts. It is good for the voice and for clear communication and expression.

Blue enhances wisdom attained through experience and brings success in legal matters, dealings with officialdom, for justice and for situations where you would like or need to take the lead.

Healing

A blue aura is often seen around healers. Blue is a natural antiseptic, soothing and cooling, relieving headaches and migraines, eye strain, earache and sore throats. It can be used in rituals to heal air pollution and polluted seas.

Gems and crystals

Blue-lace agate, laboradite, lapis lazuli, sapphire, turquoise.

Purple

Magic and psychic development

Purple represents unconscious wisdom and is used for all things of a psychic and spiritual nature and for divination. It provides a link with higher dimensions and aids meditation, past-life work, candle and mirror scrying and astral travel. It also provides psychic protection.

Healing

Purple is especially potent for healing the spirit, banishing what lies in the past. An all-healer, purple relieves allergies, asthma, sleep disorders, eye, ear, nose and skin problems and migraines, and is a natural sedative. It eases neuroses and obsessions and can aid in childbirth.

Gems and crystals

Amethyst, fluorite, kunzite, sodalite, sugilite.

Pink

Magic and psychic development

Pink encourages gentleness and kindness in family relationships and friendship. It will help with all dealings with children and to foster the growth of new love and trust after betrayal or a setback. Pink is especially good for healing past hurts, for quiet sleep and for mending quarrels. It also increases the general flow of love and compassion.

Healing

The gentle healer, pink brings relief from ear and gland problems, head pains and psychosomatic illnesses, as well as all disorders relating to children and babies. It is especially good for adolescent girls, and pregnant and menopausal women.

Gems and crystals

Coral, kunzite, rose quartz, sugilite, tourmaline.

Brown

Magic and psychic development

Brown brings physical as well as psychic protection and aids all practical matters, concerning material resources, the home, property matters and security, and learning new skills, especially later in life. It is also the colour of Mother Earth and the earth spirits and therefore is good for environmental matters and conservation.

Healing

Brown absorbs pain and sorrow, increases physical energy and primal strength, and relieves disorders connected with the feet, legs, hands and skeleton, back pain and the large intestine. It is especially good for healing animals and the earth.

Gems and crystals

Banded agate, desert rose, rutilated quartz, smoky quartz, tiger's eye.

Grey

Magic and psychic development

The colour of smudge smoke, grey is very protective against physical, mental or psychic attack. It is used primarily for neutralising or erasing negative energies or feelings. It is the shade of compromise and adaptability.

Healing

Grey is good for healing the immune system and for calming stress and fears, giving peaceful dreams and helping the subconscious mind to work though conflicts.

Gems and crystals

Apache tears (obsidian), banded agate, haematite laboradite, smoky quartz.

Black

Magic and psychic development

Associated negatively and often erroneously with evil, black is the colour not only of death, but also of regeneration. This belief goes back to Ancient Egypt when the annual flooding of the Nile carried with it black silt which brought new life to the land each year. Black can be used for banishing negativity, for leaving behind old sorrows and redundant relationships and for acknowledging grief.

Healing

Black heals the feet, legs and bones. It also helps to leave behind old stresses and anxieties, and to heal trauma. It encourages rest, cures insomnia and assists in working through loss. It is rarely used in healing, and when used it is followed by the infusion of light, as it can bring out dormant depression unless used carefully. Breathing out darkness and breathing in light or colour is very restorative.

Gems and crystals

Jet, obsidian, smoky quartz, onyx.

Silver

Magic and psychic development

Silver is potent for all forms of divination – especially for candle divination – for awakening clairvoyant powers, telepathic and psychometric abilities, astral projection, rituals to invoke female/anima power, for intuition and mysticism. It represents dreams, visions and a desire for fulfilment beyond the material world. In times of stress and sorrow, silver can remove negativity, promote inner stability and bring to the fore a person's hidden potential.

Healing

Silver alleviates hormonal problems in men and women, regularising and healing the female menstrual and reproductive system and assisting in all matters of fertility. It also helps with water retention and nightmares.

Gems and crystals

Moonstones, whose colour deepens as the Moon waxes, haematite, mother-of-pearl, snow and milky quartz, rutilated quartz.

Gold

Magic and psychic development

The colour of perfection, visions and actions that change the world, gold is also important for bringing out qualities of altruism and nobility of spirit. It is potent for worldly achievement, wealth and recognition, and fulfilling major ambitious and money-making schemes that require an instant or major return.

Healing

Gold is especially potent for overcoming addictions, obsessions and compulsions and relieving depression. It is the most powerful healing colour of all, associated with long life and immortality, and will give a surge of healing energy in any chronic or debilitating illnesses.

Gems and crystals

Amber, golden tiger's eye, topaz, citrine.

Colour in Magic and Healing

Using the above list as a guide, you may know from the nature of a physical condition, emotional problem or need which colour you should use. Or you may instinctively feel drawn to wear a particular colour, or to carry a particular crystal. You may even wish to buy a bunch of coloured flowers that would not be your usual choice, to put on your desk at work. However, there are occasions when the choice of colour is not as straightforward, and sometimes a person may need two or three colours. Whatever form of colour magic or healing you are using, you can dowse for the best colour to use. You might like to take a few minutes stilling yourself before you begin and surround yourself with light or invoking benign/divine powers to help you.

Using a pendulum

+ To find the most appropriate colour, draw a circle on stiff card, and then divide it into ten segments to represent the colours on the diagram. You can colour each segment in its own colour or write the name of the colour. Cut out the circle.

+ Begin by stating the purpose for which the colour is needed, for example 'Which colour will relieve my insomnia?' It might be caused by a digestive problem, in which case the answer would be yellow or orange.

Colour circle

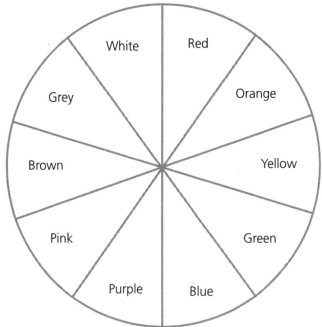

◆ Move the pendulum slowly clockwise over the circle asking it to show the colour most helpful for healing or magic.

◆ The pendulum may circle clockwise or pull down as if being dragged by gravity either over a single or two or three areas of colour.

◆ You could create a second circle chart including different methods that could be used with the colours, for example by using light from coloured candles or by adding coloured crystal water to a bath. You could then ask the pendulum to indicate the best colour treatment or stimulus.

Although I find the pendulum by far the most effective method, especially in the early stages, you could use one of the following as an alternative:

◆ Put a few crystals of each of the ten different colours into a bag and, without looking, pull out one to indicate the best colour to use. If you feel you need another colour, repeat the procedure.

◆ You can also close your eyes and visualise the colours you need, or hold the palm or index finger of your writing hand over a number of crystals placed in a circle. Your hand will be attracted by psychokinesis to the most suitable crystal for treatment.

◆ You can also rely on your inner voice to guide you to the colour.

Absorbing Colour

One of the best ways of absorbing colour energies is to keep water in coloured glass bottles. Although the water does not physically change colour, it absorbs the essential spiritual and magical energies inherent in colour.

◆ Use spring (still mineral) water.

◆ Place the water in a small, open, coloured pure-glass bottle, outdoors in a sheltered place. Leave it for a Sun and Moon 24-hour cycle (from dawn to following dawn or for the Celtic day: sunset to sunset).

◆ When the water is prepared, place a lid or cork in the bottle.

◆ Even a few drops will carry the essence – you do not need to use large quantities to achieve a greater effect.

◆ You can drink the water, add a few drops to a bath, splash it on pulse points at work or when travelling, or add a little when making tea, coffee or cold drinks. You can also add a drop or two to animal drinking bowls or when watering plants. It can be added to a polluted pond or river, or sprinkled on waste land, around your house boundaries or your workspace or even on the sea.

◆ To imbibe the energies of more than one colour simultaneously, either mix coloured waters in a bottle or place a crystal of a different colour in the closed bottle for a further eight hours.

◆ You can stand clear bottles on to coloured papers.

Crystalline Water

Coloured crystals can be added to an open clear-glass bottle of pure spring water and left outside from dawn to dusk on a single day. After this cork the bottle. You may detect a coloured aura around it after it has been energised.

While you can use absolutely any crystal to make water, in my experience the following stones are especially effective:

Agate
Whether single-coloured in blue, brown, black, orange, moss green, yellow or as banded varieties, agates bring stability, balance and reassurance in any crisis. Banded-agate water is especially good for pets, moss agate for plants and blue-lace agate water for gentle, honest communication.

Keep a dish of agates in water near your workspace to splash on your face and hands, as they are protective against industrial and any other pollution.

Amber
Water made with amber is deeply protective. Because amber is said to contain the souls of tigers and the power of the Sun over millions of years during its formation, it enables you to face obstacles and crises without panic and will, if taken over a period, increase self-love.

Amethyst
Water made with amethyst protects against and relieves stress-related conditions. It will also help to overcome food, alcohol or tobacco cravings. Added to a hot, bedtime drink it will prevent insomnia, or in a cold drink it will reduce irritability. It can also be massaged into the head and around the eyes to help a headache or migraine.

Calcite
In all its shades, transparent or semi-transparent, milky yellow, peach, green, white or clear, calcite water automatically restores harmony to the system, whether it be a person, animal or ecosystem. Green calcite is especially potent; it will detoxify people, animals, plants and places. Yellow is good for regenerating areas containing industrial waste. Use calcite water for absent healing by sprinkling it on a photograph of the sick person, animal or despoiled place.

Citrine
When made in sunlight from dawn to dusk, this Sun water will increase confidence and optimism. It is wonderful when prepared on the longest day of the year (around 21 June in the northern hemisphere and 21 December in the southern hemisphere) and then stored for dark winter days.

STEP 5

Jade

Traditionally in the Orient, water made with jade and drunk regularly will bring long life and improve and maintain health in animals and people. It is excellent poured on plants to revitalise them. Good for teenagers suffering identity crises or from raging hormones, jade water also calms fears and prevents overreaction under provocation.

Moonstone

Translucent moonstone water in gentle pastel shades is the alter ego of citrine Sun water. You can make your moonstone water by leaving a moonstone in a crystal bowl of water on the night of a full Moon so that the water turns silvery. Moonstone water in the bath is especially soothing for female stresses and mood swings, and for enhancing female fertility. Splash moonstone water in the centre of your brow to increase clairvoyant powers. For men, moonstone water encourages gentleness and the emergence of the anima/feminine energies.

Rose quartz

Rose quartz is the stone of gentle healing. Rose-quartz water can be added to a child's or infant's bathwater to reduce fretfulness and hyperactivity. In a bedtime drink the water will prevent insomnia and nightmares. Rose-quartz water opens the heart and increases tolerance, and should be added to water in drinks when families meet, to ensure that the occasion is harmonious. The water can also be drunk to counter eating disorders and other obsessions.

Sodalite

Water made with sodalite is calming, especially for alleviating panic experienced when flying, claustrophobia and other phobias.

Turquoise

Water made with this power stone can provide the confidence to stand up against bullies and backbiting. This is another stone to keep in water at work to splash on your pulse points. Especially protective of animals, turquoise water should be added to a pet bowl to prevent illness, theft or the creature straying. Take a small bottle of turquoise water when you travel, because it guards against problems, attack, accidents and becoming lost in unfamiliar places.

Colour breathing

Breathing in coloured light from different sources is a fast and effective way of filling yourself with a specific colour energy. Natural sources of prana, fruits, flowers, trees and crystals, are especially potent, as is the silver light of the Moon and the gold of the Sun (see pages 144–53). But you can also use candles or indeed any splashes of colour you see while travelling or at work. Inhaling the seven colours of a naturally occurring rainbow or those cast by rainbow crystals hung at windows will instantly revitalise the system. However, coloured lights involve electricity with all its jarring energies, so I do not recommend using them.

You can also use this method for healing the auras of others or for an absent person or animal, or place, visualising the coloured light travelling as beams of light towards its subject, and for cleansing, protecting and empowering the aura and chakras (see pages 121–24).

✦ Focus on your colour source, visualising your in-breath as spiralling coloured light beams that expand within your body (see pages 18–21 for suggested breathing patterns, or just allow your body to find its own rhythm).

✦ As you exhale, see black or grey mist being expelled, leaving your body lighter and more harmonious.

✦ Once you are filled with light you can spread it around the psychic energy field that forms an ellipse around your body.

✦ Alternatively, breathe the coloured energies towards a specific part of your body (use a mirror to help you to direct them).

✦ If you are using a candle, blow out the light when you have finished, sending radiance to wherever it is needed.

Specific colour energies produce different effects:

✦ For positivity and whole mind, body and spirit healing, inhale white or gold and exhale black.

✦ For instant energy or courage, inhale red and exhale blue.

✦ For calm, inhale blue and exhale red.

✦ For confidence, inhale orange and exhale indigo.

✦ For significant dreams, inhale indigo and exhale orange.

✦ For spiritual or psychic awareness, inhale violet and exhale red.

✦ For courage, inhale red and exhale violet.

✦ For technological expertise or logic, inhale yellow and exhale green.

✦ For connection with the natural world, inhale green and exhale yellow.

✦ For learning and memory, inhale yellow and exhale violet.

✦ For psychic invisibility, inhale grey and exhale white.

✦ For contacting higher energies, inhale white and exhale grey.

✦ For gentleness and reconciliation, inhale pink and exhale blue.

✦ For leadership and assertiveness, inhale blue and exhale pink.

✦ For power, inhale gold and exhale silver.

✦ For intuition, inhale silver and exhale gold.

Eating foods to absorb colour

Perhaps the easiest way to absorb coloured energies is by eating foods of the colour whose energies you need in your life. Attaining supernatural powers by eating was one of the earliest forms of magic, and this tradition has continued in the preparation and consumption of certain foods for festival times, for example hot-cross buns and Christmas cake.

Where possible use freshly picked, organic, natural foods that are un-cooked and unprocessed (or only lightly cooked) and as freshly prepared as possible. Try to use as many foods as possible that are grown or produced locally, as locally grown food will be available only in season, when the life-force flows at its most powerful.

Red
Beetroots, radishes, red apples, red cabbage, raspberries, strawberries, tomatoes.

Orange

Apricots, carrots, orange cheeses, oranges, orange melons, pumpkins.

Yellow

Bananas, cheese, corn, honey, honeydew melons, peaches, pineapples, yams.

Green

Broccoli, cucumber, cabbage, green apples, green grapes, green peppers, lettuce, pears.

Blue

Bilberries, blueberries, blue plums, damsons.

Purple

Aubergines, blackberries, plums, purple grapes, purple cabbage.

Brown

Brown rice, nuts, potatoes, rye bread, seeds.

White

Cream, egg white, milk, onions, white cheese, white rice, onions, yoghurt.

The Colours of Your Life

As we have seen, colours can affect our health. For example, subjects bathed in blue light for thirty minutes experience a drop in blood pressure; whereas if they are bathed in red light their blood pressure rises. Exposure to blue, often called the healing colour, also decreases perspiration, respiration and brain-wave activity, while red increases the metabolic rate. Orange stimulates the pulse. Pink can, in the short term, have a soothing effect, especially upon aggressive people.

You can decorate your home using colour therapy. Work areas and rooms where there will be lively interactions will benefit from bright colours, and gentler hues should be used to decorate bedrooms and bathrooms.

For well-being, wear a yellow scarf or tie to negotiate the darkest day with focus and confidence. Visualisation also offers the benefits of instant colour; this is especially true when based on actual experience, for example a visit to a botanical garden filled with brilliantly coloured flowers. There is no substitute for experience and whether we are city or country dwellers we can find sources of natural colour and spend some days with nature, filling our memory cells with a repository to be recalled with joy on the darkest days.

Auras

I have already referred to the aura a number of times, as it is one important way of categorising the personal energy flow. But now let me define it in terms of its place in energy work. Auras are personal energy fields that contain different colours and levels. Clairvoyants can see them spontaneously, but with practice anyone can tune into auras and interpret them.

Everything possesses an aura, even inanimate objects. Animate life possesses a stronger aura, however, because of the interactive energy flowing between it and the environment. There are of course considerable variations in what is regarded as animate life.

The Native North American and other indigenous people would argue that stones and crystals are living and their aura changes too. Therefore, they can transmit their own innate power, an amplified form of the life-force that brings healing to people, animals and places. For example, plants emanate light around their forms that can be detected by Kirlian photography, a method of capturing auras on film. Plant auras fade when the plant is cut or deprived of water. If a leaf is cut from the plant, the aura of the missing part remains.

Each personal aural field is part of the universal energy field that I have already referred to as the life-force. This can be likened to a mighty ocean where all the streams and rivers of the other personal energy fields of humans, animals, plants, crystals and rocks flow. But this is a two-way process. Because the individual aura or personal energy flow is not static, but interactive, the aura that can be seen, felt or sensed, reflects not only the essential person, but also the current emotional state, thoughts, desires, anxieties and influences, both positive and negative, from human and higher energy fields.

The Size of the Aura

The personal spiritual or bio-energetic field can vary in size and density according to our personal well-being and stage of spiritual evolution. It is estimated that the aura can extend beyond the physical body from between 2.5 centimetres (1 inch) in thickness to about 90 centimetres (3 feet), the approximate length of an adult's arm span. The size of the aura extends as you evolve spiritually and so may reach even further from the body. For example, Guatama Buddha, it is said, had an aura that extended its influence for several miles.

Reading the Aura

Although the aura contains all seven colours of the rainbow, for much of your aural work you can concentrate on the two predominant colours: the personal root aura, a relatively permanent aural colour that is visible when a subject is relaxed and there are no stimuli, and the ever-changing aura of the current mood. These will give you a great deal of initial information so that you can use aural interpretation at home, at work and during social interactions with people. As auras are read at a deeper level than body language they can anticipate the best approach in dealing with a person at any particular time. We have already discussed the areas represented by each colour on pages 95–102.

You can distinguish between the mood and permanent auras by the intensity and stability of their colours. The mood aura is much more transient and the colour more ethereal and full of movement, flickers, flashes and twinkles. However, the permanent aura colour is matt and solid. The permanent aura may contain streaks of darkness that can indicate stress or disorder not as yet manifested in the physical body and therefore preventable by cleansing the aura.

Since the ability to see auras resides not in the physical but in the psychic or inner eye, you have to learn to deactivate the conscious, analytical part of the mind and allow your psychic vision that is ruled by the third eye or brow chakra to emerge spontaneously. The hardest part is not *seeing*, but in trusting what you see with your inner eye or sense. Some people report that they initially see a white film close to the body, but others are able to see two or more colours first time.

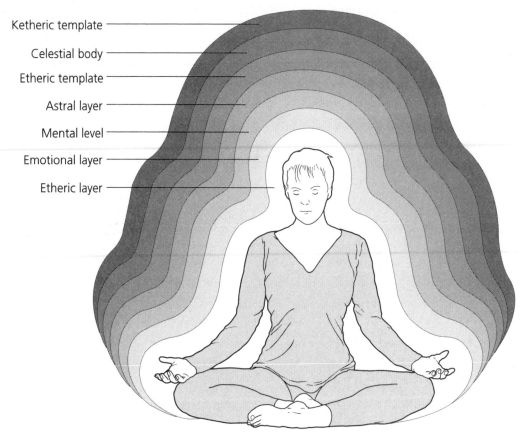

Ketheric template
Celestial body
Etheric template
Astral layer
Mental level
Emotional layer
Etheric layer

The seven auric layers

If you find it difficult, persevere and focus initially on the two main colours without trying to study any of the detail that may be seen, such as streaks. Simply look at the person, close your eyes and allow the whole picture to build up in your mind. The key is to relax. Even if you cannot identify the colours, you can heal and cleanse the aura purely intuitively or using my beloved pendulum – and ten to one when you stop trying you will find you are seeing rainbows.

◆ If you are reading for yourself, look in a mirror framed against a soft light. If reading for another, ask your subject to stand so that he or she is likewise framed against soft light (some people prefer the subject with a darker background, so experiment).

✦ Have ready a diagram of two circles, one inside the other for recording, and a set of coloured pencils that have at least three hues for each colour.

✦ Although the aura surrounds the entire body as an ellipse, look at the area around the head, where the aural impressions are strongest.

✦ Close your eyes for a few seconds, open them, blink and then you will get a vivid impression of the aura, either externally or in your mind's vision. Both are as good. The psyche is like a flashlight camera and holds intact the instantaneous image.

✦ Record your impressions quickly, colouring in the innermost circle as the mood aura. If you see any streaks, dark spots or areas where the colour is missing you can record these in felt pens over the main colour. If there are metallic streaks or the colour seems unnaturally bright, this may indicate irritability, hyperactivity or intolerance towards others; it can be recorded by colouring with a silver pen over the main colour. However, streaks are more likely to occur in the more permanent aura.

✦ If there is a mixture of colours, add them.

✦ In the outer circle, record the permanent aura, which may contain streaks of other colours and may well have holes or parts missing.

✦ Jot down notes on the side of the drawing to indicate any unusual features, holes, streaks or darkness.

✦ If you lose concentration, look at the aura again quickly and allow your hand to pick the correct colours from the crayon box automatically.

✦ Harshness or jaggedness, dark lines or streaks indicate the accumulation of negativity.

✦ Dull, turgid areas of colour or what appear to be dark knots or circles indicate blockages in one or more of the chakras that energise the aura. These will need cleansing and healing either directly through the specific chakra or the aura. As a two-way energy system, you can heal either for the same effect.

✦ A very pale shade or a missing colour needs extra energy to be directed towards that area of the aura or the relevant chakra related to that chakra to be added (see pages 123–26).

The Chakras

Chakras are energy vortexes or psychic centres that have been likened to whirling discs or channels through which life-force or psychic energy flows from the sky, earth, nature and crystals, and from other people and animals via the etheric or spirit body to the physical body. This light force flows into the individual chakras through the aura all around the body via the chakra connections.

The chakras are said to be located close to the axis of the backbone of the inner spirit body that mirrors the organs and structure of the physical body. However, they are linked with and take their name from locations on the front of the body, such as the navel, heart, throat and brow. So you can work with your chakras through the physical body. The seven chakras are set at regular intervals from the root or base chakra, located in the perineum, where we make contact with the earth and earth power, right up to the crown chakra in the centre of the head that draws in pure life-force from the cosmos.

Each of the seven main chakras corresponds to and energises one of the seven levels or layers of the aura as well as a specific area of the physical body. You will learn to distinguish these seven separate layers as you work more with the aura. Each of the chakras is related to one of the colours of the rainbow. The innermost layer of the aura is ruled by the red root or base chakra and the outermost layer by the violet/white/gold crown chakra that shares its colour. The colour of each chakra is reflected in the aura layers, as a halo around the whole body.

When the seven main chakras are open and functioning well, they receive energy and vitality from the universal life-force in its many forms. When they are operating efficiently, chakras are also able to filter out any impurities or negativity that enter our aural field or transform the negative energy into positive power.

Chakra Energies

To understand the flow of energy through the chakras, run the palm of your hands up and down your body about 5 centimetres (2 inches) away from your body. You may feel numerous gentle, vibrating channels like warm liquid ascending and descending in spiralling pathways through your body, with a sensation like an emptying bath over the areas where the actual chakra points are situated (see diagram, page 116). These psychic channels are called nadis.

Chakras and Auras

What you see in an aura reading is the energy from the chakra that is temporarily the most active at the time of the reading. This infusion of colour floods the different layers of the aura and so may be read as the mood aura that reflects the way we feel at the time of the reading. The more permanent aura colour mentioned earlier is created by the input of the specific chakra through which we most commonly operate in our lives; this colour tends to remain static even as the mood aura changes. The more spiritually evolved a person is, the higher the colour vibration reflected in the permanent aura (red is the lowest and purple/white/gold the highest). The shade and intensity are also significant, so a clear red permanent aura would indicate someone who may be content to live primarily motivated by comfort and material pleasures, whereas a harsh red might indicate a person who was angry and ruled entirely by external factors and stimuli. A very pale red with holes would indicate exhaustion, or that the person was being badly bullied either emotionally or physically.

The Seven Main Chakras and Spirit Body Layers

The etheric or spirit body has seven layers, each superimposed one upon the other in ever-decreasing density. If you looked down onto the human body from a height, you would see by clairvoyance the seven layers within and extending beyond the physical body. Each layer would appear more ethereal and misty than the one below, so that you would see the innermost layer in which the spirit organs are contained through patches of the misty layers above it.

The chakras interpenetrate all seven layers, but what we see and work with are the chakras as they appear in the innermost spirit layer. This layer is so close to our physical organs that the chakras appear as though they were part of our physical form. The aura is quite simply the overlap where, by cosmic design, the spirit body will not quite fit inside our physical form. Since each layer extends further than the last, these layers appear as seven colour bands,

The seven main chakras that we can psychically activate through advanced meditative techniques.

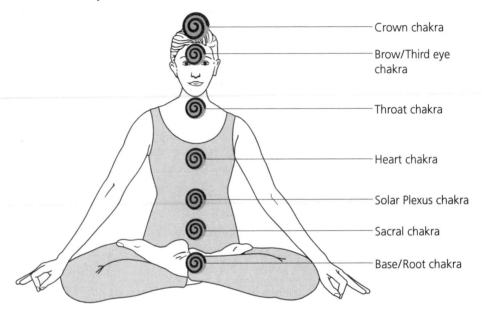

Crown chakra

Brow/Third eye chakra

Throat chakra

Heart chakra

Solar Plexus chakra

Sacral chakra

Base/Root chakra

the last joining with cosmic space. Some people can see the bands of colour also within the body and, with practice, most of us can see or sense our chakra points, helped by using a pendulum.

The root or base chakra, or **muladhara**

Its colour is red and it is the chakra of earth. This chakra draws its beautiful deep-red light upwards from the earth through the feet and through our perineum when we sit on the ground. Both these are points at which the root or base chakra can be accessed and healed. The minor chakras in the soles of the feet are also ruled by and connected directly to the root. It is linked with the kundalini or serpent energy that in Eastern philosophy is described as coiled at the base of the spine and which provides the driving power for the chakra system.

The root rules the legs, feet and skeleton including the teeth and the large intestine. Its function is survival, physical identity, self-preservation, instinctive reproductive urges, happiness and a sense of belonging, with being at home in our own body and with the earth.

Imbalances can be manifested as pain and tension in any of the body parts that the root or base chakra controls: constipation or irritable bowel symptoms, a general lack of energy and an inability to relax even when exhausted. On a psychological level, unreasonable anger or paralysing fear from trivial causes can be a symptom of a blockage.

The root or base chakra energises the innermost layer of the aura and the first or etheric layer of the spirit body (see page 27) that exists within our physical body. It is identified with the essential self that survives death.

The overlap of the spirit body at this level extends from between 5 millimetres (1/4 inch) to 5 centimetres (2 inches) beyond the physical body on which it is superimposed, following the outline of the physical form.

As the densest layer of the spirit body with the lowest vibrations and closest to the physical body, it reflects the physical condition of the body and can warn of ailments before they enter the physical body.

The sacral chakra or svadisthana

Its colour is orange and it is the chakra of the Moon and water. It is seated in the sacrum/lower abdomen, around the reproductive system, and focuses on all aspects of physical comfort or satisfaction. It controls the blood, all bodily fluids and hormones, the reproductive system, kidneys, circulation and bladder, and is a chakra especially sensitive to stress and imbalance if we get out of harmony with our natural cycles.

Its functions include childhood issues that may affect our adult lives for good or ill, the patterns of behaviour we develop and personal creativity and its expression. Some people believe personal past-life issues sit here. Blockages can show themselves as fluid retention, menstrual or menopausal problems, mood swings, impotence in men and an inability to relax during sex for women.

Disorders involving physical indulgence to seek emotional satisfaction can also result from blockages, especially food and other oral-related obsessions.

The sacral chakra controls the second band of the aura, which is part of the second emotional layer of the spirit body. It follows the outline of the body, but not as closely as the etheric layer. This is the level most subject to emotional change and can obscure the other layers with a powerful mood colour.

The solar plexus chakra or manipura

Its colour is yellow and it is the chakra of fire. You will find the third chakra above the navel and around the stomach area, or some systems locate it further up towards the central cavity of the lungs.

As there is some confusion with this chakra, you can locate this precisely in your own body by holding your palm or a pendulum 2 or 3 centimetres (¾ inch to 1¼ inches) over this area and see where you feel the pull and the swirling of the vortex in the centre.

The solar plexus chakra's function is to galvanise personal power and individuality and to integrate experience. Its body parts include digestion, the liver, spleen, gall bladder, stomach and small intestine, and the metabolism.

Digestive disorders and hyperactivity can result from imbalances and blockages. On a psychological level, a lack of self-confidence, obsessions, over-sensitivity and becoming overly emotional, finding fault with others and an inability to empathise can result from the inefficient working of this chakra.

The solar plexus chakra governs the third band of the aura, which is part of the third mental level of the spirit body that rules thought, ideas and everyday emotions. This too is a level that can flood the mood aura as it is affected by everyday interactions. It usually is most visible around the head and shoulders as a yellowish light.

The heart chakra or anahata

Its colour is green or pink and it is the chakra of air or the winds. It is situated in the centre of the chest, radiating over heart, lungs, breasts and also hands and arms. There are minor chakras in the palm of each hand and these are the outlets for healing powers that stem from the heart chakra, which in turn draws power from the higher centres (see pages 118–20).

Compassion and transformation of our everyday lives through connection with our still centre of being are results of a clear heart chakra. Constant coughs, breathing difficulties and allergies can be a result of blockage or imbalance, as can over-sensitivity to the problems of others that leaves us anxious but unable to offer real help.

The heart chakra rules the fourth band of the aura, which is part of the fourth astral layer of the spirit body. It is at this level of awareness that we move from our personally orientated world and can link to higher dimensions.

When this chakra is open, we reach the vibrations of people who have lived in the past and so, if this chakra is active, you may experience some mediumistic powers and an awareness of past lives and worlds. Gifted healers invariably have very open heart chakras.

You may experience increased healing energies derived from natural sources such as herbs or crystals.

The throat chakra or vishuddha

Its colour is blue and it is the chakra of sound. The throat chakra is situated close to the Adam's apple in the centre of the neck. As well as the throat and speech organs, the throat chakra controls the mouth, the neck and shoulders and the passages that connect to the ears.

Its function is to enable us to instigate meaningful communication with others and with devas and personal spirit guides and for creativity and self-expression. When our throat chakra becomes fully operational, this is the stage of our spiritual evolution where out-of-body experiences, divination, dreams of other dimensions and clairaudience become possible. For this is the level at which the collective unconscious or cosmic memory bank can be accessed; the boundaries of time lose their meaning at this gateway.

Blockages may be manifested as sore throats, swollen glands in the neck, mouth ulcers and ear problems. On a psychological level, confusion and incoherence and an inability to speak the truth that is in your heart may result if the chakra is not working efficiently.

The throat chakra controls the fifth band of the aura, which is part of the fifth level of the spirit body, the etheric template that holds the potential for what we could become in our present lives.

The third eye or brow chakra, or savikalpa samadhi

Its colour is indigo and it is the chakra of light. The brow chakra is situated just above the bridge of the nose in the centre of the brow. It controls the eyes and ears, and both hemispheres of the brain and radiates into the central cavity of the brain.

You may find your channelling abilities evolve, perhaps through automatic writing or psychic artistry, once this chakra is fully active in your life. Similarly, your prophetic abilities may increase.

Blockages in the brow chakra can result in blurred vision without reason, headaches and migraines, and blocked sinuses, as well as earache. On a psychological level, insomnia or nightmares can result from blockages.

The third eye or brow chakra fuels the sixth band of the aura, which is part of the celestial body that holds the potential for our emotional growth in this life.

The crown chakra or nirvakelpa samadhi

Its colour is violet merging with white or gold as rays from the cosmos pour in. It is the chakra of spirit or pure aether. The crown chakra is situated at the top of the head. It extends beyond the crown and some systems locate the centre about three finger-breadths above the top of the head. It rules the brain, body and psyche. In this chakra resides our personal core of Divinity, which ultimately connects to the source of Divinity itself. Its function is to allow the merging of the individual with cosmic consciousness and connection with archangels, ascended beings and the source of Divinity through mystical or peak experiences – whereby we sense unity with all creation and with the source of Divinity.

Blockages in the crown chakra can result in headaches and migraines, in inefficient functioning of the immune system, a tendency to forgetfulness and in minor accidents. On a psychological level, blockages are manifested as a sense of alienation from the world.

The crown chakra controls the seventh band of the aura, which is part of the almost formless seventh layer, the ketheric template. This area holds the model of what we can achieve through our mental and spiritual explorations in our present life.

Healing the Chakras

In time you may spontaneously perceive all seven layers of the aura, which will indicate the functioning of the ruling chakras. A number of people use inner vision or the hand to trace energy blockages, and then direct energies through the fingers to heal the chakras (for healing using higher energies, see page 118). Equally, you can visualise rays of healing light filling individual chakras or the whole system.

Using a pendulum

Some healing methods are suggested here, and in Further Reading (see page 242) I have listed books on the study of this very detailed field. However, I have found in my own work and in teaching situations that the most accurate and straightforward method is with the third psychic hand – the pendulum. You can work directly with the chakras by using a crystal pendulum to trace the energy flow and to cleanse and heal the aural field. You may wish to begin with an aural reading. Follow it with direct chakra intervention that will heal any holes, darkness or paleness in the aura as you clear the chakra causing the blockage – a bit like psychic drain cleaning.

◆ Hold the crystal pendulum in your power hand, a few centimetres away from your body.

◆ Begin at your left foot and trace an energy path upwards through your body to your head and then down again out of your right foot.

◆ Let the pendulum trace its own path up the front of your body, down the right arm and hand, then up the left hand and arm.

◆ You may feel a sensation in your fingers similar to when you hold your hand over the plug hole of an emptying bath. This is a chakra point.

◆ Allow your pendulum to descend down your spine, spiralling again to the right foot.

◆ The pendulum may swing gently in a clockwise direction as it follows its spiralling path, and anticlockwise if it reaches a blockage or knot.

◆ The pendulum may also feel heavy, seem to vibrate out of rhythm or become stuck at one of the points of negative energy.

◆ If you encounter a knot or blockage, circle the pendulum gently anticlockwise until you feel the tension loosening.

◆ If you lose the energy source – this may be indicated by the pendulum ceasing to swing – then retrace your path until you reach the area where you last felt it. If the area lacks power, energise it with clockwise rotations of the pendulum. Healing and diagnosis go hand in hand in chakra work.

✦ Cleanse your pendulum by plunging it into clear water, preferably in sunlight, shaking off the water and allowing it to dry naturally. This action will empower as well as cleanse it.

✦ This is a good exercise to carry out weekly or when working with others' chakras for the first time to trace their unique energy flows.

Using chakra crystals

If you are healing a person or animal that is not present, you can create a diagram of their outline and, while closing your eyes, visualise the coloured energy centres (see page 124 for animal chakra positions). Alternatively, you can hold an image of the person or animal in your mind, and colour in the outline with rainbow colours. Include any streaks or blockages while you are colouring. Let your fingers choose the colours and do not try to analyse or second guess them, as even if you know a person's symptoms the blockage may stem from another area.

Use a chakra crystal from the following list and, holding it in your power hand, pass it anticlockwise in circles over the blocked or malfunctioning chakra and then clockwise to restore energy and well-being. You can choose a gentle crystal for relatively gradual healing with children, the chronically ill and very old people. For rapid relief, use a creative or powerful chakra crystal.

You can circle the chakra crystal over the head of the person in a diagram and energise a specific aural layer. For whole mind, body and spirit healing, circle a clear crystal quartz or your pendulum anticlockwise and then clockwise over the crown of the head. Whether you work primarily through aura or chakras, the effect is the same. For any harshness or jaggedness that may suggest imbalance use a gentle chakra crystal first anticlockwise then clockwise.

If you want to heal a place or species, use gentle heart chakra crystals over a picture, moving first in anticlockwise and then in clockwise circles, seeing life, fertility and love returning.

The root or base chakra – red

For power Bloodstone, garnet, jasper, ruby, tiger's eye or iron pyrites (that when polished is a beautiful red/gold stone), bloodstone, garnet, ruby.

For gentle healing Earthy red opaque stones, such as banded red/brown agates, red tiger's eye, smoky quartz, black obsidian.

The sacral chakra – orange

For power Orange glowing crystals such as carnelian, amber, rich opaque jasper or silvery haematite.

For gentle healing Banded orange agate, calcite, moonstone, rutilated quartz.

The solar plexus chakra – yellow

For power Sparkling citrine, sunstone, topaz, yellow zircon.

For gentle healing Agates of any yellow or golden-orange shade are especially good for balancing and stabilising energies.

To soothe Gentle-yellow crystals, fluorite or calcite.

The heart chakra – green

For power Green aventurine or malachite, pink rhodonite, rhosochrite or sugilite.

For gentle healing Green jade or moss agate, pink rose quartz.

The throat chakra – blue

For power Azurite, lapis lazuli, turquoise.

For gentle healing Aquamarine or blue-lace agate.

The third eye or brow chakra – indigo/purple

For power Sodalite, sugilite, peacock's eye (bornite).

For gentle healing Amethyst, kunzite.

The crown chakra – violet/white

For power Clear crystal quartz, clear fluorite, purple sugilite.

For gentle healing Purple fluorite, white calcite.

For either energy Banded purple and white amethyst.

Contact healing with chakra crystal

Chakra crystals can be used for absent or distant healing and also when the patient is with you. Sit in front of the patient with a dish containing a power and gentle crystal for each of the chakras. Allow your hand to select a chakra colour and, as you hold it over the chakra it rules, let it guide you whether to move anticlockwise to remove pain or tension or clockwise to infuse light and healing.

As you work, you can visualise beams or rays of light, coloured spheres or sparkling filaments of colour, allowing the colours of the crystals to penetrate every fibre of the patient's body. Talk to the patient of natural images associated with the crystals: the green of the hills, the purple-headed mountains. The words will flow with the rhythm of your hands. Continue until your hands no longer reach for a crystal; you may have used four or five.

Chakra healing for animals

Animals have three chakras: the root or base ruling the legs and tail, the sacral ruling the reproductive organs and the solar plexus ruling the remainder of the body. However, those who have worked with animals for a long time say that they have also a heart chakra that extends from the chest upwards and accounts for their altruistic attitude towards humans.

Some pets are happy for you to massage their fur gently with a crystal, but others, if they are old or sick, prefer to have a crystal gently circled over them. Any agate, jade or amethyst can be circled first anticlockwise then clockwise over the chakra points of the animal's body with special attention over any area of pain or injury.

To ease a dying or very old pet, use a smoky quartz and make gentle spiralling movements over the chakras to help them to close. Alternatively, you can hold the pet in your arms and send it love and light.

Cleansing, healing and protecting the aura and chakras by smudging

This method works with both aura and chakras and is my own favourite. It can be carried out weekly or whenever you feel stressed.

✦ Begin with an aura reading to identify any problems.

✦ It is best to work with a dual cleansing and empowering herb. White or grey sage or any of the sagebrushes are excellent for all forms of healing, as is cedar. These can be bought as smudge sticks. You can also use a sage, cedar, pine or juniper incense stick.

✦ You will need a candle to light the smudge stick. If outdoors I use one of the garden torches containing a safety candle, as this can stand directly in the ground.

✦ Light the smudge stick from the candle or garden torch in the centre of a visualised circle, creating a clockwise circle of smoke around you.

✦ Standing in the centre, face the east and extend your smudge stick in that direction in greeting, then do the same in the south, west, and north.

✦ Face east once more and raise the smudge stick skywards, and finally point it towards the earth.

✦ If you are healing another person, he or she can sit in the centre facing west.

✦ A partner or friend and yourself can also mutually smudge each other. Initially stand side by side, holding your smudge sticks to greet the directions. Use the east/west axis and face each other as you smudge, with yourself facing east.

✦ Since the aura you see is an extension of the spirit body that is within the physical one, it is best to start with a general cleansing of the aural field.

✦ Smudge anticlockwise from the top of the body down in spirals, remembering to extend the smudge as far outwards as you can detect the aura. Then go down a second time, now swirling over the specific chakras, with extra smoke over any chakras related to known problem areas.

✦ You may find that at certain points the smudge stick feels resistant. This is due to a blockage, and you may need to make several anticlockwise swirls. As you work, visualise darkness and heaviness flowing from the body into the earth.

✦ You may find that you are swaying or almost dancing; some people play drum music while flowing with the energies.

✦ Allow the smudge stck to guide and flow its own path.

✦ Next, you are going to restore the energies by smudging upwards from the feet, this time with clockwise spirals, following the aura outline and ending with a clockwise circle over the crown of the head.

✦ Returning to the feet, spiral upwards clockwise a second time, pausing and smudging an extra clockwise circle over the chakras and any areas of discomfort. Fill in any holes or missing parts of the aura with the smoke. See light in rainbow colours flowing from all around, energising and enriching.

✦ End with a final clockwise circle around the crown of the head.

After the ceremony, extinguish the smudge stick by tapping it in a bowl of sand or against the edge of a fireproof ceramic dish.

The Next Step

By now you should be buzzing and humming like a well-tuned engine. Remember, the best treatment of all for your own and others' psychic energy fields is to spend time in the open air, even in the smallest city square, breathing, grounding, centring, stilling and visualising your chakras turning in harmony and filling you with rainbow light. I have talked in this section and earlier ones about drawing power from the earth and from the cosmos. In the next section, we will work with those all-powerful earth energies and the elements that are the component forms of our psychic development, each fuelling different psychic powers and in their unity taking us beyond time and space to other dimensions.

STEP 6

Working with Earth Power and Elemental Energies

I
N STEP 4 I TALKED ABOUT linking our personal psychic development with the energies inherent in nature as a way of amplifying our innate powers and tapping into the cosmic bank of human experiences and symbolism. In Step 5 I linked the personal energy fields with universal energies and described how the higher chakras and aural levels enabled us to move from the immediate beyond parameters of time and space.

Now it is time to connect our personal psychic energies with the powers of the earth and the ancient elements that have been associated with the human personality and psyche from ancient times. Imagine standing in a place of great antiquity where people have worshipped for thousands of years or where nature has never been built upon. Now imagine feeling through your feet and your skin the power of the rain or sunlight, the wind blowing and the earth pulsating.

Those powers are, according to the ancients, the source of our personal energies. If we are to move from the personal psychic explorations to linking with the greater powers of the earth and elements, we need first to make the connection with the forces of nature. This link was spontaneous in childhood but in adulthood it gets lost, especially in urban life. We need to stand in the rain or paddle in the sea, feel the warmth of the Sun beating down, be buffeted by the wind, climb rocks or walk over grass or sand so that we are part of the interconnected web of existence.

Earth Energies

When writing about the root or base chakra (see page 116) and about grounding our energies (see page 23) I described the powerful earth energies pulsating beneath our feet that can be felt even beneath city streets. Indeed many old towns in eastern and Western Europe, the Mediterranean and Scandinavia are built quite deliberately along psychic or ley lines of earth energies. You will identify these by walking them, whether by using your pendulum to tune into the energies or by relying on your feet, whose chakras link to each individual's root or earth chakra. Furthermore, if you study a map, you will see that a number of old churches and chapels are positioned in a straight line. This is because, until the 14th or 15th centuries, craftspeople and clerics recognised the power of the earth and almost every Benedictine abbey, for example, is built on a line of earth power.

Working with Sacred Sites

Certain places on earth have especially powerful energies where the earth and sky meet, and these were used for worship from time immemorial. They include the sites of stone circles and dolmens (ritual burial or initiation chambers), and later the sites of temples, abbeys and cathedrals.

If you are standing on an ancient site, your pendulum (if you are holding one) or your whole body will often identify an energy vortex where underground earth power, perhaps focused on an underground spring, meets with a shaft of sky power. You will sometimes find a sacred well nearby. These places of energy may be several feet in circumference and the energy will be concentrated in the centre. As you stand there, your feet will feel hot, your pendulum will spin as if going into orbit and you will feel as though you are taking off in an unpressurised aircraft.

Notre Dame Cathedral in Chartres, not far from Paris, is perhaps the most remarkable and a relatively accessible example of a site where connecting with the surge of the sacred earth is almost guaranteed. The cathedral became a Christian pilgrimage site because it holds the relic of the chemise in which the Virgin Mary was said to have given birth.

Many of the earth sites, like Chartres, have enduring connections to the earth mother. Even before Christianity, at Chartres the druids created an underground shrine and wooden statue of the Black Madonna and her child close to a healing well dating from time immemorial. This well may still be seen in the cathedral crypt and retains healing powers for Christians and pagans alike. Black Madonnas are a pre-Christian version of the Virgin. Made from dark wood, they are sometimes associated with the Egyptian mother goddess, Isis, and her son, Horus, or the earth mother in her winter aspect.

So if you want to feel earth energies, go to almost any European, Mediterranean or Scandinavian cathedral and somewhere you will find an underground sacred water source in the crypt. If you scratch deep enough into the mythology you will uncover a whole history of pre-Christian earth worship and healing. In the open countryside you can feel the earth energies when you are close to ancient sites, such as menhirs or monoliths (single standing stones, sometimes dating from the 3rd millennium BC); figures etched into the chalk hillside; early rock sculptures or paintings in caves; ancient barrows or burial mounds where the Neolithic peoples buried their dead. Often the barrow and burial mounds were identified in Celtic lands as fairy hills. Around the world, earth energies are at their strongest at sacred and ancient sites such as the numerous stone circles in Sweden – for example, Ale Stanen near Malmo, which is set on a clifftop – the pyramids of Ancient Egypt or Ayers Rock in Australia, said to be the navel of the world.

Ley Lines

Psychic lines of energy that run beneath the earth and which carry a concentrated form of earth energy are known as ley lines. Sacred places have been built along them for thousands of years, to take advantage of their power. For example, Notre Dame Cathedral at Chartres is situated on a ley line linking Glastonbury, Stonehenge and the pyramids of Egypt.

Many lines of psychic energy originally formed ancient traders' tracks, perhaps because of their easily identifiable landmarks. Ghost legends are often located close to ley lines; it is hypothesised that ghosts draw energy from the lines to manifest themselves on the earth plane. But for living people too, and especially those who want to develop psychic powers in any way, ley lines are a repository for energy that we can absorb and store.

We can then use our mind-power in all kinds of amazing ways, from remote viewing to seeing other dimensions. If you want to see ghosts, for example, find places in your own area in which there have been sightings over many generations – the white ladies, phantom coach and pair – and if you look on a map you will often find that the sightings follow a straight line across the country and that there are sites of antiquity close by (see pages 184–86).

True ley lines – the straight ancient traders' tracks, first identified by Alfred Watkins in the 1920s – are the most stringently defined as possessing at least five aligned pre-Reformation sacred sites within a relatively short distance, say ten miles, that can be measured as straight to the standard of an H-pencil line on a 1.25,000 scale map. However, such strict definitions may actually exclude many existing ley lines, for example in the United States, where Native American sacred sites may have been destroyed. In Australia, New Zealand and America, sacred sites tend to date from the post-Reformation times of the settlers. However, even more recently constructed sacred buildings through-out the world are usually instinctively created on a site of spiritual power. In countries of a greater size than England, sacred sites may be hundreds of miles apart.

Some energy ley lines, even in the United Kingdom, are not marked by places of power at all. You can detect these quite spontaneously as you walk across vast open tracts of land; you may see natural markers, a huge rock on top of a hill, a pond or clumps of hawthorns that were tended by secret village guardians to guide travellers. These areas have not been built on, except by Mother Nature. If you stand in an open hilly region by a rocky outcrop, you will feel the energy vibrating beneath your feet.

Ley lines have been identified throughout Europe, Scandinavia, India and the United States. For example, the Cree Indian trails of North America invari-ably followed straight tracks. In Chaco Canyon, New Mexico, long, straight tracks were laid down by the Anasazi peoples. In ancient Egypt cairns were set up on hilltops as markers for the caravan trails and it is hypothesised these were ancient markers of ley energies. From the Sun Temple that was built in the middle of the city of Cuzco in central Peru, 41 lines radiate into the sur-rounding countryside. Along them lie shrines, temples, graves, sacred hills, bridges and even battlefields.

In Further Reading (see page 243) I have listed some books which will direct you to ley lines in various parts of the world. There really is no substi-tute for walking the leys, and because there are so many you may discover new ones in your own region by using your feet and pendulum. One final clue is to read local legends – you will find that many of the local fairy and giant sites are in fact aligned.

Negative Earth Energies

Places with strong earth energies were never intended to be used as dwellings or workplaces. In countries such as Iceland and Ireland, where awareness of earth powers still exists among the population, no one would build along what is called a 'fairy path' between the ancient burial mounds or fairy forts, or over the straight paths along which it was believed spirits travelled. But modern industrial builders have no such qualms when creating huge office blocks or vast housing estates on green fields or ancient monastery lands. This can make a building seem dark and cold even on a summer's day, leading to inexplicable tension, minor illnesses or malaise among residents or workers. These are often called negative earth energies.

True negative energies can be caused by major construction works, such as mine workings, or building a motorway that can sour the earth energies. It is said that not only people but also animals and plants can be adversely affected; even telegraph poles seem to corrode faster over such spots.

There are various theories about geopathic stress that can cause disturbances in energies close to ley lines, and of the nature of black streams. Black streams form a vast network of underground veins of water that have become soured or polluted psychically by negative earth energies, and sometimes physically, for reasons I have listed above. Because this is quite a complex and controversial area, I have suggested books and societies where such concepts can be explored. For the purpose of psychic development work, it is important to detect the presence of negative earth energies and to neutralise them.

Detecting and neutralising negative earth energies

If your workplace or home seems gloomy and dark or there is a bad atmosphere, try to locate the spots at which the negativity is strongest.

✦ Walk around with your mind blank and slowly identify the places where you feel uneasy. If you move around again with a pendulum, it will swing anticlockwise and feel heavy as if it is trapped in a vortex that pulls downwards, rather like holding your hand over the plug hole of an emptying bath that opens on to a very wide drain hole.

✦ Plot these spots on a diagram. You may find that they form straight lines. This might indicate that they lie on or close to a ley line at an intersection where two leys cross or where several adopt a grid formation. One theory identifies Hartmann and Curry grid lines with problems wherever they intersect: a more undulating path might indicate a black stream. These grids are named after their discoverers, who were researchers into earth energies, and are said to divide the earth into square lattices.

✦ One of the easiest ways to neutralise these dark spots is by using a pointed amethyst crystal as a pendulum. Stand over each spot swirling your crystal first anticlockwise then clockwise until you sense the tension from the vortex atmosphere lifting; this feels like a snagged reel of cotton or a cog with wire tangled in it (you can check the energy has cleared later with your pendulum).

✦ Identify the negative spot nearest to an external wall and then the other end of the negative energy trail. Once you have cleared the dark energies away, you can block the flow of negativity regardless of which way the negativity is flowing. You may of course have two streams crossing the workplace or house, in which case you need to block the end of each.

✦ Place a large stone, containing quartz if possible, next to the spots on the external wall through which the negative energies are entering. Alternatively, you can block the flow with a dobbie stone. Dobbie stones are stones in various sizes containing a small, hollowed indent. They come from the Anglo-Saxon and Viking traditions of East Anglia and Scandinavia. They are traditionally placed near entrances to farms and where tracks intersect, and filled with honey or milk as offerings to the earth spirits (see page 180). You can make dobbie stones from small stone urns. Flowers or herbs can be planted in them to ensure the flow of positive energies.

✦ Check your home or workplace regularly for the return of negativity, and repeat neutralising when necessary.

✦ You can hammer protective iron staves into soil outside the four corners of your home and also at gateposts and boundaries, to divert any underground dark waters.

Negative Energies from Unfriendly Ghosts

Negative energies may be caused by ghosts who are locked in your home, perhaps by the trauma of their death, or because they cannot see the light because of their own negativity. You may be aware of shadows or voices in the places where there is coldness; animals may growl or their hackles rise in the room; and children may talk about a frightening dark figure. These are very different from the friendly ghosts who may be former inhabitants who are just happy or come back to see children and the current residents from time to time.

You may find the above remedies will work to neutralise these energies, but if not, use salt and water, as your ancestors did, to restore positivity to your home. However, as you become more psychically aware you may become more conscious of bad atmospheres. Nevertheless, you can light candles and visualise the light necessary to allow the escaped paranormal energy to move on.

A simple protective salt ritual

This can be used either for a particular room or a whole apartment or house. Rituals are an important way of focusing psychic powers so that by following steps, however simple, you are creating a channel through which your personal energies can operate.

✦ Put a few pinches of sea salt crystals into a crystal dish, and add some pure spring water, rainwater that has not touched the ground or sacred water from a holy well (some clear mineral waters come from sacred sources, so read the labels before you buy them).

✦ Sprinkle a few drops of salt water in the four corners of the room. If you want to cleanse the whole house of the phantom, mix a larger quantity of salt water in a metal or unglazed pottery bowl, and scatter it around each room beginning at the front door, going upstairs and working down to the back door, if you have one, or out of the main entrance.

✦ As you sprinkle the water, say: 'By salt and water, purify this home, bless all who dwell therein and may only light and love remain.' This blessing will include your ghost.

✦ You can, if you wish, also say, 'Friend, if it be right, depart in peace or remain as guardian and benign protector of all who share this sacred space with you.'

✦ You can then burn scented candles in lemon, pine, lavender or rose.

✦ Then open all the doors and windows and visualise your phantom leaving through one of the exits and travelling upwards in a shaft of light and fragrance.

The Elements

For thousands of years in both Eastern and Western societies, people have organised and analysed the energies of natural phenomena – the continuous cycling and recycling of different energies as elemental forces emanating from earth, sky, seas and rivers, from the lightning and the Sun.

Earth, air, fire and water are part of our psychic and psychological make-up and each offers us qualities and strengths that we can use at different times in our lives to make us operate more efficiently in the everyday world. We contain all the elements within us as part of our psychic nature and we can plug into the wider forces to strengthen those aspects, or in this case elements, of ourselves that are needed in our lives.

Your own core element is the one that rules your Sun sign, since each of the zodiacal signs is ruled by an element:

EARTH rules Taurus, Virgo and Capricorn.

AIR rules Gemini, Libra and Aquarius.

FIRE rules Aries, Leo and Sagittarius.

WATER rules Cancer, Scorpio and Pisces.

Working with the Elements

Spend a little time working with each of the elements in turn: fill your special place with the different elemental materials, hold elemental crystals and burn candles in the elemental colours, inhale the different energies, and allow visions and images to form. Go to places where each element predominates, and using psychometry and clairsentience allow yourself to merge with and thus absorb the manifested power. Become pure air, fire, earth or water, and monitor the different emotions and powers you feel.

You can use any of the symbols listed below to add the qualities of the particular element to a room, your workplace or your life. Meditate by a pool or to the sound of flowing water, maybe from a water feature, or sit by an open window, lifting your face to the breeze. Visualise the hot desert in the noon sun, for fire and earth.

The elements can help in your everyday life. For example, you might need the practicality of earth to put your finances in order, or the fluidity of water to help you through a period of emotional change. Rooms too can be modified in this way, for example temporary water symbols can be placed in the living room if difficult relatives are calling, or additional air symbols could be placed in your workspace if you have an urgent project to finish or are being bullied by an employer. I have listed the psychic powers below each element that stimulates them.

Earth

Representing north, midnight and winter.

Colours Green or brown.

Psychic abilities it increases Clairsentience, psychometry, pendulum work, divination with natural materials such as herbs, past lives, ancient wisdom.

Qualities Stability, common sense, groundedness, practical abilities, caretaker of the earth, protectiveness, upholder of tradition, love of beauty, patience and perseverance, generosity, acceptance of others, nurturing powers.

Rules over Abundance and prosperity, fertility, finance, law and order, institutions, authority, motherhood, the physical body, food, home and family, animals, the land, agriculture, horticulture and environmentalism, womb and tomb.

Deities All earth goddesses (see pages 232–33 for examples), the Virgin Mary, Mother Earth.

Elemental creatures Gnomes. Originating in Northern European folklore, these are ancient, dwarf-like creatures who live mainly underground or in deep forests for a thousand years.

Crystals Agates, emerald, jet, obsidian, rose quartz, rutilated quartz, tiger's eye.

Places: Megaliths, stone circles, groves, forest homes, temples, the crypts of churches and cathedrals, ley lines, caves.

Power animals Bear, bull, serpent, snake.

Zodiacal signs Taurus, Virgo, Capricorn. Earth signs can use an air symbol to bring innovation, fire to burn away inertia, and water to connect with others' feelings.

Substances and symbols Salt, herbs, flowers, trees, coins, bread, corn and wheat, nuts and seeds, clay, grass and sand, berries, potpourri, cauldrons, dishes.

Sacred substance Salt is the traditional magical substance of earth. You can carry empowered salt in a twist of foil (see page 71). Place a twist in each corner of a room, or sprinkle a circle of salt around your workspace for protection, to attract abundance and to banish negativity. You can also make a salt-and-pepper protective wash for doorsteps; it should be applied before dawn. Carry a tiny purse of salt with a coin added for prosperity and for tangible rewards at work.

Ways of increasing the earth element in your life

✦ Work with clay to form pots, figures or the elemental creatures.

✦ Work with wood, twigs and branches and a knife to create shapes, animals or people.

✦ Walk across grass or sand barefoot, or dance on the beach or in your garden, allowing your feet to follow the spiralling rhythm pulsating within the soil and sand.

✦ Dance or walk a turf labyrinth or create your own in sand or on soil (see page 196).

✦ Sit in a grove of trees and place your back against one of them, allowing it to fill you with pure earth power.

✦ Walk along ancient tracks or ley lines (see page 129) and visit ancient standing stones or sites.

✦ Find a large stone or unpolished crystals to form the focus for earth meditation.

✦ Surround yourself with plants at home and work and absorb their energies by opening yourself up to the freshness of the greenery.

Air

Representing east, dawn and spring.

Colours Yellow and grey.

Psychic abilities it increases Clairaudience, clairvoyance, psychokinesis, astral travel and out-of-body experiences, channelling wisdom from angels, etc., mediumship, spirituality.

Qualities Logic, clear focus, an enquiring and analytical mind, the ability to communicate clearly, concentration, versatility, adaptability, quest for truth, commercial and technological acumen, healing powers through channelling higher energies.

Rules over New beginnings, change, health and healing, teaching, travel, house or career moves, knowledge, examinations, the media, science, ideas, ideals, money-spinning.

Deities Sky gods and goddesses, messenger and healing deities (see pages 232–33).

Elemental creatures Sylphs are the winged air spirits who live for hundreds of years and can, it is said, attain an immortal soul through good deeds. They never age and live on mountain tops.

Crystals Amethyst, clear crystal quartz, citrine, diamond, lapis lazuli, sodalite, sugilite, sapphire.

Places Mountain tops, hills, towers, steeples and spires of churches and cathedrals, the sky, pyramids, open plains, tall buildings, balconies, roof gardens.

Power animals Eagle, hawk and other birds of prey, white dove.

Zodiacal signs Aquarius, Gemini, Libra. Air signs can use earth symbols to prevent fickleness or unwillingness to stick at a task, fire to avoid ambivalence and water to soften criticism or contempt of those with less ability.

Substances and symbols Four winds, clouds, balloons, kites, swords, knives, feathers, air-borne seeds and spores, incense, smudge sticks, smoke, mist, oils, storms, boats with sails billowing in the wind, weather vanes.

Sacred substances Incenses and oils. Herbs are available as incense sticks or cones, or can be burned as smudge sticks. You can burn incense or oils in these fragrances to increase the air element in your home and your life, using fragrances that symbolise specific needs. Books on incense burning and oils are suggested under Further Reading (see pages 243 and 244); for information about specific oils, see page 241.

Ways of increasing the air element in your life

+ Create or buy a simple weather vane. You can then work with a keen east wind to bring change, a warm south wind for abundance or fertility, a gentle west wind to bring love or reconciliation or a fierce north wind to blow away destructive influences or sorrow in your life.

+ Walk in fierce winds, gentle breezes, winds full of rain, through mist into sunlight, and allow the varying intensity of energies to flow through you, releasing stagnation and untying emotional knots.

+ Stand on top of a high hill on a windy day or in the middle of a windy plain and, while opening your arms wide, spin around calling out your desires, dreams and frustrations to be carried into the cosmos and transformed into positive action.

+ Write the ways in which you wish to free your life of stagnation or attachments to destructive people or situations on to string luggage tags or paper streamers. Attach them to the string of a kite or a balloon. Fly the kite or balloon high into the air.

+ Climb high hills at sunrise and open yourself to the light, then run downhill.

Fire

Representing south, noon and summer.

Colours Red, orange or gold.

Psychic abilities it increases Prophecy, magic and spellcasting, visualisation, mysticism, astrological interpretation, connection with Divinity.

Qualities Fertility in all aspects of life, creativity, light-bringing, power, passion, joy, initiating, transformation, courage.

Rules over Ambition, achievement, illumination, inspiration, all creative and artistic ventures, poetry, art, sculpture, writing, music, dance, religion and spirituality, psychic powers – especially higher ones such as channelling – innovation and sexuality. It is also potent for destruction of what is now no longer needed, for binding and banishing rituals and so for protection.

Deities All fire gods and goddesses, deities of light (see pages 231–32).

Elemental creatures Salamanders are the legendary fire lizards who live in volcanoes and lakes of fire, and are said to have originated in the Middle East in desert places. They are also seen as elongated wand-like beings in the shape of flames and in forest fires.

Crystals Amber, bloodstone, boji stones, cornelian, garnet, lava, iron pyrites, ruby, topaz, turquoise.

Places Hearths, bonfires, deserts, volcanoes, sacred festival fires, hilltop beacons, all conflagrations, solar eclipses.

Power animals Stag, lion, dragon, ram, the legendary golden phoenix. The latter is a symbol of transformation and rebirth; it burned itself on a funeral pyre every five hundred years and a young phoenix rose golden from the ashes.

Zodiacal signs Aries, Leo, Sagittarius. Fire signs can use earth symbols to give their ideas a solid foundation, air symbols to focus unrealistic expectations and water to soften a dogmatic approach.

Substances and symbols Candles, beeswax, flames, ash, fibre-optic lamps, the Sun, lightning, wands, spears and lances, fire, torches, jack o'lanterns, clear crystal spheres, mirrors, suncatchers, sunflowers and all golden flowers.

Sacred substance Burn candles to increase the fire element in your life or home at any time, using different colours and fragrances according to the specific quality you wish to invoke. Focus on a specific need by burning a candle of the appropriate colour (see pages 95–102). You can also use a candle to represent the fire element in any ritual or empowerment, and you can scry for images in the flame, especially for past-life work (see page 177). Use the flame to draw psychically what you need towards you, for example a specific lover or money, visualising it in the candle.

Ways of increasing the fire element in your life

✦ Walk in the sunshine, especially in sandy places, up steps or along a path suffused in sunlight to fill yourself with light.

✦ When it is dark or cold, use golden candles, mirrors, rainbow crystals or optic-fibre lamps to create pools of light. Surround your bath with candles or allow the sunlight to filter in so you can bathe in its radiance.

✦ On the summer solstice – around 21 June in the northern hemisphere, 21 December in the southern – keep a vigil from solstice eve at dusk through to dawn.

✦ Have a rest and then climb a high hill to greet the Sun at noon.

✦ Storms with lightning are a way of connecting with natural fire power, as are sites of volcanic activity.

✦ Light huge orange candles in a dish, a cauldron or a pot of sand, or light a bonfire, a small fire in a metal tray or even a barbecue, and move slowly around the source of heat and light at a safe distance, allowing your body to sway like the flames, so that you connect with the power of the flames.

Water

Representing west, dusk and autumn.

Colours Blue and silver.

Psychic abilities it increases Intuition, healing, divinatory powers especially water scrying, dream interpretation and incubation, seeing ghosts.

Qualities Empathy, inner harmony, peacemaker, unconscious wisdom, ability to merge and interconnect with nature, the cycles of the seasons and the life cycle.

Rules over Love, relationships, friendship, dreams, the cycle of birth, death and rebirth, purification rites, healing, using the powers of nature, especially crystals and sacred water, all water and sea magic, Moon magic, travel by sea.

Deities All sea and Moon deities (see pages 231–34).

Elemental creatures Naiads, who according to myth originated in the Aegean Sea, are said to live in coral caves under the ocean, on the shores of lakes, banks of rivers, or on marshlands; they shimmer with all the colours of water in sunlight.

Crystals Aquamarine, calcite, coral, jade, moonstone, fluorite, pearl, opal, tourmaline.

Places The ocean, rivers, lakes, pools, sacred wells and streams, marshland, flood plains.

Power animals Frogs, dolphins, all fish especially the salmon.

Zodiacal signs Cancer, Scorpio and Pisces. Water signs can use earth to prevent the squandering of time and resources, air to counter over sentimentality and conflicting aims and fire to channel dreams into action and bring them into reality.

Substances and symbols Milk, water, blood, sea shells, kelp, wine, cups, chalices.

Sacred substance Water. You can create sacred water for sprinkling around rooms at home or at your workplace for protection, or for healing by anointing the brow of yourself or a patient with a cross. Also use sacred water for cleansing artefacts. You can make it by leaving pure spring (still mineral) water in a crystal or clear glass container in the sunlight and moonlight for a full 24-hour cycle from dawn till dawn the following day. This is best performed on the night of a full Moon so you can combine solar and lunar energies. A quicker method is to leave a clear crystal quartz and an amethyst in spring water for eight hours.

Ways of increasing the water element in your life

✦ Spend time by the sea or on the shore of a tidal river, letting the surge of the waves in the shallows flow around you. When the tide turns, write with a stick in the sand whatever it is you wish to be taken by the sea: an empowerment, a desire or urgent need, or whatever you wish to banish from your life. Allow the tide to carry the wish away at its most powerful moment. When the seventh wave breaks, cast the stick on to the sea calling out your empowerment.

✦ Visit the local swimming pool in the early morning or evening and swim or float in ever-widening circles, pushing away whatever you wish to banish, and drawing in fresh water to fill you with potential and hope.

✦ Swim in the sea at dawn or in full moonlight.

✦ Create or buy a small water feature, adding crystals, shells, plants and a small pump so that you can hear water flowing whenever you feel you are trapped or stagnating in old emotions and worries.

✦ An indoor fish tank or garden pool, especially one containing goldfish, which are Oriental symbols of prosperity, can offer a living source of meditation; outdoors you can use the reflection of the Moon in the garden pool as a source of inspiration and for scrying.

The Next Step

In the next section we will add to our psychic treasure store the powers of the Sun, Moon, and planetary influences to boost innate strengths and qualities, and also learn to use dreams as a means of accessing unconscious wisdom and moving beyond the physical body. Our ancestors tapped into all of these to increase their own psychic abilities. By working with them we can connect with powers beyond the world as well as those within nature that will expand the horizons of possibility, both spiritually and in our daily world.

STEP 7

Working with Cosmic Energies

I N THE PREVIOUS CHAPTER WE looked at the power of the Earth. The Sun and Moon also exert a direct and enduring effect on our psyche, and with the pulsating powers of the Earth they form the triple gateway to other dimensions.

Generally people are primarily Earth, Sun or Moon directed. If you love gardens, crystals, forests, ancient stones, animals and children, spring and autumn, are gifted in psychometry, dowsing or clairsentience, then the Earth moves strongly with you. If you love sunny places, open spaces with the sky all around, brilliant-coloured flowers, sunlight shimmering on water and the summer, and are gifted in clairaudience, clairvoyance, and in channelling angels, then you lean towards the Sun. If, however, you are a creature of the night, loving shady pools, hidden groves, moonlit seas, walking in the rain and winter evenings, and are gifted in scrying, dream interpretation, past lives and prophecy, then the Moon is your motivator.

However, although one element may predominate, we are usually creatures of all three. As you work with their energies you will find that the higher dimensions automatically open, so that your dreams become more meaningful and prophetic, and that you can travel either in your mind or spirit body to other times, places and dimensions.

Moon Power

People throughout the ages have been aware of the cycles of the Moon and have linked them with their own fertility, the growth of crops and the earliest calendars. The Moon, which governs tides and the growth of plants, has traditionally been associated with the female menstrual cycle, with human emotions and with our inner psychic nature. It is reflected in our dreams and daydreams, our intuitive awareness and our ability to live, not in a straight linear path but recognising the ebbs and flows in our energies.

The Triple Cycle

The Moon was regarded as the mother of all, long before written records. For psychic purposes, her cycle is seen as possessing three phases: waxing or increasing, full and waning or decreasing. Men as well as women often find that by tuning into this natural cycle of rising and falling psychic, emotional and physical energies their lives become more harmonious.

Working with the Phases of the Moon

It can be helpful if you relate your psychic Moon work to what is happening in the sky, which can vary from month to month due to the Moon's irregular orbit. There are eight astronomical phases of the Moon. However, for the purposes of psychic work, if the Moon is increasing in size, it is waxing until the point of the full Moon and the light increases from right to left. Then follows the day of the full Moon, and from that point, the energies are waning and the light decreases from right to left until you are back where you started.

Sometimes the Moon and Sun are in the sky at the same time, and so you can work with both solar and lunar energies. During the later waning phase you may see the previous day's Moon still in the sky the following morning. This time is good for transitional work – moving from one phase of your life to another.

The waxing Moon

The more the Moon increases in size, the more powerful its energies to draw down what you desire from the dreaming plane to actuality. So if a need was urgent, you might visualise or use symbols to represent it. For example, lighting a candle in the appropriate colour on the two days leading up to the full Moon, with the final ritual or empowerment on the day of the full Moon itself.

✦ For a gradual increase in love or money, or to galvanise your energies to initiate necessary changes, begin on the crescent Moon, having meditated on each of the two nights from the new Moon itself.

✦ Light a small silver candle. Around it set symbols of what powers or results you need, and as you inhale the silver light and exhale the darkness, see the silver sphere enclosing you and drawing your desires closer.

✦ Make a declaration of intent, blow out the candle and send out the silver charged with your essence into the cosmos.

✦ Each evening until the full Moon (the number of days will vary slightly each month, so use your Moon diary and your observation) light an extra candle and add another symbol, replacing any old candles that are burned out. Breathe in the light and repeat your declaration of intent before blowing out the candles.

✦ On the night before the full Moon, allow the candles to burn until they are gone. Remember: never leave a burning candle unattended.

In your personal and work life, you can use the waxing period to initiate and develop ideas and projects, especially money-spinning ideas and creative ventures, learn new skills, make new relationships or deepen existing ones.

The full Moon

Although strictly speaking there is only one day of pure full-Moon energies, the days on either side are also very powerful. It is a time of both fulfilment and change, since its astrological opposition to the Sun causes instability.

In formal magical covens, drawing down the full Moon to receive wisdom from the Great Goddess is usually practised by the high priestess. It is also a potent method for those who do not practise witchcraft as it can be used to expand the horizons of our psyche and link directly into wisdom from higher sources. The powerful full-Moon energies are used as a direct route to these higher sources, whether or not they are attributed to the wisdom of the Moon Goddess.

Some practitioners focus on Gabriel, archangel of the Moon. But the sheer beauty of a full Moon, whether seen in the garden, from a balcony, rising over the trees or over my own favourite, a sandy beach, is so magical it would be hard to remain disconnected.

The idea of drawing down the Moon is to merge with its energies, by visualising it coming nearer and nearer until it surrounds you. Some believe that we use mind-power or psychokinesis to draw down the essence of the Moon, merging with a natural force. In the same way we scry with a crystal by channelling energies through and with it.

The following technique is one I discovered quite by chance on the beach at the bottom of the cliffs near my caravan, as my daughter Miranda, my son Bill and I were drawing labyrinths in the sand.

✦ If possible work barefoot and draw, smudge or visualise a large circle around yourself that will become the focus for Moon power.

✦ Face the Moon and, while extending your arms wide, spin round fast anticlockwise nine times then stop suddenly, facing the Moon.

✦ The Moon will appear to physically rush towards you and this physiological trigger offers a psychic springboard for feelings of pure joy and excitement.

✦ When the world steadies, maintain the connection. With your arms still extended, breathe in the moonlight deeply (nasal breathing seems to work best), and on the exhaled breath push anything that is not the silver Moon away with your arms.

✦ Continue until the boundaries have melted between your conscious self and the silver sphere. With hands by your sides, sit or stand, and in the stillness allow the lunar wisdom to enter. Listen and you will hear the Moon goddess or its spirit speak to you, perhaps as a rich female voice or maybe your own inner voice, or as images, sensations, sounds, or a momentary peak experience when you are one with the whole cosmos. For a second –

a tantalising but life-changing second – you will know all the secrets of the universe and will be filled with a certainty that whatever is happening in your life, all shall be well.

✦ Allow the sphere of light to recede, and sit quietly, perhaps watching the Moon casting light on the trees or water, or making even urban rooftops temporarily attractive.

✦ Draw or paint your Moon wisdom in your psychic journal and you will be rewarded over subsequent nights by rich dreams in which you may travel to other dimensions.

In your everyday world, full-Moon energies can be used for making a major leap or change in your world, for speaking what needs to be said, whether 'I love you,' 'I am sorry,' 'I am no longer afraid of you,' or 'Goodbye'.

It is also a time that is traditionally good for conception, and once you start to live by the Moon energies you may find that your own bodily cycles will become better attuned to the natural ones. Make beautiful love, dance, run, send your typescript to the publisher, your CV to the managing director of the firm you hope one day to run. If you ride the instability of the time like the crest of a wave, you can use it to carry your intentions to their target.

The waning Moon

The more the Moon decreases in size, the more the potency decreases. So the pull that keeps whatever it is that is in your life that is destructive, is also decreasing. In fact, waning Moon powers are like an emptying bath that washes away all the bad things into the cosmos or the earth, to be restored and reformed into positivity.

I often make Moon water by leaving spring water in a silver dish in the full moonlight and using the water for healing or empowerment throughout the month. This is a very powerful method, but you can also make waning-Moon water that you can use for banishing sorrow, or the influences of destructive people or habits.

The waning Moon is in many ways the most psychic of all the phases, for as you move away from earthly activity and frantic schedules, conscious development will slow down and your innate powers will guide you. The result of this will be that your dreams become richer, your meditation quieter, your inner imaging richer, and your scrying work more spontaneous. Choose a night or early morning before light when the Moon is still shining, and use a mirror to direct the light into the water. Alternatively, you can choose a clear night and leave your bowl out for eight hours from moonrise. Unlike full-Moon water, I would not suggest keeping it for more than a day, as its banishing powers may sap your determination.

✦ If possible, find a source of running water, the ebb tide, a fast-flowing river or stream, or use water in a bath and add a few drops of lemon, tea tree or pine essential oil, or bath foam.

✦ Work when you can see or know that the waning Moon is in the sky.

✦ Find a symbol for whatever it is you wish to banish: a few drops of alcohol; cigarette ash; dying flower petals for a lost love or destructive relationship or one that has run its course; a fallen leaf for the need to accept change in your life; mouldy breadcrumbs for anxieties about food or an opportunity that failed to bear fruit. Alternatively, you can burn incense, myrrh, eucalyptus or cypress or any other purifying fragrance and collect that ash in a container.

✦ Name what it is you wish to decrease or lose from your life, focusing on banishing the destructive emotions rather than releasing negativity to the person, no matter how unkind (leave that to the natural forces of justice).

✦ Then, crumb by crumb, or petal by petal, repeat as you cast the negativity away: 'Go flow from me, go from me, no more to see, go in peace, destruction cease.'

✦ Now add the waning-Moon water drop by drop from a dark bottle until it is gone, saying: 'Moon of wisdom, Lady Crone, carry away, what cannot stay.'

✦ If you are working with a bath, take out the plug and stir the water anticlockwise, visualising the silver Moon water carrying all the darkness away.

In your everyday world, waning-Moon energies can be used to cut back on unnecessary activity, encouraging rest and time for focusing on your inner world, especially through scrying and dream interpretation. It is a good time to begin a healthy diet, or to cut out unnecessary stimulants, to clear clutter both physical and emotional, and to finish either a stage or a project you began on the waxing Moon.

Sun Power

Solar energies are as important as lunar ones in psychic development and magic, because they contain direct, dynamic, concentrated rays of light for empowerment, psychic energy, cleansing and healing. They supplement the cyclical ebbs and flows of the Moon, and both solar gods and goddesses are portrayed as concentrated light sources who bring the life-force as sunbeams on their daily journey across the sky to revitalise, illuminate and inspire.

What is more, Sun power concentrates within a single day the energies to attract abundance at dawn; the sudden blast of pure power to achieve any goal or overcome any obstacle at noon; the banishing of sorrow with the falling of dusk; and a fourth phase of transformation and regeneration at midnight. These energies are especially concentrated on the four annual solar festivals. These festivals are:

The spring equinox – around 21 March in the northern hemisphere, 21 September in the southern hemisphere – when equal day and night mark the triumph of light and warmth over the dark winter days and the time of new beginnings.

The summer solstice – around 21 June in the northern hemisphere, 21 December in the southern hemisphere – when just about anything is possible as the Sun reaches the highest point in the year.

The autumn equinox – around 21 September in the northern hemisphere, 21 March in the southern hemisphere – the time of reaping abundance.

The mid-winter solstice – around 21 December in the northern hemisphere, 21 June in the southern hemisphere – that promises the rebirth of light and hope even on the darkest, coldest day.

Since each of the four solar marker-points of the day corresponds and shares energies with the four solar festivals, you can adapt the daily activities I suggest for those four special occasions.

Sun Times

Dawn times vary each day and can be found in a diary or the weather section of a newspaper. Unless you live on the Greenwich meridian, the Sun will not be exactly overhead at noon, so work either with your own local noontime or when the Sun is above you. Dusk also varies each evening.

Dawn

This corresponds with the spring equinox and is represented in ritual by facing east. However, since the Sun only actually rises true east (and sets in true west) on the equinoxes, because of the tilt of the earth, you may wish to work with its actual position in the sky when dawn breaks. It is worth rising early to meditate with the ascending light, to walk in the quiet of the city before it wakes, or in the countryside, or to watch the darkness receding over the sea, leaving scarlet-tinged waves. It is also a good time to send healing.

Use the following exercise for a new beginning, a new project or simply to restore hope and stir up positive energies at a time when life is going badly. Work either out of doors, if it is warm enough, or in a room from which you can see the sunrise.

✦ While it is still dark, place a symbol that represents the new beginning that is needed on a table, rock or tree stump. Stand in the darkness picturing in your mind the new beginning you need, and either name your intention or the name of the person who needs healing.

✦ Place next to it a golden-coloured bowl filled with spring water.

✦ As the light breaks through, hold up your symbol so that it and you absorb the rising light, chanting slowly: 'Light of dawn intensify, flood the earth, the sea, the sky-life and loveliness, hopefulness and healing, fill I ask this symbol of... and my heart and mind with the promise of new beginnings.'

✦ Stir the water three times clockwise with a clear crystal quartz, saying: 'Bless, purify, sanctify, Mother, Father,' (or you may wish to invoke an archangel or the more abstract power of goodness and light).

✦ Sprinkle a few drops of the dawn-tinged water either on to or around the symbol, repeating your intention and adding: 'Bless, purify, sanctify, from the earth to the sky.'

✦ Leave the water until noon and then you can use it for drinking, adding to baths or to send to someone who is sick. Water made on the solar festivals is especially powerful, as is that made on a solar eclipse.

Noon

These energies are a concentrated form of solar energies that can be used when there is a sudden or urgent need for power, confidence, strength or an unexpected need for a fast injection of money. Noon on the day of the full Moon will give you more enduring power. Noon is also an excellent time for absent healing of serious or acute conditions, perhaps on the day of an operation or when medical tests are taking place. It is also a good time for galvanising psychic powers if you have hit a period of stagnation or uncertainty. You can also heal war-torn lands or polluted places by this method.

✦ Work with a clear crystal sphere, your crystal pendulum or a large piece of crystal quartz. (Many indigenous cultures believed that the power of light itself was concentrated and held frozen in crystal quartz.)

✦ At noon, face the direction of the Sun.

✦ If possible, stand within a circle of sunlight.

✦ Hold your crystal so that the light is reflected within it and name the purpose of the noonday ritual, but avoid looking directly at the Sun or its reflected sphere.

✦ Now move clockwise around the Sun circle, or visualise one instead, still holding the crystal so that it is full of light. Chant: 'Noon power at this hour, bring to me what I see.'

✦ Chant and move faster so that the sunlight sparkles, and allow your feet to guide you in what may be a spiral as you connect with earth energies.

✦ Visualise the light getting brighter. Within the sphere, visualise whatever you want or whomever you are healing, bathed in pure gold.

✦ You may find you are stamping or singing.

✦ When the light and motion increase no more, cry: 'So shall it be as I count three. Three, two, one, it is done. Peace come,' and, dropping to your knees, place the crystal before you and sit quite motionless, using your mind to project the light to wherever it is needed.

✦ When you are ready, whisper: 'Go in peace.'

✦ Sit quietly. When it feels right, carry out a positive task, such as planting a few seeds, tidying an unattractive place, making a phone call, or sending an email to someone who needs cheering up.

Dusk

This is a good time to retreat to your special place, if only for a few minutes. If you are with other people you could slip outdoors and let the evening empty away all the tensions of the day, the regrets for what was done badly or not done at all. It is a time consciously to lay down your burdens. Night workers may prefer to reverse the dawn/dusk energy patterns, although dusk can bring a wonderful calm for those who work while others sleep.

The following is a good ritual to practise standing on a bridge over water; urban parks can sometimes have quite ornate water gardens. If you cannot, visualise a really spectacular bridge and yourself with total access to it, such as Tower Bridge in London or the Golden Gate Bridge of San Francisco, or a bridge over a tiny Japanese water garden overhung by cherry trees.

✦ Fill a small bowl with a mixture of your favourite nuts and/or seeds and wait until dusk begins to tinge the sky and the water (or your visualised water).

✦ Take a nut or seed, and state in your mind or aloud what went well during the day or any pleasure you derived, however small. Eat the nut or seed.

✦ Take another nut or seed and name something that went badly, a task you did not finish or a worry you still have relating to the day. Cast this nut or seed into the water (or into a second bowl if you are visualising).

✦ Taking another nut or seed, name or think of a person who was kind or made you laugh or with whom you had contact during the day, even by email, or of whom you thought positively. Eat the nut or seed.

✦ Take another nut or seed. Recall someone who was critical, who failed to contact you as promised or about whom you worried during the day. Cast that into the growing dusk.

✦ Continue comparing positive with negative, eating and casting away until it is all resolved. Try to end with a positive thought or affirmation about the past day (sometimes I really struggle with this).

✦ Then bury any remaining seeds or nuts where they may grow into new tomorrows. If you collected cast-off regrets in a second bowl, bury those too, even if only in a plant pot.

✦ Watch the light fade, welcoming the dark and consciously pushing away any tensions or worries about the day that try to return.

Midnight

This is the quiet time when, if we cannot sleep, we can light a candle and allow the magical images to heal and transform our lives. It is a time to recall deceased family members with affection or forgiveness, and to send healing thoughts to living friends and family members. We should especially remember older ones who are far away or ill, or those who are in war-torn lands or places damaged by pollution.

Although regarded traditionally as a time for psychic as well as physical and mental rest, natural regeneration and transformation, midnight can also form the focus for active psychic work to break the barriers between the here and now and other dimensions.

✦ Work at midnight, in total darkness, near a window or in the open air, except for the single light of a tall, slender white candle.

✦ Look into the external darkness and focus on the exact place the visualised Sun will occupy. Picture a single dot of light in that position.

✦ Concentrate on that spot, visualising the blazing ball of fire building up from the spot of light.

✦ Now transfer your gaze to the candle flame and see that too as a blazing sphere of light.

✦ Return to the visualised Sun in the sky and ever more rapidly transfer your gaze between the actual and ever-growing and pulsating perceived light source.

✦ When you can feel power and light throbbing within you, move so that the candle is between you and the window. The two light sources can then more easily join in the final phase.

✦ Raising your hands high over the flame, cast them down towards the ground as though you were holding a sword or knife in each, and then sharply lift them up again so that they are parallel with your waist. Cast the final blaze of light along the blades towards the Sun at Midnight, so that the image in the sky flares and momentarily fills the whole sky. If you are comfortable doing so, you can use paper knives or small ornamental swords set alongside the candle during the visualisation.

✦ Call on the Divine forces to send aid wherever it is needed.

✦ Afterwards you may see the golden glow temporarily in the sky.

With practise, you will find that it takes less time to transfer the light source. The Sun will remain longer in the midnight sky and will gradually make it light as opposed to the glowing sphere set against blackness.

As you become skilled you can make the candlelight source even smaller until you are working in total darkness. In time you may also experience travel to other dimensions.

The Power of the Planets

Traditionally, only the five ancient planets, Mercury, Mars, Venus, Jupiter and Saturn plus the Moon and Sun, are used in psychic work and magic. One reason is that all these are clearly visible with the physical eye without the aid of a telescope. A good way of focusing on planetary energies is to use a computer programme or sky map to plot where each is located in the sky at a particular time.

As with the elements, the ancient planetary powers are present in everyone's birth chart and so they have at least a symbolic influence on us all. The later planets, Uranus, Neptune and Pluto, take so much longer to move around the Sun and are so much further away, that their influence is more pronounced on the generations than on individuals. The powers of the seven traditional planets (which include the Sun and Moon even though they are not planets) can be used at times when you need their specific strengths. You can work with their crystals, trees and incenses, for example to increase the desired planetary qualities in your life temporarily or permanently. You could paint or engrave a planetary glyph on the relevant crystal or a piece of wood and wear it as a pendant or carry it in a purse or pouch. A few of the dried herbs associated with the planet could be added to the purse or pouch to act as a protective amulet or to give you power. Or you could carry the planet's symbols as amulets or talismans (see below).

These associations have become entwined throughout the centuries in different lands. For example, a number of people have discovered that burning frankincense oil increases energy and gives the confidence to strive with every sinew to achieve any ambition – these are the qualities associated with the Sun. What is more, it would seem that you can use the symbols as keys to open the store of qualities that have accumulated over centuries psychokinetically, by people using them for that specific purpose. Planetary strengths can help not only in your psychic work but also in your everyday life.

Working with the Planets

Each planet is linked to a day of the week when its energies are symbolically especially strong. So, for example, if you wanted to ask for promotion or increased responsibility at work, a Thursday would be a good time, as this is the day of Jupiter who rules all matters of increase. You might also carry a lapis lazuli stone, or a tin coin and perhaps light a blue candle and burn sandalwood oil in the early morning. All these invoke the strengths of Jupiter.

I have listed specific herbs, oils and incenses you can use, or you can refer to the more detailed list of herbs on pages 76–81. You will find details of the archangel powers that are linked with each of the planets in Step 10.

The Sun

The Sun is mainly the focus for yang/male/animus energies in both men and women. The Sun deities are usually male, though in a number of traditions, from the Celts to the Baltic lands and Japan, Sun goddesses are important. Use the Sun as a focus for personal fulfilment and ambition, power and success, for increasing the flow of the life-force, asserting or strengthening your identity and individuality, for innovation of all kinds and new beginnings. It is potent also for energy, joy, health, prosperity, spiritual awareness and self-confidence. It will bring or restore prosperity when fortunes are low and will break a run of bad luck. The Sun is also potent for all matters concerning fathers.

Element Fire.

Colour Gold.

Crystals Amber, carnelian, diamond, clear crystal quartz, tiger's eye, topaz.

Trees Banana, bay, chestnut/horse chestnut, laurel, orange, date palm.

Herbs, incenses and oils Benzoin, copal, frankincense, juniper, rosemary, saffron, St John's wort.

Metal Gold.

Day of the week Sunday.

Archangel Michael.

The Sun rules Leo and the planet is especially potent for those born under it and for anyone during the Sun sign period 23 July–23 August.

The Moon

The Moon is mainly the focus for yin/female/anima energies in men and women. Moon deities are predominantly female, though there are Moon gods in the Slavic, Viking and Oriental traditions. Use the Moon as a focus for home and family matters, mothers, children and animals, for fertility and all the ebbs and flows of the human body, mind and psyche. Also use it for protection, especially while travelling, for psychic development, clairvoyance and meaningful dreams, sea and gardening rituals and concerns, and for herb magic and healing; also for keeping secrets.

Element Water.

Colour Silver or white.

Crystals Moonstone, mother of pearl, pearl, selenite, opal.

Trees Alder, coconut, eucalyptus, lemon tree, tamarind, willow, and any other trees that grow by water.

Herbs, incenses and oils Chamomile, jasmine, lemon, lemon balm, lotus, mimosa, myrrh, poppy, wintergreen.

Metal Silver.

Day of the week Monday.

Archangel Gabriel.

The Moon rules Cancer and the planet is especially potent for those born under it and for anyone during the Sun sign period from 22 June–22 July.

Mars

Use Mars energies for courage, change, taking the initiative, independence and establishing the boundaries between self and others. Mars also represents aggression, competitiveness and anger, all qualities that can be used positively for altruistic purposes, when standing against injustice and protecting loved ones and the vulnerable when under threat. This is the lifeblood planet and so can be used to overcome seemingly impossible odds – to defeat opposition, to survive and thrive, for physical health and vitality – and so its rituals are always dynamic. Mars also rules passion and the consummation of love.

Element Fire.

Colour Red.

Crystals Bloodstone, blood agate, garnet, ruby, jasper.

Trees Cypress, hawthorn, holly, palm, pine, rowan.

Herbs, incenses and oils Basil, coriander, dragon's blood, garlic, ginger, mint, pepper, tarragon, thyme.

Metal Iron and steel.

Day of the week Tuesday.

Archangel Samael.

Mars rules Aries, 21 March–20 April, and is the co-ruler of Scorpio, 24 October–22 November. It is most potent during those Sun sign periods and for those born under Aries and Scorpio.

Mercury

Use Mercury as a focus for money-making ventures, for clear communication, persuasion, adaptability and versatility. Its powers are also used for improving memory and sharpening logic, for learning, examinations and tests, for mastering new technology, for short-distance or short breaks, and for conventional methods of healing, especially surgery. It is also potent for divination, business negotiations and overcoming debts, and for repelling envy, malice and spite and those who would deceive.

Element Air.

Colour Yellow.

Crystals Agate, citrine, falcon's eye, jasper, malachite, onyx.

Trees Almond, ash, hazel, sycamore.

Herbs, incenses and oils Dill, fennel, lavender, lemongrass, lily of the valley, mace, parsley, valerian.

Metal Mercury or aluminium (occasionally platinum).

Day of the week Wednesday.

Archangel Raphael.

Mercury rules Gemini, 22 May–21 June, and Virgo, 24 August–22 September, and so it is most potent during those periods and for those born under Gemini and Virgo.

Jupiter

Use Jupiter as a focus for all forms of increase and expansion, whether improving fortune or career prospects, or obtaining promotion, power, and joy through fulfilment of ambitions. Jupiter is also potent for leadership, for conscious wisdom and creativity, for extending one's influence in the wider world and for idealism, matters of justice and the law, authority and altruism. It increases what already exists and so can bring greater prosperity and abundance, or success and good fortune. Jupiter also rules marriage, permanent relationships – business and personal – fidelity, loyalty and male potency in both the human and the animal kingdoms.

Element Air.

Colour Blue/purple.

Trees Beech, cedar, oak, redwood.

Crystals Azurite, laboradite, lapis lazuli, sodalite, turquoise.

Herbs, incenses and oils Agrimony, borage, cinquefoil, coltsfoot, honeysuckle, oakmoss, hyssop, mistletoe, sandalwood, sage.

Metal Tin.

Day of the week Thursday.

Archangel Sachiel.

Jupiter rules Sagittarius, 23 November–21 December, and is co-ruler of Pisces, 19 February–20 March. It is therefore especially potent in the period of Sagittarius and Pisces and at all times to those born under these Sun signs.

Venus

Use Venus as a focus for love and all forms of love magic, especially to attract love. Venus is also invoked for beauty, the arts, crafts and music, relationships, friendships, blossoming sexuality, the acquisition of beautiful possessions, harmony, the mending of quarrels and the slow but sure growth of prosperity, for Venus rules all matters of growth. Like the Moon, she can be invoked for fertility and for women's health matters, for horticulture and the environment; also for healing using herbs and crystals.

Element Earth.

Colour Green, pink.

Crystals Amethyst, calcite, emerald, fluorite, jade, moss agate, rose quartz.

Trees Almond, apple, birch, cherry, olive, peach, pear.

Herbs, incenses and oils Echinacea, feverfew, geranium, lilac, mugwort, pennyroyal, rose, strawberry, vervain, yarrow, ylang-ylang.

Metal Copper.

Day of the Week Friday.

Archangel Anael.

Venus rules Taurus, 21 April–21 May, and Libra, 23 September–23 October, and so is especially potent during these Sun sign periods and for those born under Taurus and Libra.

Saturn

Use Saturn as a focus for unfinished business, endings that lead to beginnings, all slow-moving matters and for accepting limitations, as well as for overcoming obstacles that are long-standing or need careful handling. It can help to relieve pain, lift depression or doubts, and in meditation, long-term psychic protection, locating lost objects, animals and people and for regaining self-control whether over bad habits or emotions. It is also the planet of mystical experiences, for exploring the unconscious depths of the individual and collective psyche, and for past life work. Saturn can be used to slow down the outwards flow of money and to encourage those who owe you favours or money to repay them.

Element Earth.

Colour Black/grey.

Crystals Haematite, jet, lodestone, obsidian, smoky quartz.

Tree Aspen, blackthorn, cypress, rowan, yew.

Herbs, incenses and oils Aconite, bistort, comfrey horsetail, patchouli, Solomon's seal, vetiver.

Metal Lead or pewter.

Day of the week Saturday.

Archangel Cassiel.

Saturn rules Capricorn, 22 December–20 January, and is co-ruler of Aquarius, 21 January–18 February, and so is especially potent during this period and for those born under these signs at all times.

Working with Your Dreams

As you develop psychically and connect with the forces of the Moon, Sun and Earth, you will find quite spontaneously that your dreams become more vivid and filled with symbols. You may also find that your recall improves and that you become aware that you are dreaming while you are asleep. Later in this section, you will work with lucid dreaming, discovering the ability to change or use a dreamscape by being aware that you are in the dream state; these techniques mirror those of astral travel.

Dream analysis is an important form of divination as it offers access not only to your unconscious mind, but also to the universal symbol system and to higher forms of consciousness that enable us to interpret our own experiences in the context of a world not bound by material limitations. Dream analysis is not bound by time, so we can often see in our dreams future paths that may be fruitful, and warnings of less advantageous actions or ventures. All we have to do is to understand the symbols in which the deeper mind operates. As we work with scrying and tap into the symbolism associated with the planets, we can interpret the psychic code, so that we can make wise choices in the light of day.

Recalling and Re-entering Your Dreams

To work with your dreams, it is first important to improve your dream recall, so that you can interpret them as any other form of divination or counsel from the collective store of wisdom. As you work through your dreams, you will find that you can receive messages from higher beings, such as angels, and access future as well as past knowledge.

✦ Keep a notebook, pen and bedside light or torch close to your bed. When you wake from a vivid dream, allow the dream to re-run as though you were watching a video screen. Write down absolutely every detail in any order or draw images – this is like emptying a bottle so you tip out the last drop.

✦ When you have finished, close your eyes and reconnect with the last image before you woke.

✦ If you want to re-enter a dream, leave something behind in the dream, such as a piece of luggage or an earring. You can then re-enter your dream by looking for the item and by that means you can often retrace your path.

✦ Alternatively, visualise something of yours on one of the dream paths, and moving via the last image you recalled, draw yourself towards it by visualising your boundaries melting and the dream world enclosing you.

✦ If you do not want to return, push the image away gently on a boat down a stream to return to the dream plane. Then float on pink fluffy clouds or in a warm blue ocean until you drift off again (or take advantage of the early morning for some dawn magic or meditation and take a siesta later).

Creating a Dream Dictionary

In Further Reading (see page 242) I have listed books in which there are dream meanings and also information on the mechanics of how we dream. However, it is far more important for you to create your own dream and divinatory symbolism. You will find that the same symbols occur in both dreams and scrying/divination. You have already been keeping A–Z entries from your scrying work and this will form the core of your dream dictionary.

✦ As you did for scrying, after a vivid dream select one or two symbols you noted down and visualise the image as though on a screen, or use a purple candle as a focus. A whole mythology may embellish it: elements of half-remembered tales from childhood, or of strange lands or past places you may meet in your future astral travels (see page 164). Add these insights to your alphabetical list. There may be an overlap of dream and scrying images. These usually represent those that have deep significance for you and that will unfold with your psyche over the coming months.

✦ A dream symbol may appear spontaneously in the external world by the process the psychologist Jung called synchronicity, or meaningful coincidence. This is where the image appears in an unexpected place or time in your life shortly after the dream.

✦ It can then be helpful to see what is going on in your life to which the symbol is referring. The personal significance of the symbol will indicate the best action or way forwards and is where a personal dream list is more helpful than one given in a book.

Creative Dreaming – Dreaming True

It is quite possible to use the dream state to give answers or creative solutions to questions or dilemmas, by casting the topic into the dream sea and trusting cosmic wisdom to provide the solution. You can even gain either a healing remedy or actual healing in the dream state by focusing pre-sleep on the specific problem. In ancient Egypt, this was called 'dreaming true'. Seekers went to a cave that faced south and sat in the darkness gazing at the candle flame until they saw a deity in it. They would then sleep, and it was said the god or goddess would come to them in their dreams and provide the answer to the problem. This method can easily be adapted to the modern world.

✦ Set a deep-blue candle, for quiet meditation, on a metal tray. Light it before sleeping and recite the question as a silent mantra for two or three minutes only.

✦ Write the question down on paper, then safely and carefully burn the paper in the flame, this time reciting the question or dilemma aloud.

✦ Collect the ash from the tray, and scoop some of it into a small purse to keep under the pillow with a few grains of lavender or rosemary for meaningful but gentle dreams.

✦ Blow out the candle, saying; 'Light of love, light of hopefulness, carry the answer on the sea of dreams.'

Dream healing was practised by the ancient Greeks through a process known as dream incubation. This process resembled the Egyptian dreaming true. Most famous for dream incubation were the Aesculapian temples in the Classical world, which were sited at sacred wells and springs. You can adapt the above technique for dream incubation by focusing on the illness or emotional distress and stating it as above. With this technique, when you dream it may be a healing angel or deity who appears, or you may dream of particular plants or places where you will find relief.

Working with the Etheric Self through Lucid Dreaming

In your dreams you can visit other realms. Lucid dreaming can be defined as dreaming while knowing that you are dreaming, so it can be used as a gentle introduction to out-of-body or astral travel to explore the astral or dream planes when we are most relaxed and least connected to the material world.

The astral planes are akin to the realms accessed by shamans – the magical priest/healers of indigenous cultures from Siberia to Africa – and are called the lower realms. These realms are reached through sleep or light trances and are approached by different routes: through holes in the earth and along tunnels; while riding spirit horses across plains; when coursing along rivers in spirit canoes; or when diving deep into oceans.

The lower realms, which bear no relation to the Christian Hell, are the places where healing or wisdom can be experienced by communicating with talking animals or the Master or Mistress of the Herds and Fishes, who controls fertility and abundance. Also present are magical forests containing fruits and plants that bring wisdom and healing, and rivers and seas with fabulous creatures.

To the uninitiated this may seem like reliving a fairy tale, but as an adult we can connect with the core of this archetypal wisdom. By working within the framework of the astral planes that can also be accessed through meditation and out-of-body experiences, we can receive meaningful symbols. These will help us to resolve dilemmas and will provide understanding about the deep spiritual nature that connects us not only with the past and future, but also with the unseen world of spirit.

The higher realms are traditionally the home of the wise ancestors, who include our deceased grandmothers who may come to us in dreams if they are concerned that we are not caring for ourselves properly. Ancestors, perhaps from other lands, with whom we have specific spiritual kinship, will also reside there. Mediumship can also be used to access this realm, as can channelling (see page 200).

Lucid dreaming techniques

You can develop the dream-directing techniques you began on page 163. You will then be able to explore the astral realms as well as being aware that you can fly, float, or cross the Atlantic Ocean or the Milky Way in seconds by the powers of thought control.

Eventually you will be able to visit these places in dreams and be aware that you are as fully in control of your spirit body as your physical one. You can then transfer this ability to waking out-of-body travel, regression or progression work (travelling backwards or forwards through time). With time, advanced meditation and visualisation work will enable you to channel wisdom from higher forms, such as angels, and even momentarily to access the source of Divinity (see pages 189–92).

You have already practised dream recall and re-entering dreams in the half-dreamful early morning state. The next step is to practise creating dream scenarios immediately before sleep and then to re-enter a dream experienced just before waking.

Recently I have discovered that the fastest way to experience lucid dreaming is to create a really vivid dream state, either based on a book rich in otherworldly images, for example a section from Tolkien's *Lord of the Rings*, C.S. Lewis's *Narnia Chronicles* or one of myths from around the world. Alternatively, watch a video about a particularly powerful indigenous group.

There are a number of evocative films about the Native North American world. You might also find a fantasy about other galaxies stimulating. Any of these will reconnect you with the archetypal symbols of the dream world. After a while you will not need such triggers.

✦ When you are relaxed, re-create in your mind scenes from the stimulus that were especially positive, or focus on a character with which you can readily identify.

✦ Now, while in this visualisation, create a dream sign that is linked with the stimulus, something that would not readily happen in the everyday world, such as a talking animal, a brilliantly coloured flower or the sensation of flying.

✦ When this sign appears, say out loud: 'When this… appears I will know I am dreaming,' and continue with the reconstruction.

✦ Evoke the symbol two or three times in your myth weaving, repeating each time: 'When this symbol appears, I recall that I am dreaming.'

✦ Let yourself drift into asleep, but keep your dream symbol in your thoughts. As you drift, recite the intention to know you are dreaming slowly as a mantra, so that these are the last remaining thoughts in your mind before falling asleep.

✦ If you do not enter the desired scenario or see your symbol in your dreams that night (it may appear in another context or dream, in which case go with that dreamscape), as you wake re-enter the desired dreamscape and deliberately evoke the symbol so that you have a half-waking lucid dream.

✦ The next evening re-read or watch the stimulus, visualise the scene and repeat the lucid dream mantra night and morning.

✦ Continue this process using the same dream symbol until it finally appears. You may even gain your first experience of lucid dreaming in an entirely different dreamscape from the one you planned.

Moving into other dimensions in sleep

Once you are in a dream, and are aware of yourself reacting as in meditation when you watched yourself meditating as though you were sitting above yourself on a cloud (see page 52), you can experiment, creating doorways into other realms: diving into underwater worlds; exploring jewel-encrusted tunnels; walking through enchanted forests and talking to nature spirits, or climbing the cosmic world tree to the stars. You can try flying or floating across space to realms where deceased family members, wise ancestors, angels and beings of light can offer wisdom. Or you can travel to Atlantis or Lemuria (see pages 234–35) or forwards to the realms of future potential, where prototypes of future experience may be found, to be shaped by the choices and actions of the present generations. You can explore these worlds by relaxing just before sleep and allowing your mind to float.

After a few weeks of lucid work you will find waking visions and out-of-body experiences, as well as past and future life work, entering your quiet psychic times quite spontaneously.

The Next Step

There are also other ways of communicating with the world of spirit. In the following chapter we will continue the work you began in your dreams in other contexts and meet some of the helpful beings who inhabit higher realms. You will meet your guardian angel or guide, travel to other realms while you are awake and relaxed, explore past worlds and the future, talk with devas and other nature spirits, connect with ghosts in a positive way and link with the wisdom of your personal ancestors.

Connecting with the Spirit World

THERE HAVE BEEN COUNTLESS speculations about the nature of spirit realms. Some people believe that they are arranged in order of ascending spirituality, with the higher ones having a higher rate of vibration than those closer to the material plane of existence. It is hypothesised that these higher realms, or planes, can be contacted the more spiritually evolved we become. The lowest of the spirit realms or planes are inhabited by spiritual essences from devas or higher nature spirits. Then, ascending through the planes are spirit guides, angels and archangels up to the Godhead or source of Divinity, whether this is perceived as God or the Goddess.

In this belief system, the highest realms are only rarely accessed by mortals and then only after several lifetimes of increasing enlightenment. However, there are others, myself included, who are more egalitarian. I would echo the sentiments of the poet William Wordsworth, who wrote in his poem, 'Ode on the Intimations of Immortality', that a child possessed the most spiritual nature of all humans, having existed in heavenly realms before birth. He believed we move away from this spiritual nature as we become adults. He wrote:

> *Our birth is but a sleep and a forgetting*
> *the soul that rises with us, our life's star*
> *hath had elsewhere its setting and cometh from afar…*
> *trailing clouds of glory from God who is our home.*

Young children can happily converse with angels, fairies, the Virgin Mary and God/the Goddess, and I believe that once we have rediscovered our forgotten powers and spiritual nature, we too can talk directly to spirit beings, right up to the Godhead. As long as we do not expect to see a burning bush, but are content with a humbler but equally precious sign, we will be protected.

As discussed in the previous chapter, we can travel to these other realms when asleep and also when awake. First, however, it is important to contact what may be your first spirit being, one you may recall from childhood or a dream. He or she will protect you as you travel to the other places and always bring you safely home.

Guardian Angels – Discovering Your Astral Guide

Once your astral travel and contact with other realms begins to take form, you may be aware of your guardian angel or wise spirit guide, who will protect and return you safely to the material planes.

Your astral guardian may be someone who has appeared in your dreams for years, perhaps a wise druidess, an Oriental sage, a Native North American chieftain, a wise Hindu priest, an ancient Egyptian scribe, an African medicine man or woman, or your personal angel. You may even know their name and, as you develop mediumistic abilities, you may see him or her hovering at your side. If you wish, this guide will also act as an intermediary to help you to become a channel for even higher forms of wisdom (see pages 229–30).

If you have not yet made contact, try the following exercise. It may take a while to get the weather conditions exactly right for it to be a success, but when you can achieve it you will find it very rewarding. If you can find your water source with overhanging trees that will make your reflection quite shadowy, so much the better.

✦ Work on a day when there is sunshine and clouds.

✦ Find a pool, a lake, or even a swimming pool.

✦ Sit or stand so you can see your reflection.

◆ Gaze into the pool and ask your special guardian to make him or herself known if the time is right.

◆ When a cloud obscures the Sun, wait until you can see the Sun beginning to emerge and stir the water with a branch.

◆ At the moment the Sun breaks through you will see a figure, albeit dimly behind you.

◆ Blink to bring it momentarily into sharp focus and you will perceive your guardian. You may hear a voice or sense him or her brushing against your aura, like a gentle breeze, even on a windless day.

◆ Still facing the water, visualise the figure standing protectively with arms or wings outspread behind you.

◆ Touch your third eye and then your heart chakra with your right hand, and the guide or angel will touch his or hers with the left. This will complete the union and establish a sign that you can make unobtrusively whenever you feel the need for your guardian angel to move close and offer wisdom or protection, whether you are asleep or awake.

◆ If you carry out this ritual regularly, you will find that you see your special angel or guide in more detail. You may also hear a soft but clear voice that is your own and yet richer, and calmer, and one you have heard a thousand times in your dreams or on the wind.

◆ If you ask, he or she will tell you their name. You can call this before you go to sleep and when you practise out-of-body or past-life work.

Out-of-body Travel

To many indigenous peoples throughout the world, out-of-body travel, also known as etheric or spirit body travel, is a reality both in sleep and during waking hours. Even in Westernised society, about a third of people have reported such experiences – as a child you may recall the sensation of floating or flying downstairs.

Etheric projection is strictly defined as the ability of the spirit body to travel beyond the confines of the physical body, although it may be the mind that is projecting. In contrast, astral travel is said to be closer to the shamanic and dream travel that you may have experienced as you worked with your lucid dreams when you visited fairy-tale-like realms in sleep. In practice, out-of-body travel is no different from astral travelling and waking out-of-body travel; just as in lucid dreams you can define your destination, whether it is for present, past, future or mythological realms.

Using Tattwa Cards as a Focus

By far the most effective method I have used and taught for out-of-body work involves using the Vedantic tattwa cards that were introduced into the West by the theosophists and the magical order of the Golden Dawn at the end of the 19th and early 20th centuries. Using these cards prevents the sensation of floating above and looking down on the physical body that some adults do not like, although children usually love dancing in front of their physical body.

The cards consist of five basic shapes that correspond to the four elements plus the fifth quintessential aether or akasa. I have found that if you visualise yourself moving in ascending order of vibrations from earth right up to spirit, you can quite naturally attune your spirit or etheric body to the vibrations of aether or *akasa,* which is the same vibration as that of the dream and astral planes.

The easiest way to explain this is if you think of the ascending levels in terms of the gears of a car. You are using the higher gears or spiritual part of your body to reach the higher realms. You are still in your physical body, just as you are still in the car when in top gear. But because you are operating on a higher level than you do in the everyday world, you can move beyond the confines of time and space while at the same time the lower reaches of your mind are totally relaxed within your physical body.

I have found that if you move through the realms in ascending order of vibrations, which correspond with the descending order of mass, you can quite naturally attune your spirit or etheric body to the vibrations of aether or akasa. So if you are interrupted, your spirit will not be left floundering in, say, Tokyo but will transfer the necessary attention, losing the connection with the higher dimensions but not vice versa.

Making your out-of-body stairway

Using tattwa cards can help form a stairway to lead us to out-of-body travel. They can easily be made from card. Create the geometric shapes from card or draw and colour them framed on a square background. Each shape should be about 15 centimetres (6 inches) square. Using fluorescent colours can make them even more powerful. The Sanskrit names are generally used.

◆ First, make *prithivi*, earth, which is a yellow square, set on purple to give a three-dimensional effect. Imagine this as a block of ice, that is solid.

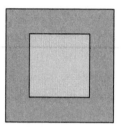

prithivi, earth

◆ Next, create *apas*, water, a crescent lying on its back, in silver on a black background. That represents the melted ice.

apas, water

✦ Then comes *tejas*, fire. In some systems it is the mover/creator/destroyer element, and it is pictured as a red triangle on a green background. When this fire is applied to water, steam is produced.

tejas, fire

✦ The steam gives rise to *vayu*, air, a blue circle on a red background.

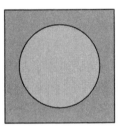

vayu, air

✦ Finally, air diffuses into the aether or spirit, called *akasa*, represented as an oval black or indigo – the cosmic egg on a yellow background.

akasa, aether or spirit

The backgrounds are optional. You can just work with the coloured shapes.

✦ Attach just the shapes without the backgrounds to a cord or string with *akasa* at the top, then *vayu*, then *tejas*, then *apas* and *prithivi* at the bottom.

✦ Alternatively, staple your cards to a medium-thick cord and hang this from the ceiling.

✦ By varying the size of each shape, you can superimpose them one on top of the other on to a single piece of white card, so that you walk horizontally through each level to the next. Make *prithivi* the smallest of all at the front and then graduate the sizes so that *akasa* is the largest at the back. Paste the cards in descending order on to *akasa*. Arrange them so that they share the same centre and the edges overlap, so that you walk in your mind through *prithivi*, then *apas* and so on to *askasa* as though you were walking through a tunnel.

Making the journey

Now all you have to do is to decide where you wish to travel. It can help to hold a symbol, perhaps of the person you intend to visit, a shell for an under-sea realm, a picture of an exotic land or a tiny angel statue if you wish to visit higher planes.

✦ Light rose or frankincense incense and work in pink or green candlelight.

✦ Ensure that your candles are positioned safely in case you fall asleep (night-lights or enclosed containers are the safest).

✦ Lie with your head propped up so you can comfortably raise your glance from the bottom card to the top one without straining your neck. If the cards are hanging from the ceiling they will be easy to see; alternatively, prop the cards in ascending height, one slightly behind the other on small tables or stools, so that you can view them all from where you are lying. They can also be piled on the floor so that you can hold one at a time, discarding each as you walk through it in your mind. Experiment for the best effect.

✦ Focus first on *prithivi*, then close your eyes so that you can see the glowing square in your mind's vision.

✦ Open your eyes and focus next on *apas*, then picture that with closed eyes.

✦ Progress through the other levels, lengthening the time you spend on each until at last you have the glowing *akasa* in your mind. Focus on the open doorway through which only your inner or spirit part is insubstantial enough to enter.

✦ You may see your guide waiting, but if not, call his or her name and they will appear. Allow them to guide you, holding your hand as you are flying.

✦ Remember nothing can hurt you, for you can confront any demons created from your own fears. Nothing can entrap or possess you or come back to haunt you in the everyday world, for you are viewing the scenes from the safety of your own psychic bubble and are protected by your guardian. Some believe our guardians are the higher essence of ourselves.

✦ Your guardian will know when you wish to return, and will guide you back to the indigo doorway.

✦ Thank your guide and ask if he or she has a special message for you.

✦ With your eyes still closed, descend the shimmering tattwas and, when you are ready, open your eyes to the candlelight.

Other Ways of Travelling

Although tattwa cards are my favourite method, there are many others. You can do a visualisation or meditate with your eyes closed and create a pathway down steps that lead you into a garden, up a hill or along a river. You could also travel on a magic carpet. Alternatively, count slowly from 1 to 30 or downwards from 30 to 1, as you walk in your mind along a road or through a forest until you reach a doorway in a high wall, a house or even a tree. You could also position a light on a high shelf and visualise yourself moving towards and through the curtain in it again by counting.

Experiment with different foci, including actual sensory experiences, such as lying on grass or sand, or near banks of fragrant flowers. The only limit is your imagination. You might also try shaman-style dancing out of your physical body to the rhythm of drum music, or drumming or playing a rattle to rise on the sound, or ride a spirit horse across the skies.

Shamans are the magical priest-healers who perform rituals in tribes across the world, from Siberia to Africa. They use drumming, dancing and the rhythmic sound of rattles as a way of moving beyond everyday consciousness, and this can be a good way of initiating out-of-body work if you find it difficult to relax sufficiently to travel to other realms in your mind.

Discovering Past Lives

It is also possible to experiment travelling to past worlds. There is evidence, much of which has come from the experiences of young children, that suggests that we have lived before.

What is not certain is whether when we regress or go backwards in time as adults we are accessing lives that belong to us, or whether we link into the lives of our ancestors or those whose worlds have special relevance for our current life path. We can all recreate events in vivid detail from years ago and relive the emotions in our present lives as though they were yesterday. So take a moment to recall a particularly happy event as far back as you can remember, complete with the touch of fabrics, fragrances, tastes and sounds, as well as words or images. We can seem lost in such past worlds for hours, so vivid are they, although in fact only minutes may have passed.

You will use exactly the same technique for recalling a past life, although this time you will be stepping back to the time before your present childhood.

◆ Begin by focusing on a period to which you are instinctively drawn. We are all fascinated by some historical link and place, whether druidic, Elizabethan or the colonisation of a new land. This interest may seem to have no genealogical basis, though we all have roots in cultures apart from our current one. It may be a place with which you feel kinship – ancient Egypt or Tibet – perhaps a fascination that began in childhood, or with a visit to a museum.

◆ Before you begin your past-life work immerse yourself in the chosen culture. Especially helpful would be psychometric work at a museum or an ancient site (see page 35).

◆ If you want to let your unconscious wisdom select a period, hold a fossil, a dinosaur bone or an organic gem such as amber or jet that is many millions of years old.

◆ Focus on your tattwa cards, perhaps naming a significant date in your chosen period.

◆ Allow yourself to walk through the *akasa* doorway and greet your guide. They will take you to the place where you can observe what you need that will be of help to you now.

◆ You may identify someone who resembles you, perhaps yourself in an earlier life or an ancestor. Usually with this method you experience a single cameo. Although you are an observer, if you wish you can momentarily focus your attention intensely on the character with whom you identify. Then, as you would with a close friend or relative, use telepathy to share their emotions.

◆ Remember that you cannot and should not try to change the past, but only learn from it. If you become uncomfortable, withdraw from the figure gently and watch, knowing that nothing can hurt you.

◆ When you have understood the message the past holds for you, follow your guide back to the doorway and thank them.

If you prefer, you can discover past lives without using the tattwa cards:

◆ Burn cypress, frankincense or myrrh incense, which evoke past-life visions. By the light of a single beeswax candle, sprinkle a few grains of dried lavender in the flame, saying, 'I am five years old,' then 'I am four years old,' continuing to sprinkle the lavender and counting backwards. You will then experience a slight inner bump as you become aware that you have moved to a time before your present childhood.

◆ Now the candle flame will seem to expand and enclose you.

◆ You may experience a sense of floating downwards and of looking up from a cradle. Begin counting forwards and sprinkling lavender once again, this time being aware of a series of images like a fast-moving film until you reach one that slows and is in clear focus in the candle flame.

◆ This is the cameo that will answer what it is you need to find out from the past world. As with the *akasic* door, when you are ready your guide will know. The guide may leave you with a final message before you move out of the candlelight into the fragrant room.

Past-life work should not be carried out more than once a month. You can continue to work with the same period or experiment with others.

Visiting Future Worlds

Because future worlds exist only as potentialities, they are very different from those in past lives. By this I mean that it is quite possible to tap into a hypothetical future world in which you are reborn, or you may see descendants, who resemble you closely because they carry your genes. However, some visionaries have seen very accurate visions of the future. For example, the Renaissance Leonardo da Vinci drew startlingly accurate flying machines centuries ahead of the times they were finally invented. But for most of us it is the people and the relationships that predominate in future intuitions.

The most successful technique I have discovered is ascending steps in sunlight. I originally worked with this technique as a way of opening my crown chakra and discovered the effectiveness of spontaneous future-life visions as a bonus.

◆ On a sunny day, find a flight of steps, perhaps in the grounds of an old house or cathedral, or the steep part of an old town or an old botanical garden.

◆ Work out in advance how you will divide your timeline according to the approximate number of steps and how far forwards you wish to travel. Begin by moving forwards one or two lifetimes.

◆ Walk upwards towards the increasing light, counting for each step, 'I walk forwards ten/twenty/thirty/forty/fifty years,' and focusing on the shimmering haze.

◆ As you ascend, blend into the sunlight so that your body is shimmering inside, and keep counting, focusing on nothing except the warmth and brilliance.

✦ You may be aware of your guardian walking just ahead of you. At the transition points between lifetimes there may be extra brilliance and a sense of lightness.

✦ Sit at or near the top of the steps and, using the haze in front of your eyes as a screen, allow a scene to form and people to move into focus, one of whom you will identify as yourself or your linked descendant in this future age.

✦ Because this is only a speculative world, the focus may be quite soft and at times hazy. However, you may also hear words and experience emotions, although you will not be able to merge with your future alter ego as you did in the past life, as it is too ethereal.

✦ When you feel the thread weakening, turn to your guardian, who will be sitting beside you, and ask if they have a message for you that will help in your future decision-making.

Do not explore future worlds more than once a month unless you have a major decision to make.

Earth and Nature Spirits and Devas

Throughout the book I have emphasised the living energies manifest in the natural world. Few people who live close to nature or spend time at sites of great antiquity can remain unaware of the presence of spirit beings. They resemble and may merge with the specific forms of the plants, trees or stones they guard and in which they make their homes. Because they are formed of an essence higher than the vibrations of our material body, we become aware of them as we become more spiritually evolved (or with the open vision of childhood). For it surely is human vanity that dismisses the possibility of a parallel universe or universes and insists that we are the most evolved form of life.

Because the bodies of nature spirits are less dense in matter than our own, it is easy to miss them. We may mistake them for a ripple on water or a face in the trees caused by the movement of the leaves.

Higher nature spirits are called devas, which in Sanskrit means shining ones. Devas are akin to angels and are opalescent beings who watch and direct the natural world. They are more accessible than angels, however, because they make their homes in the natural world. Devas communicate with people through channelling or psychic communication or directly through the healing and restorative properties of herbs, flowers and trees.

Communicating with Devas

Devas are said to be aware of the thoughts of humans and can channel messages to those who are sufficiently sensitive to hear them. Using clairaudient and telepathic channels, especially when a person is in a state of meditation close to the natural world, enables them to receive the messages. Devas are frequently described as taking the form of beautiful humans who can change size and appearance almost instantly. This may be so that they will harmonise with the image and belief system of the perceiver.

Some devas assume the role of sacred guardian at ancient sites. They have been described by different people, not only by those with clairvoyant sight, as huge brown shadows that appear near ancient circles as dusk draws in, or as silver columns of light at dawn. In the Icelandic and Scandinavian traditions that spread to other parts of Northern Europe, including Britain, the land wights, or *landvaeitir,* acted as guardians of villages and settlements, passing along the fairy paths at dusk and enclosing the area in their protection. Certain fields and hills were declared sacred to them.

As you walk the ancient ley tracks, visit stone circles or single standing stones at twilight, or sit by a fast-flowing river, you may have an overwhelming sense of being in the presence of a sacred power and beauty. Or, as you walk along an ancient track, you may see out of the corner of your eye the measured tread of a figure so old that it seems formed from the loam. You should not be afraid, for these beings are always benign and will bring blessings. You will find after you have experienced such a presence that you instinctively know the right crystal to soothe a headache, or the herb to place in a healing sachet.

Devas are also associated with one of the four elements: earth, air, fire and water. According to their elemental bias, they control different aspects of nature, for example forests – transforming them from a single acorn to acres of dense woodland – protection of wildlife and the seas. It is unsurprising that their communication has become ever more direct and prevalent as we increasingly despoil the planet. Their message is primarily of the need to conserve and protect our natural heritage. They will also be wise teachers of healing, empowering those who listen to them with healing powers through using crystals and herbs (see pages 121–23 and 76–81).

Channelling the wisdom of the devas

As you walk or sit quietly in places of natural sanctity, you will hear quiet, measured words in your head. If you have not already made contact, the easiest connection comes with the devas of the flowers. You may also detect the flower fairies captured so brilliantly by the Edwardian Cicely Mary Barker, moving like so many brilliant butterflies. The secret is time and patience.

✦ On a bright, warm day, find a flower garden; wildlife gardens are being created even in the centres of cities. Flowering herb gardens can also work well.

✦ Spend time walking around alone or with a friend or family member who will not chatter or make demands, and attune yourself to the energies.

✦ When you find a large flowerbed, preferably full of butterflies and humming insects and surrounded by other flowerbeds, sit on the grass so that the earth energy flows through your perineum.

✦ Focusing on a particularly dense bank of colour, allow first eyes then a nose, mouth and hair to separate out. The face may be old, young, beautiful, beyond conventional beauty, or perhaps brown and wrinkled like a being who lives close to the soil.

✦ You may not perceive your deva very clearly – in a mist of a paler shade or as a patch of brilliance or pure white light.

✦ Any or all of these may be perceived with your inner or external eye.

✦ You may hear, either within your head or externally, a disembodied voice, or the communication may be filtered through your own voice and thoughts.

✦ Do not ask any questions, but wait. You may hear a line of poetry, a phrase, a story or see images. The communication may be complex or, like many profound experiences, remarkably simple. There may be a sense of peace and warmth, and of being loved, rather than words or pictures.

✦ After a few minutes, you may feel a sudden breeze or chill, or you may hear someone approaching; this is the time to close the channels.

✦ Let the face fade, and as it does so visualise the colour of the flowers as a sphere – surrounding, protecting and enclosing you as though in soft, coloured mist.

✦ Silently thank the deva and visualise a flower all around you, enfolding you in its petals as your psychic energies close.

Walk quietly around the gardens, allowing any excess energy to flow through your feet into the earth. You can talk to the devas of the hillside, the lakes, the sea, stone circles or forests, and you may discover that one particular setting gives you the clearest and most profound contact.

Ghosts

In many indigenous cultures, for example among the Australian Aboriginal peoples, in the African continent, among the Maoris of New Zealand and in the Orient, ghosts are not the subject of fierce scepticism or terror, but are a reality. They represent the continuing presence of the wise ancestors who are welcomed on special festivals as well as the anniversary of their death.

In Celtic times, Hallowe'en was the first of the three-day Festival of the Dead when the dimensions parted and the family dead were welcomed at the domestic hearth with their favourite food and drink. In France and Mexico, as well as many other Catholic lands, the dead are remembered at the beginning of November with flowers, food and family togetherness.

Family Ghosts

Most contact with deceased family members is very subtle: perfume or pipe tobacco of a loved grandparent when we feel sad; a dream in which the deceased relative may return to hug you or to complete unfinished business; a light touch on your hair; or a sudden sense of a presence out of the corner of one eye. For every person who sees, touches or hears the voice of a loved one there are a hundred less intense but equally meaningful expressions of love. I have listed books, including my own, that contain ghost encounters of all kinds in Further Reading (see page 243).

Anyone who feels unloved because a favourite grandparent has not manifested him or herself to them, should not despair as this does not mean the relationship was not special. If you are patient you may have an experience similar to that of Rebecca, on her thirtieth birthday.

Eighteen months after her grandmother died, Rebecca was unable to get home for her birthday from a business trip because of a train strike and had to stay over in a town a hundred miles away. She took what she thought was a wrong turn on her way to the hotel and, as she passed an antique shop she saw in the window an unusual and distinctive tea jar that was identical to the one her grandmother had kept spare money in when Rebecca was a child. She bought it and was immediately flooded with an overwhelming sense of joy; she then felt a light touch on her hair. In her mind she saw her grandmother smiling and knew she had not been left alone on this special day.

Honouring the wise ancestors

Whether you wish to feel close to a deceased relative or to contact an ancestor from your roots hundreds or even thousands of years ago in another land, work at one of the transitions of the year. These are New Year's Eve, Hallowe'en, the beginning of the Celtic year and winter, May Eve, the beginning of the Celtic summer, or one of the Sun festivals (see page 149). Sit close to an open window as night falls and place a protective clove of garlic on the window ledge saying: 'Welcome all who come in love and peace.'

✦ If there is a particular deceased relative you would like to contact, work on their birthday rather than the anniversary of their death. Smell their favourite perfume or hold a ring, a scarf, a pipe, or a book they loved, or softly play a CD of a favourite song from their youth (many revamped recordings are widely and cheaply available).

✦ Close your eyes and wait, speaking in your mind words of love or welcome. You may sense a presence and will understand the purpose of the contact without words, and will sense the positive inflow of love into your heart from past generations. You may sense more than one person.

✦ If you suddenly open your eyes wide, you may catch a fleeting glimpse or a flash of light or see the whole person in front of you. The less you actively seek, the more you will get; welcome any contact for the wonder that it is.

✦ When you are ready, thank the ancestor/s in your own words and say: 'Go in peace.'

✦ Sprinkle salt and water on the window ledge and door entrance, saying: 'May only love remain and blessings.'

✦ Close the window and bury the garlic outdoors or in a plant pot.

After carrying out this exercise, you may dream of the person or of places you do not know but which seem very familiar and welcoming.

Ghosts of the Place

Many apparitions are attached to a specific place and may be seen by different people over a number of years or even centuries. For this reason, these phantoms are more amenable to formal investigation and measurement than family ghosts who may appear only once, often without warning. Ghosts that are attached to specific places may seem unaware that they are perceived. They perhaps exist like photographic impressions etched on a location by the strong emotions that prevailed at the time of their death, or during a trauma or great happiness. However, some phantoms do interact with observers, and this suggests the survival of the essential person, who either chooses to stay at, or feels unable to leave a specific location that was of significance during their earthly life.

Following a ghost's path

You are unlikely to see a ghost in the most haunted house in England or any other land for that matter, as tourists shuffle around with noisy children and cameras. Ghosts are sensitive to disturbances of their energy field and, furthermore, are not performers for curious onlookers. We need to display towards ghosts the same good manners we should extend to the living, especially when entering their homes. Similarly, a ghost walk around an old part of town is unlikely to be fruitful, although it can be a useful way of finding out about the local legends, and it is likely to follow or cross over an urban ley that seems to energise apparitions.

Ghosts exist not primarily to satisfy ghost hunters, but may still follow the paths they took in life. Because they operate on a higher vibrational level than we normally do, we need to attune ourselves to them through being quiet and still, and using our clairvoyant rather than our physical eyes.

You can quite easily tune into ghosts at a site impressed with strong emotions, for example a battlefield, a place where there was a massacre or the site of former gallows, but these tend to be suffused by sorrow. This can be quite overwhelming unless you are experienced in ghost encounters. It is better to begin at a site where many feet have walked over the centuries, and where emotions were stable for long periods, such as a ruined abbey, a rose walk, a long gallery in a stately home or a cathedral aisle, where people walked while experiencing strong emotions.

Two or three hundred years is quite sufficient time for a location to build up memories, but you can also visit a sacred site where indigenous peoples held ceremonies to celebrate the seasonal cycles. Avoid burial grounds and graveyards, as these are resting places that are not for interaction with the past.

Your best tools are your feet and your pendulum (see below).

Make your first pass relying on your feet alone. Walk along a straight natural pathway in an old house, cloisters or a garden where people would have paced up and down over time, while lost in thought or trying to calm strong emotions, thereby leaving a strong imprint.

We have chakras in the soles of our feet that are powerful transmitters of psychic energy (see page 116).

You can also work in old labyrinths. There are magnificent medieval labyrinths in some European cathedrals and churches, as well as numerous outdoor turf labyrinths in the United Kingdom, and stone ones in Scandinavia. Because these have primarily been used for spiritual purposes, you can absorb vivid impressions via your feet chakras of those who walked, thought and dreamed. You do not need to use a pendulum, but walk barefoot if possible.

When exploring ghost paths, you can follow your initial walk by using a pendulum to amplify impressions. While the swing of the pendulum is important, it is the amplification and transmission of the energies as feelings, images and words that is its chief function. There are many similarities to clairsentience at old places, and indeed if you can find a bowl of dried lavender or smell the roses in an arbour, this will make the connection easier.

♦ Let your pendulum swing vertically and quite naturally as you walk.

♦ You may find that your pendulum swings a different way from the normal positive/negative circling. It may form ellipses or even swing strongly from left to right or vibrate in the presence of the ghost.

♦ Do not worry if it makes an anticlockwise swing – it is not detecting evil, rather a blockage in the energy that indicates that the ghost does not wish you to continue on that particular part of the path. Step aside as you would for a living person and rejoin the trail a little further along the path.

♦ If the pendulum ceases to swing, look for an obvious focal point, such as a fireplace, and you will pick up the track diagonally.

♦ If you make contact with the ghost, you may feel the hairs on the back of your neck tingling or a sudden drop in temperature. This will occur as you come within the aura of the ghost and it may extend several feet.

♦ Half-close your eyes and look in the area surrounding the pendulum; you will become aware of a misty shape enclosing the pendulum. You may see a momentary flash of light as you catch a brief picture of your ghost either externally or in your mind's eye.

♦ Move a few inches away and the reaction will cease, in which case thank the ghost and say: 'Go in peace.' Because the ghost is so attached to the place, it is unlikely that it would follow you but it is important to mark the beginning and end of paranormal contact so that your energies are not receptive to less benign influences.

♦ As you leave the gates, thank the ghost, sprinkling a little sacred water from a bottle at the entrance.

✦ When you get home wash your pendulum under running water and have a ritual bath.

Ground yourself before you sleep and surround yourself with earthing banded or moss agates or jade. Do not be tempted to return to the site to contact the ghost. We all have our family ghosts or maybe there is one attached to your home; it is they who watch over us and with them that we should establish loving links.

The Next Step

Angels and archangels have become an increasingly important focus for spirituality in the modern secular world, and you may find that through your guardian angel you already see and talk with other angelic powers. If you want to read about angels and archangels, see pages 222–28. I have written about them in Step 10 when I talk about channelling their wisdom. The next section focuses on developing your channelling and mediumistic skills so that you will be able to communicate more clearly and understand these beings.

Expanding the Higher Self

A s you move from step to step, many of the psychic processes you learned early on in the book will have become automatic. This section explores ways in which you can, if you wish, try some of these familiar processes in a more advanced form. The main emphasis is on directing your growing awareness of the closeness and accessibility of other dimensions to discover particular psychic gifts. These can be used in the service of others, whether informally or as part of therapy.

Altered States of Consciousness

In meditation, visualisation and ritual we can attain what are called altered states of consciousness. These operate through the higher chakras and levels of the aura and make us sensitive to other dimensions so that we can act as a medium. We can benefit from this whether we are channelling messages from those who have died, or from angels or higher beings.

Some people believe that what we access is not an externalised spirit being but the evolved part of our soul that we may carry with us from previous lifetimes. We can reach this higher inner wisdom when we have opened channels from our conscious mind during this lifetime, so that we can access what we previously learned spiritually but cannot now recall.

An altered state of consciousness is linked to the slower, deeper alpha and theta brainwaves that are associated with meditation and light trance states, and through which healers operate when channelling powers from a higher source. Internal and external foci merge into moments of timelessness in which anything is possible and we become one with the universal consciousness (more of this in the next section).

What might you feel in this state? Certainly not spaced-out or detached from reality, but you will feel a lovely warmth. You may see colours in your mind's vision or in actuality and you will feel gentle vibrations like a well-tuned engine. You will not even need my beloved third hand, the pendulum, to know the rightness of decisions and a sense of being in the world, and you will be able to touch and communicate with other worlds.

If you ever feel as though you are losing control or are uncertain or afraid, just visualise yourself as a tree and push down into the earth with your feet to return to rootedness, then dig your real garden for a while, cook, tidy a cupboard or sort accounts – reality is always waiting.

Advanced Meditation

There comes a point in meditation when you lose awareness of the process and slip quite naturally and effortlessly into an altered state of consciousness. At this stage mantras evolve into internal affirmations such as: 'I am in all, all is in me, the cosmic sea embraces all.' In Zen Buddhism, a single phrase or sentence called a koan is used, which may be a riddle like, 'What is the sound made by one hand clapping?'

Some people find it helpful at this stage to meditate facing a mirror, focusing on the reflected wall just above the head. Reflect the light from beeswax candles on a horseshoe behind you, and you may find your focus changes and you are viewing the scene of your body in meditation pose from inside or above the mirror. You can flit from one to the other, tossing your consciousness like a silver ball.

Advanced Chakra Work

According to early and indeed prevailing Eastern chakra tradition, each yogi or adept creates the chakras within his body by powerful visualisation and meditative techniques, thereby attaining transcendental awareness. By meditation on the chakras, it was believed that siddhis, or supernormal powers, could be attained by dedicated yogis.

Activating the chakras

The following exercise attempts to create or at least activate through visualisation the chakra energies, and it is a good method of self-healing and restoration of inner harmony, as well as opening higher channels of awareness. Carry it out for seven consecutive days or once a week for seven weeks, preferably at the same time each day. You may see the chakras – which is Sanskrit for wheel – as some ancients did, as whirling multi-coloured lotus petals around a pulsating gem of the main chakra colour. Other people visualise them as spinning discs or coloured cones.

✦ Sit in a comfortable position with your eyes half-closed, if possible in a natural setting with perhaps the background of buzzing insects or birdsong; the muted roar of traffic can be equally soothing.

✦ Focus on the area around your perineum as you sit and allow the root or base chakra to unfold and whirl round. However you see it, visualise a red ruby in the centre becoming luminous.

✦ Focus on the root or base chakra animals and create in your mind the roar of the bull, the hiss of the serpent and the surging power of the fiery dragon, stirring within you as your innate survival nature wakes.

✦ Concentrate next on the mighty snake goddess, Kundalini the empowerer, as she uncoils from around the base of your spine.

✦ See the serpentine channels of energy rising through a central tube or channel of red light with two other main channels coiling round her like the snakes around the staff of the ancient Egyptian healer-god of wisdom, Thoth, that later became known as the staff of the Greek messenger and healer-god, Hermes.

✦ As the central column ascends through the chakras it assumes their rainbow colours in turn. Visualise the two spiralling columns, *ida* and *pingala*, the left lunar and right solar channels of energy, as silver and gold liquid snakes, spiralling upwards, coiling rhythmically around the *sushumna* central energy column – a dance that will continue up to the brow. Here, as the channels merge into the central column, there is a surge of power that has been described and depicted as the head of a magnificent rearing cobra reaching the crown of the head or as a golden eagle's wings spread wide.

✦ But that ascent is yet to come. From the root or base chakra move next to the sacral chakra in the centre of the lower abdomen. Allow the petals to whirl around the amber gem, a glowing orange sphere of desire and sensuality, filling you with warmth and satisfaction as the blue dolphin – its power creature – leaps through shoals of golden fish over a crescent Moon, scattering sparks of silver Moon water.

✦ Next, open the solar plexus, situated above the navel. See that opening and the whirling yellow around the rich topaz core – fuelled from below by orange light – filling you with power, confidence and focus, as its power icons – the salamander, elemental fire lizard and the golden phoenix – blaze glorious in the dancing flames.

✦ Move upwards to the heart chakra in the centre of the chest. Allow its petals to open and whirl around a flawless emerald, energised like the lower chakras by the triple columns that criss-cross and meet in the centre of each chakra. Feel the fountain of love and understanding cascading as pink and green light droplets, while a flock of turtle doves – symbols of the goddess of wisdom, Sophia, and the Virgin Mary – symbol of the chakras – ascend in the growing light.

✦ Move upwards and allow the throat chakra around the Adam's apple to open as the swirling petals reveal a rich sapphire. Ganesha, the elephant-headed god of wisdom, learning, prosperity and good fortune, sits enthroned with blue gems as an icon of this chakra, and the light ascends ever upwards.

✦ In the centre of the brow see the two spiralling columns merging with the central one as a pulsating indigo-violet jewel, around the huge, deep-purple amethyst, the heart of the swirling chakra flower. Now the snake, its powerhouse, is transformed into a magnificent rearing hooded cobra ready to strike, and through death to offer immortality.

✦ Finally, the column emerging from the crown as a pure white dazzling diamond, whose radiance mingles with cascading white/gold from above, as the eagle of pure gold – the supreme chakra icon – touches the Sun through skies filled with rainbow birds of paradise.

✦ Now allow the whole body to become a rainbow firework display of those magical birds, as light enters through every chakra, cascading from above and below until the external body frame melts and there is only a single golden circle. This sphere of pure gold represents your unchanging essential self.

✦ In their own time allow the colours to separate to form once more the seven separate chakras. One by one from the crown see them slowing and closing like flowers in the evening sunset and the life-force descending gently until there is only a faint red glow around your perineum. Then finally embrace darkness and the slumbering Kundalini, though you are still part of the golden sphere within that is your indestructible soul.

Sacred Geometry

The enclosure of a sacred space with geometric shapes and principles that have spiritual as well as mathematical significance is known as sacred geometry. Sacred forms are very important for attaining states of altered consciousness as they provide an area of power and protection. Because of its perfect geometrical nature, this area of power is in harmony with the higher energies of the universe. It has been described as the area in which dimensions meet, with the centre as the doorway to enlightenment.

Quite as important as working within these forms is their creation. That in itself raises the level of awareness and focuses the psyche on these other worlds, just as when you were a child colouring complex patterns you were transported to other lands and totally unaware of the everyday world clattering around you. As an adult, meditation is especially powerful within a sacred enclosure.

You have already worked with the circle. This forms the basis of the mystical mandala, which is Sanskrit for 'circle'.

Mandalas

A mandala is a geometric pattern that represents the sacred sphere – the union of the self with the universe. Mandalas originate from Hinduism and Buddhism, and are an important feature of both religions, especially in Tibet. They are used as a focus for meditation and as a sacred space for ritual.

Mandalas can be used in personal development in the traditional manner, whether they are visualised in the mind for meditation, created on paper, or drawn on sand or earth to create a temporary enclosure for personal psychic work. They are completely destroyed after the ceremony or work has finished.

Mandalas are also said to be the formal geometrical expression of sacred vibration or sacred sound, and mandala patterns have been produced using a device called a tonoscope from the sound waves created by chanting: 'Aum' (pronounced 'om'), the sound Buddhists believe brought the universe into being.

Working with mandalas

Many beautiful mandala reproductions can be found in books or on the World Wide Web. You can also buy posters of mandalas from shops that sell Asian goods. You will probably need to study and draw a number of your own if you are to visualise easily one in your mind for higher meditation.

My own favoured method is to either colour an intricate black-and-white photocopy or draw and colour a less intricate one while meditating. In this way the creation is an integral part of the meditation. You can alternatively draw a mandala in the sand or earth with a stick or on a paved yard or patio with chalk. You can create one from stones or large shells in the garden from a master drawing.

If you have created a mandala in your garden, do not destroy it, but decorate it with crystals and perhaps plant flowers or herbs in the circles. You can then literally walk or spiral dance your mandala as you would a labyrinth.

Whether you move within your mind, with your fingers tracing the design of a painted or drawn mandala or in actuality with your feet, as you work from the outside through the different segments to the centre, you will enter an altered state of awareness through contemplation. You will travel inwards to the sacred centre, the heart of silence. Here, you can make an affirmation or recite a prayer in each of the sections. If working outdoors, you could scatter seeds along your path.

You can contemplate mandalas while meditating and may find that you connect with the most wonderful worlds that seem to spiral inwards in rich colours, patterns and ever-changing perspectives, like sitting inside a kaleidoscope.

When you have finished working with your mandala, remain in the centre and then return slowly to the perimeter, carrying within your own centre, the still point of what T.S. Eliot called 'the turning world'.

Making a mandala

Even a child can draw a simple mandala – the key is symmetry, not complexity – and it is the repetition of a pattern that has meaning for you that makes the mandala form a very personal sacred tool. You can use a basic geometrical compass and pencil to mark out your design, ready to colour. Below is a simple design you can use as a basis, but there are many excellent sites on the Internet that will teach you more elaborate forms of this art. Begin by drawing a small mandala, and you can then use a simple design as a template for a sand or earth one.

✦ Use white paper or card and colouring pens in jewel-rich colours.

✦ Create a large circle by drawing around a dinner plate, or use a geometric compass to create an outer circle that fits within the page comfortably.

✦ Mark the centre of the circle, then draw a horizontal and a vertical line through the centre, to give four segments.

✦ Draw a single equal circle in each of the quadrants.

✦ In the centre of the main circle draw two smaller circles with the same central point and make the larger one pass through the centre of the four outer segment circles.

✦ Keep your design symmetrical, i.e. each part balanced, and use repetitive patterns to establish a rhythm that enables you to slip into a light trance state.

✦ To make a star mandala, create two concentric rings. Inside the second, draw a six-pointed star. Inside the star, draw another circle. Although this is not a true mandala, in practice it is very effective for meditative work and ritual.

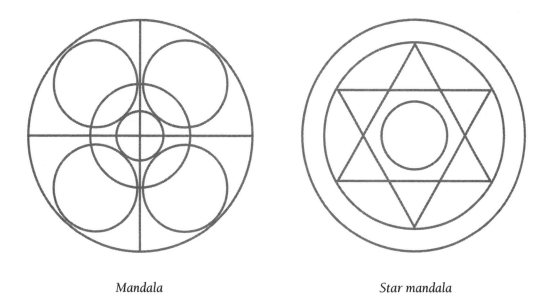

Mandala   Star mandala

Labyrinths

The labyrinth is based on one of the most ancient Mother Goddess symbols, the spiral, and is a sacred form found in every part of the world except China and sub-Saharan Africa. It dates back to at least 15,000 BC. The associations with the earth mother, whose womb labyrinths represent, are almost universal. Labyrinths differ from mazes in that there is a single circuitous path to the centre, representing not a puzzle but the journey to the inner psyche and enlightenment. In parts of Germany and Scandinavia, labyrinths can be found where the path does not end in the centre but, having reached the centre, leads out again.

Labyrinths are found with anything from three to seventeen coils as well as more complex sacred geometric formations. They can be built of turf or small boulders as found in Scandinavia and Finland (some dating from the Bronze

Age). Some, made from tiles, are located in medieval churches, like the magnificent eleven-coil labyrinth in Notre Dame Cathedral in Chartres. The latter labyrinth acted as a substitute for a pilgrimage to Jerusalem during the Middle Ages and was danced by the priest and the people at Easter to celebrate the Resurrection.

Seven-coil labyrinths were carved on small pebbles sometimes known as serpent stones, for use in daylight, and the more mysterious moonstones for meditation by moonlight; these may be druidic devices. It is my own belief that temporary labyrinths, made from stones or drawn in earth, were like some of the medicine wheels created by Native Americans wherever they made their camps, made by indigenous peoples throughout the world.

The seven-coil design is the most prevalent, and some say the most magical and sacred, since it is frequently linked with the seven traditional planets (which include the Sun and Moon). You can walk to your centre, Earth, via the planets. Because you begin on the third circuit (see diagram, page 197) and follow a spiralling path, the first planet you walk will be Mars on the third coil, then Jupiter, Saturn, the Sun, the Moon, Mercury and finally Venus, before reaching the centre, the Earth.

Most famous is the legendary Minoan Cretan labyrinth that held the fabled Minotaur – half-man, half-bull, who was slain by Theseus. The seven-coil labyrinth is called 'mother within the earth' or Mother Earth by the Hopi Indians.

Identifying the pathways

From the inside:

8 Earth

7 Moon

6 Mercury

5 Venus

4 Sun

3 Mars

2 Jupiter

1 Saturn

Making a seven-coil labyrinth

To create a seven-coil labyrinth carefully follow the sequence of diagrams on pages 198–99.

✦ Practise drawing the shape on paper until it is second nature.

✦ You can make temporary labyrinths in the sand (try walking one on the shore by full moonlight) or in the earth, or draw them with chalk in a yard.

✦ For a more permanent result, paint the labyrinth design on a floor and cover it with a rug when not in use.

✦ Alternatively, you can create a labyrinth with stones in your garden on grass, using large marker stones for the central cross and building it up stage by stage. Keep a diagram handy in case you go wrong. Make each path wide enough to walk around.

✦ You can draw a labyrinth for meditation by day on a white stone or clear crystal quartz. Make this at dawn. The summer solstice is the most magical day and its dawn the most magical dawn.

✦ For night-time meditation, use a grey stone or a moonstone and create the seven-coil design on it on the night of the full Moon.

Using the labyrinth

Walking or dancing labyrinths creates an altered state of consciousness, akin to a light trance. What is more, the action is said to activate the inherent magic in this sacred geometric form and in the energies within the earth. Make affirmations at each curve, perhaps based on planetary energies, meditate in the centre, make love, say: 'I love you' or 'Goodbye'. Leave flowers or seeds to be carried away by the sea on your shoreside labyrinth, leave sorrows or talk to the wise ancestors in the centre.

When you wish to meditate draw and then trace the pattern of your seven-coil labyrinth on paper with your finger, allowing the design to guide your hand around the circuits to the centre. Visualise yourself walking around the spiral, perhaps deep beneath a palace, on a shore or between green hedges, your feet moving rhythmically along the well-trodden path of the ages.

Step 1 To create the classic seven-circuit labyrinth, first draw an equal-armed cross, with an 'L' shape in each corner, and a dot in each of the 'L' angles.

Step 2 Starting at the top of the cross, create an arc up from centre to the right and end your line at the top of the 'L'.

Step 3 Start next at the top of the 'L' just to the left of the last step. Make an arch over to the dot on the right. Continue to start on the left, and arch over to the right.

Step 4 The rule is always to work from the nearest dot or line to where you finished and follow that round to the next logical point, even if you feel you are going back on yourself (see diagram below). Move the drawing instrument to the first available starting point on the left (the dot) and arch it over to the first available open spot on the right (the other end of the 'L').

Step 5 The next marker is the other end of the 'L' angle.

Step 6 Now progress to the left arm of the cross, and curve around to the open end of the lower 'L' angle.

Step 7 Continue to move to the next free starting point on the left, arching over and around to the next free spot on the left until you complete the labyrinth on step 9.

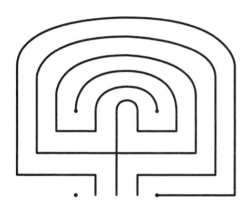

Step 8

Step 9

Channelling

Once you are regularly experiencing the connection with the higher powers, you can begin to channel the higher energy into your life in a number of ways. You have already worked with the devas so are familiar with the technique.

Mediumship

This is the process in which a sensitive person, called a medium or channel, is used by spirits to communicate with the living, and for relatives to ask questions of the spirits via the medium. It is also a method used to obtain wisdom and information about the higher planes of existence from evolved spirit guides, who assist the medium in his or her work.

Mental mediumship

This involves a medium relating information through thought transference from the afterlife, and therefore usually takes place while the medium is conscious. The medium may talk to a spirit guide, who acts as an intermediary, or communicates directly with the spirits of deceased loved ones. The messages from the spirit world are transmitted in words generally using the medium's own voice, and the medium can simultaneously communicate with the living person seeking the contact. The deceased person will offer idiosyncratic or personal information, so that the recipient or sitter can identify the spirit who is making contact. The mental medium may see the spirit through clairvoyance, or *hear* the spirit through clairaudience, but the sitter, unless clairvoyant, will not.

Physical mediumship

This involves the manipulation and transformation of physical systems and energies. This form of communication comes via a spirit operator, often a spirit guide, and the results can be seen and heard by the sitters as well as the medium. For physical mediumship you must be properly trained, as this form of mediumship involves quite deep trance states.

Beginning mediumship

To learn mediumship, whether mental or physical if you intend to work either professionally or on a regular basis, I would advocate training through one of the spiritualist churches or a healing organisation (see pages 248–49). Since mediumship with the afterlife is a very powerful form of communication, you can attract negative energies if you open yourself without the protection of an experienced co-worker or earthly teacher. However, after calling upon angelic protection (see pages 65–68) and stating that you will only be using mediumship for transmitting light and goodness, you can help your own family, friends and acquaintances to contact deceased family members. This is safe because you are contacting specific spirits who have a link of love with the people who wish to contact them.

◆ Ask your special guide or angel to protect and assist you. Communication with spirits is at best like using a mobile phone in a poor area of reception, so if you do receive a single symbol or phrase, accept it with gratitude. Symbols are a common form of spirit communication.

◆ Hold an item belonging to the deceased person between your hands to open a channel, close your eyes and let words flow.

◆ If your mind goes blank, do not panic as that will block communication. Visualise a sea or riverbank and symbols being washed up on the shore.

◆ Symbols are usually the first mediumistic contact, but as you hold the item, you may see in your mind's vision cameos of people (sometimes just a head and shoulders), or perhaps hear a distinctive voice or phrase. In time you may see the people next to you or hear their voices externally (this is definitely a point to seek training).

◆ Describe the face or faces, any distinctive clothing, mannerisms or speech patterns and any phrases, however odd or unrelated. These idiosyncratic connections are the real jewels that enable a person to know that their relative is present.

◆ If you get nothing, say so. Even experienced mediums may receive only a single symbol or message.

✦ When you sense any connection fading, thank the spirit and ask the sitter if he or she has any message to speak to the deceased loved one. This can be very healing even if no specific proof was obtained.

✦ Thank your spirit guide and say: 'Go in peace.'

✦ Afterwards have a bath to which pine or tea tree oil has been added and smudge the room.

✦ Visualise your chakras. Beginning with the crown and moving downwards close them one by one like stars going out in a velvet sky. This will avoid energies and possibly spirits buzzing around you all night.

Automatic Writing

Traditionally, automatic writing is regarded as a tool of mediumship, whereby, it is believed, information is channelled from a spirit, whether that of a deceased close relative or someone who needs to communicate to the living. Through automatic writing the spirit will pass on information about the manner of its death or unfinished business during life. However, more recently it has become popular as a personal art for the purpose of receiving angelic communication and channelling from other higher beings of light.

You can define the purpose for which you are carrying out the session and either ask questions to set up a question and answer response or simply allow your mind to go blank and allow wisdom to flow.

Beginning automatic writing

Keep a special pen and paper for automatic writing and, when not in use, keep them wrapped in white silk. Immediately before a message is received, you may experience a tingling sensation in the arms or writing hand. For people who use this technique regularly, this can be a signal that the time is right. However, if you are feeling negative or tired, run the hand under cold water and leave the exercise until another time.

Protect yourself as you would for any other psychic work, asking the protection of your special guide and that only goodness will be transmitted. Light pure white candles and breathe in the light.

✦ Sit quietly with your pen and paper and either allow a question to form or still your mind and just wait.

✦ Before long you should begin to write spontaneously; keep writing until you can no longer either hear the words in your head or your pen just stops writing, whichever way works for you.

✦ If nothing seems to flow, this may not be the right time, so put your pen down and just sit quietly, perhaps looking into a candle flame or holding your favourite crystal. Automatic writing should not be forced. Some people do not find it a helpful psychic tool.

✦ If a message seems negative, distressed or overpowering, put down the pen and say, 'Go in peace' and after a bath, carry on with a physical earthly activity to ground yourself.

Automatic writing tends to be faster than conscious handwriting and generally very prolific, with thousands of words produced in a short time with seemingly little awareness. You may feel as though you are in a light trance.

You may find that your handwriting temporarily improves, with some messages being transmitted in a wonderful copperplate script. Sometimes you can identify the script as that of a deceased grandparent, or you may recognise it unexpectedly in a museum or library as belonging to someone from another age. The content will often establish the source.

The communication may be in verse or contain complicated biblical quotations, or occasionally foreign languages that are not spoken by the receiver. This does not necessarily indicate the presence of spirits but shows that you are delving into the cosmic memory bank.

You can ask the transmitter for a name and who he or she is, whether an angel, a higher being or your own higher self.

Prophecy

Inspired utterances, either about a specific present or future event or more global wisdom, are known as prophecies. They also include channelling about future events, personal as well as more general, that can be altered by a change in attitude or perspective. I have chosen the I Ching and tarot cards to act as a focus for prophecy in this section.

Choose an I Ching hexagram or a tarot card and allow words to flow as you gaze at your focus. Let the basic core meanings I have given expand and act as a channel for the ancient wisdom you carry in your veins. This ancient wisdom connects you to the same cosmic flow that prophets and prophetesses have used for millennia, whether in the name of a deity or not, to predict and suggest solutions for future events.

Your prophecies may be expressed almost entirely in symbols and may seem unrelated from day to day. However, if you tape record your words, record them in your journal and read in a single session the prophecies you have made over a period of weeks, you will detect a pattern.

The I Ching

I Ching divination in its purest form dates back about 5,000 years to the time of the Chinese ruler Fu Hsi. This emperor was said to have first read the prophecies from the shell of a tortoise. Therefore, the 6th century BC philosopher Confucius, who is often credited with the creation of this most profound form of divination, was a comparative newcomer, although it is his form and structure that has been most influential. The essence of the I Ching also reflects the Taoist belief that we are not separate from nature and the universe, but a part of it. Life, natural forces, people, and even food are made up of yang, the original Sun concept of light, power, masculinity, assertiveness, logic and action, which is depicted as:

Yang ▬▬▬▬▬▬▬

The opposing force is yin, the Moon, representing darkness, receptivity, femininity, intuition, acceptance and inaction.

Yin ▬▬▬   ▬▬▬

I have suggested in Further Reading (see page 243) a book that would be helpful if you would like to use the I Ching for divination. Here, I have given the eight basic trigrams, or three lines of yang and yin that each represent a natural force. You can combine two trigrams to form a hexagram (six lines giving two natural forces in different combinations). Making hexagrams gives you a deeper understanding of an issue in question by providing a more detailed image, made up of the interaction of two forces, for your psyche to interpret.

Chi'en, Heaven/Sky

This is the trigram of pure power and energy, of personal identity, assertiveness, directed power and success. As an indicator of action, it advises aiming high, developing potential and being confident and single-minded.

Attributes Strength, focused energy, creativity, logic, courage.

Animals Horse, tiger, lion.

Body Head, mind, skull.

Family Father.

Roles Sage, military commander, philosopher, elderly men.

Associated images Outer garments, cold and ice.

Direction Northwest.

Season The approach of winter.

Colour White or gold.

Plants Chrysanthemum, herbs.

Trees Fruit trees.

K'un, Earth

This is the trigram of pure receptivity, of considering the needs and feelings of others, of relying on intuition, unconscious wisdom and waiting rather than acting.

Attributes   Docility, receptivity, intuition, nurturing, patience.

Animals   Ox, cow, mare, ant.

Body   Stomach, abdomen, womb, the unconscious mind.

Family   Mother.

Roles   Wise woman, old women, ordinary people, especially in crowds.

Associated images   A seamless cloak that envelops all things without question, an old cart that carries everything.

Direction   Southwest.

Season   The approach of autumn.

Colour   Black or dark brown.

Plants   Potatoes, all bulbs.

Trees   Tree trunks of all kinds.

Li, Fire

This is the trigram of illumination and of clinging to whatever fuels it, whether the fire of the great solstices where the Chinese emperor made offerings, or the ritual fire that cleansed what was imperfect or no longer needed.

Attributes   Clarity, illumination, cleansing, communication, inspiration, clinging.

Animals   Pheasant, sacred turtle, goldfish.

Body   Eye, the blood, speech, heart.

Family   Middle daughter.

Roles Artists, young women, generous people, craftsmen.

Associated images The Sun, lightning, objects with holes, such as shells and armour.

Direction South.

Season Summer.

Colour Orange.

Plants Tomatoes, red and yellow peppers.

Trees Dry trees, hollows.

K'an, Water/the Abyss

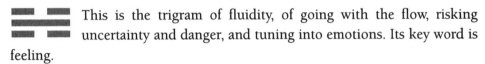 This is the trigram of fluidity, of going with the flow, risking uncertainty and danger, and tuning into emotions. Its key word is feeling.

Attributes Desire, emotion, instinct, fearlessness, danger, hardship.

Animals Pig, rat, wild boar, bat.

Body Ear and kidneys.

Family Second son.

Roles Young men, the sick and troublemakers, fishermen.

Associated images Wells, Moon, the deep, rain and rivers, floods.

Direction North.

Season Winter.

Colour Blue.

Plants Reeds, water lilies and lotuses.

Trees Willow, alder.

Chen, Thunder

This is the trigram that represents renewal of life; in Chinese mythology thunder came from the earth at the beginning of summer, liberating the seeds from the earth womb and scattering them to generate new life and growth. The sudden dramatic thunderstorm, which Chinese mythology claimed was made by dragons fighting, can be both creative – in bringing refreshing rain – and also destructive.

Attributes Arousal, renewal, surprise, spontaneity, initiative, male sexuality, fertility.

Animals Dragon, eagle, swallow.

Body Voice, foot.

Family Eldest son.

Roles Men up to middle age, princes, inventors, musicians.

Associated images Thunderstorms, hurricanes, volcanoes.

Direction East.

Season Spring.

Colour Yellow.

Plants All blossoming flowers.

Trees Evergreens, blossom trees, bamboo.

Sun, Wind/Wood

This is the trigram of gentle but persistent change – the slow but enduring growth of a tree or the wind that can move mighty objects in its path. It is associated with incense-giving trees and the peach tree, as these were believed to be life-giving manifestations of the Mother Goddess.

Attributes Gentle but determined progression to overcome any obstacles, adaptability, flexibility, endurance, justice.

Animals Cockerel, snake, tiger.

Body Thigh, legs, lungs, the nervous system.

Family Eldest daughter.

Roles Women up to middle age, teachers, travellers, people engaged in business.

Associated images The tree, fragrances, clouds, ropes and webs.

Direction Southeast.

Season The approach of summer.

Colour Green.

Plants Grass, poppies, lilies.

Trees All tall and high trees.

Ken, Mountain

This is the trigram of waiting, solitude and a desire to rise above material and daily concerns. According to Chinese mythology, ascending to the Jade mountain was one way whereby immortality might be reached.

Attributes Stillness, withdrawal, silence, meditation, spiritual aspiration.

Animals Dog, bull, leopard, mouse.

Body Hand, back.

Family Youngest son.

Roles Boys under sixteen, prisoners, the faithful and sincere, priests and monks.

Associated images Door, opening, narrow path, walls, watchmen and watchtowers.

Direction Northeast.

Season The approach of spring.

Colour Purple.

Plants All mountain plants.

Trees Nut trees, gnarled trees.

Tui, Lake, Marsh

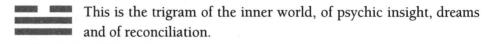 This is the trigram of the inner world, of psychic insight, dreams and of reconciliation.

Attributes Pleasure, joy, inner tranquillity, healing, magic.

Animals Sheep, birds, deer.

Body Mouth, lips that smile.

Family Youngest daughter.

Roles Women under 16 and daughters, concubines and sorceresses.

Associated images Valleys, mist, the harvest, low-lying land.

Direction West.

Season Autumn.

Colour Red.

Plants Magnolias, gardenias, all lake plants, spices.

Trees Trees bleached with salt from the sea and salt marshes.

Making basic I Ching stones

I Ching stones made from jade are especially powerful as a divinatory tool, but you can equally use stones collected from a beach, riverbank or any place that has positive associations for you. I Ching Stones have a yang – an unbroken line on one side – and a yin on the other. By choosing three of these stones at random you can create trigrams, and by choosing six, hexagrams.

Yang ▬▬▬▬   *Yin* ▬▬ ▬▬

◆ Take either six oval pieces of jade or stones about the size of a medium coin, with a flat surface on either side. Use paint or a water-resistant permanent marker in a clear colour to mark the yangs and yins. Alternatively, for more permanent markings, etch out the yang and yin signs with a sharp metal object and then paint the indented shape.

◆ Mark each of the six stones with a broken line, yin, on one side and an unbroken line, yang, on the other (see diagram on page 210).

◆ Use a drawstring bag or a purse to hold the six stones.

Using I Ching stones

Both trigrams and hexagrams are created and read vertically from bottom to top. The top line is the last stone you put down and read.

◆ When you want to make a trigram or hexagram, pick a stone from your bag and cast it on to the table or a flat surface.

◆ Place this nearest to you with the side that fell uppermost, yang or yin, at the base of the column. This is the first line of your trigram or hexagram.

◆ Continue to throw until you have a vertical row of yangs and yins. The top one will be the last pebble you threw.

Interpreting the trigrams and hexagrams

◆ Work at first with trigrams, casting only three stones and using the basic symbolism given for each.

◆ When you have made your trigram, close your eyes and allow words and images to form in your mind.

◆ Once you are familiar with the trigram meanings, cast two trigrams to give you a more accurate picture.

◆ Although you have two trigram images you do not read them separately. Close your eyes and create a picture in which the two forces are interacting.

◆ In the example below, Tui – lake or marsh – was the second hexagram to be cast. This, combined with the trigram Sun, gives an image of wind beneath the surface of the water, creating a whirlpool. Sun here has no connection with the Sun or sunshine but is the Chinese word for 'wind' or 'wood'.

✦ In this interpretation, the answer to your question might be that you have a great deal of untapped power at your command and that the time is coming when you will change the status quo by persistence.

✦ However, if you see in your inner picture, the trigram Sun as wood, you might just as validly evoke an image of trees underneath the water, perhaps after a flood. In this case the same hexagram would tell you that you may feel overwhelmed. If you wait and let the floods recede, you will achieve your goal, whereas you would fail if you were to rush ahead when circumstances were against you.

✦ There are no rights or wrongs, as these are your interpretations. The selection you made was influenced by psychokinesis, the power of your mind to choose unconsciously the basic templates that hold the key to your question.

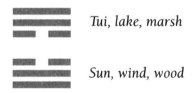

Tui, lake, marsh

Sun, wind, wood

Tarot Cards

Another powerfully prophetic device is the tarot pack. The origin of the tarot is uncertain but it was probably a medieval Italian creation, although the images and themes are much older and universal, hence the huge variety of packs. For prophecy, choose a highly illustrated pack. My own favourites are the Morgan Greer and the Rider Waite packs, which both have jewel-like images. Go into a store rather than buying by mail order so that you are able to handle different cards and see which feel right for you.

Types of tarot card

Work with the 22 major arcana (which means secret wisdom) picture cards, numbered either 1–21 or 0–20, according to your system. These major cards begin with the Fool and end with the World. Create a story in which they all take part, beginning perhaps with the Fool going to the Magician, the second card, for advice on his journey. You may find that this story reflects aspects of your own life, especially your inner world.

After you have studied or meditated on each card look at my very brief meanings below. When you feel familiar with the cards, shuffle the pack and place it face down to form a circle of cards. Take a single card from the circle of cards, and allow it to speak to you. It may address your present life, your dreams, and all those questions of mortality, love, survival after death, the purpose of the cosmos and global issues present and future. Keep a page or more in your journal for each card and note any that appear regularly.

Fool
The cosmic egg/inner or divine child. Representing untapped potential, a step into the unknown that will bear fruit spiritually or in actuality.

Magician
The alchemist, transformative agent. Representing the creative spark, originality, versatility.

High Priestess
The divine virgin/priestess/druidess. Representing spirituality, detachment from trivial concerns, independence from the need for approval by others, incorruptibility.

Empress
The earth mother. Representing fertility in ventures as well as human reproduction, nurturing those who are vulnerable, acceptance of the weaknesses of self and others, unconditional love.

Emperor
The sky father. Representing the life-force, focused energy, willpower, demanding highest standards.

Hierophant

The priest/guru/prophet. Representing a card that indicates evolving prophetic powers, the need to seek wisdom from a wise source – whether a person or book, adhering to traditional values.

Lovers

Representing sacred sexuality and the sacred marriage between earth and sky, the union of male/animus and female/anima energies even in single-sex relationships, emotional or love choices.

Chariot

The hero/heroine/warrior. Representing courage, overcoming obstacles, taking control of one's destiny, integrating opposing factors and pressures.

Justice

The seeker after truth. Representing a desire for justice and a fairer world, principles, ideals, integrity, the need to speak the truth that is in one's heart.

Hermit

The solitary seeker. Representing sanctuary in the inner world, withdrawal from the world's demands for creative renewal, and the creation of inner space and silence to let the answers or wisdom flow.

Wheel of Fortune

The hand of fate. Representing the external shaping of the life path, the power of natural and cosmic forces, accepting one's place as part of a wider pattern, interconnectedness with all other forms of life.

Strength

Primal survival instincts. Representing going back to one's roots, patience and perseverance under difficulty, hidden strengths, the strength of gentleness.

Hanged Man

The willing sacrifice/saviour that underpins many spiritual traditions. Representing making a long-term advantageous plan or commitment that will require great input or short-term loss, giving up unrealistic plans or redundant ways of living, unselfish actions.

Death

Representing transformation (never physically dying), the cycles of the year, the seasons and stages on the life path, natural change points, endings that if accepted will lead to new beginnings, indications that decisions or changes that have been deferred can now be made.

Temperance

The healing angel/spirit guide. Representing healing, whether of people, animals, places or nations, finding balance and avoiding extremes of emotion, inner control rather than the control of the external world.

Devil

The shadow self. Representing acceptance of darkness as well as light, and acknowledgement of our own negative aspects that when no longer repressed can form the catalyst for positive change.

Tower

The cleansing fire/lightning flash. Representing liberation from restrictions, not least those imposed from within, necessary cleansing and purification of what is redundant or destructive, opening to the light.

Star

The visionary. Representing the unconscious mind and the cosmic memory bank, ability to experience other dimensions, bringing wishes, desires and thoughts into actuality.

Moon

The mystic. Representing wisdom through dreams, visions and psychic insights, mystery, magical powers, harmonising with the natural ebbs and flows of energies to know the right time to act and to wait.

Sun

The triumphant hero. Representing illumination, rebirth, birth, regeneration, the free flow of the life-force, realising potential, joy.

Judgement

The merciful judge/angel of judgement. Representing reassessing priorities, letting go of the past, acceptance of what cannot be changed, forgiveness of self as well as others, determining what is of worth, setting the parameters for future wise action.

The World

The cosmic dance/dancer. Representing reaching the still point of the turning world, experiencing moments out of time, expanding spiritual and physical horizons, applying spiritual wisdom to the everyday world.

The Next Step

Because this has been quite a large step in terms of spiritual evolution, you may wish to wait a while before taking the final step. In the meantime, perhaps spend time counselling friends, family and colleagues or incorporating your new skills into existing professional work, if applicable. This may be the point when you consider future courses and paths and whether you want to use your psychic gifts professionally to help other people. Some highly gifted psychics do not want to charge for their skills, although in one sense it is like charging for any other enterprise where time and effort are expended. On a personal level, you now have your new-found wisdom to help answer your questions, although sometimes the answer will simply be to wait and allow the path to unfold.

STEP 10

Experiencing the Divine

I

N HIS POEM 'LITTLE GIDDING', T.S. ELIOT referred to the 'condition of complete simplicity' that was the result of a lifetime of spiritual explo-ration. The more we learn and the wiser we become, the humbler we should be in many ways. For while we think we know a great deal, our ego protects us from the vastness of the universe.

I have often found that those self-styled gurus with their apparent knowl-edge of every complex term and method from Eastern philosophy are not actually very spiritual or compassionate. Some of the best healers and miracle workers I have known are ordinary men and women, sometimes with little formal education, who open their hearts to others and their spirits to whoever they call their god or goddess.

Healing is a central strand throughout this final section, although in a sense the process of self-healing began when we first opened ourselves to universal energies in the earlier sections and learned to trust our inner wisdom. As we have learned more about our own nature through dream interpretation, through scrying and meditation, so we have been able to heal our own spirits bruised by the harshness and brashness of the modern, frantic and sometimes uncaring world.

We have used herbs, colours and crystals, breathed in light and exhaled darkness, connected with the natural cycles of the Sun and Moon and gradu-ally have practised using our emerging healing powers to help others. In this section, we move towards healing using higher energies and establishing our connection with higher forces and beings of goodness and light.

Healing with Higher Energies

There are few healers who would not attribute their abilities to divine power or light, although there are many ways of identifying the ultimate source of goodness. Healing organisations from many disciplines and cultures offer training in channelling higher energies through your hands and voice. The method below does not belong to a specific healing tradition, although it has similarities with a number including some schools of Reiki. It is one I learned from a wise old healer and that I have adapted to my own healing work.

You can draw light and healing power from cosmic sources, for example a deity figure to whom you pray, Raphael the healing archangel or another angelic being or evolved spiritual essence. Since we all possess a divine core, this connection with higher spiritual energies is a natural one, but we cannot recognise it easily until we become more aware of our own spiritual nature. Healing passes in from the crown via the higher energy centres and out through the hands, which are ruled by the heart chakra.

The voice is also a powerful healer. As you heal, you can allow your voice, via your throat chakra, to become a channel for the wisdom of the source of healing power.

◆ Prepare the healing room so that it is framed in natural sunlight or candle-light.

◆ Prepare yourself by sitting quietly and asking for help and guidance from the form of divinity you work with, or a more generalised power of goodness and light.

◆ Ask the patient to select a crystal from a selection of amethyst, rose quartz, jade or a clear quartz sphere and sit with this between you, both touching it.

◆ Allow time for talking to establish a rapport so that the energies will flow between you.

◆ If you see or sense the other person's guide or angel, describe it and welcome your own healing guide.

✦ As the patient sits or lies while holding the crystal, allow words of healing to begin to flow.

✦ Move your hands gently over the aural field around the head of the patient as you speak, allowing your fingers to untie any tangles, and use circling movements to push away any darkness. This attunes you to the vibrations of the patient and makes your fingers part of the circuit of light and power.

✦ Now make an arc with your hands and hold your fingers up to the light, visualising the angelic force or radiant light transmitting pure gold and white liquid power through the crown of your own head, down through your brow, spiralling as it reaches each chakra, through the throat chakra, into the heart and thereby through your arms to your fingers.

✦ As the light enters your outstretched fingertips, you may be aware of tingling or faint golden sparks.

✦ Describe the process to the patient, who may be able to see the light or feel the warmth radiating.

✦ Transfer your hands to the crown of the patient's head. As the light and words flow, slowly move your hands from the crown chakra to the root, working with each chakra in turn.

✦ Afterwards, return to any chakra that seems to need extra healing or untangling. At each position, hold your hands for about a minute, although you may feel the need to work longer with some areas. Be guided by the flow and not by the clock.

✦ At the crown chakra, hold your two hands facing downwards and close together, fingers pointing downwards, about three fingers breadth above the front of the fontanelle of the person you are healing.

✦ Allow the light to flow downwards and inwards and to flow in and around the crown chakra, clearing, harmonising and empowering.

✦ Next, hold your hands 2 or 3 centimetres (about an inch) from the eyes with your hands towards them as though covering the eyes. Feel the light flowing into and around the brow chakra.

✦ Move downwards to the throat chakra; cross your hands over the centre of the throat or hold your hands about 2 centimetres (¾ inch) from the throat on either side, fingers pointing downwards.

✦ Move down to the heart chakra and again cross your hands, this time over the centre of the breast or chest, 2 or 3 centimetres (about an inch) away from the body.

✦ Continue to feel the light flowing and continue to describe and flow with the energies. Once the channel is open, light will flow until you have completed healing.

✦ Direct your hands now towards the solar plexus chakra, with your fingers still pointing downwards and not touching the body, around the waist and between the navel and the chest so that your hands almost touch.

✦ Next, point your hands downwards to form a 'V' just below the navel towards the sacral chakra. The energies of the two hands will merge and form a single beam of healing light.

✦ Finally, work first with the left and then the right foot. Cupping your hands around the sole of each, allow the energies to rise up each leg and converge at the base of the spine and perineum area.

✦ Return to any chakras that need attention or to the specific areas where the patient feels pain.

✦ Thank the angels and wise guides, or the power of light that has filled you with healing, and plunge your hands into water in which an amethyst and clear crystal quartz have been soaked for eight hours.

Healing Animals

When healing animals, work with the heart chakra, concentrated around the heart area, the solar plexus for the stomach, the abdomen for the sacral chakra and the four paws for the root or base chakras. When working with birds, the root chakra will be in the claws.

Healing Places

Use the crown chakra movements over a picture or photograph or when standing in the actual location. Raise your arms in an arc to replenish the power if you are working with a picture of war or famine. Surround the picture with alternate crystal quartz and amethysts to amplify your powers.

Healing an Absent Person

To help someone who is absent, work from a photograph to visualise each chakra point. Alternatively, you can draw a large outline on paper or model one from clay and work with that. Afterwards, keep the picture or clay model of the absent person on your altar and burn a white candle over it. You can work with pictures of endangered species or absent animals in the same way. You can also heal yourself using this method.

Hands-on Healing

Some healers use hands-on healing, especially of shoulders and head. If you have a patient you know well or are related to, this can be very effective. However, some people find the physical closeness intrusive, so it is important to be sensitive to the person and the situation so that you will strike the appropriate note of intimacy that can be achieved with the lightest touch or none at all.

Working with Universal Light and Cosmic Energies

We work within the framework of our humanity and so we interpret higher powers within our own cultural context. This will be affected by childhood religious teachings and later through the writings of others, such as mystics and saints, as well as by philosophers who have attempted to categorise and describe what they have felt, seen and heard in visions, dreams and altered states of consciousness. Inevitably, because humans categorise such experiences in hierarchies, there are numerous divisions hypothesised between planes of experience and ranks of heavenly beings.

It may be that you have discovered a framework of religious or philosophical belief through which you can conceptualise and direct these energies. But other people find the divisions artificial and unnecessarily complex, and they prefer to make their own contact with divine powers. I will briefly describe some of the ways these higher powers have been visualised and how to tune into their vibrations and ask for help and guidance. You may like to try working with these concepts or reading more about a particular topic.

Angels

Emanuel Swedenborg, the 18th-century scientist, Christian mystic and visionary, believed we all have the potential to become angels. Swedenborg taught that all people are born to become angels, whatever their religion. If they choose the path of virtue, they can continue on an angelic path after death.

Personal angels are sometimes regarded as an externalised form of the individual's higher self and archangels as the archetypes of spiritual qualities and powers. However, the more traditional view is that angels are separate entities who have never lived on earth. They are of a higher order of existence, and some of them choose to guide a particular person or act as guardians of a city or even a nation.

Although angels are often envisaged with huge feathery wings and long flowing robes, such perceptions are influenced by the cultural and religious background of those who study and believe they have seen angelic beings.

Many ordinary men, women and children not only see angels at times of crisis but develop an ongoing relationship with one who acts as counsellor, friend and guide. Indeed, you may have an angel as your astral spirit guide (see page 169).

As the world becomes more dangerous, materialistic and polluted, and loneliness increases, so angelic influences are increasingly necessary to restore meaning and beauty into the environment. Increasingly, too, in modern times the angel offers a personal path towards awakening the Divinity within us all and recognising that we are connected to a universal life-force that extends beyond conventional parameters of time and space.

Angels are traditionally found in the Judaic, Christian, Islamic and

Zoroastrian religions. The word angel comes from the Greek *angelos*, which is a translation of the Hebrew word *mal'akh*, meaning a messenger. In formal religion angels are regarded as intermediaries between God or the gods and humankind. Angels are associated with almost every quality, heavenly body and zodiacal sign.

If you want to read about specific angels there are many angel sites on the World Wide Web, and I have also suggested books in Further Reading (see page 241), but many people find that initially they need to begin with the personal level of the guardian.

Guardian angels

Credited with clarity of vision, guardian angels can divert you from danger, guiding you to love, health and happiness, if you can just recognise their call. Equally, if you can learn how to reach across the barriers of logic and disbelief, you can contact your angel guide and other angels in times of need.

We would seem to have a guardian angel from the moment of birth, perhaps even before, although if you choose not to contact him or her, the guardian will not appear in your life except if you are in danger. These guardians can be seen as a best friend who is always available and always forgiving, someone who will gently lead us to greater spiritual awareness and the right course of action, if we choose to take it. For angels will not interfere with free will, although now and again they may indicate a path where we will not stumble.

Some people are aware of this personal angel from early childhood, but the presence may fade if we become preoccupied with other issues. Many people report seeing their angel in the last moments of life and realise that he or she has always been with them throughout their life. As well as having a guardian, we may see different angels at different stages of our life, and these may help us through each stage.

Some people close their eyes and can visualise their angel. If you find this difficult, try the following method.

✦ To work with, choose from: a rutilated quartz containing golden filaments; a moss agate; a piece of uncut amethyst or rose quartz with imperfections; or amber – an organic gem whose inner treasure may be millions of years old. Alternatively, use a clear crystal sphere or a crystal pyramid.

◆ Hold your crystal so that you can see the full Moon reflected in it or the early morning sunshine casting sunbeams and rainbows.

◆ If you want to see your angel at night and the Moon is in another phase, light a silver candle – the Moon's own colour – and hold your crystal so that the candlelight shimmers through it.

◆ As the light moves, you may briefly see your angel.

◆ Breathe slowly and deeply. With each exhaled breath, visualise the light expanding so that the angel fills the crystal and then moves beyond it.

◆ You can now talk to your angel and may hear a soft and gentle voice answering within your mind.

◆ When you have finished your dialogue, reverse the ritual so that as you inhale, the angel can, if it wishes, return to the crystal – its special sanctuary.

Keep the crystal wrapped in white silk when not in use. If you contacted your angel by moonlight, place the crystal under your pillow while you sleep. Children love this ritual and feel safe with their angel under their pillow – you can let them choose their special angel crystal, which need not be at all expensive. It can be especially useful if you or they have to be away from home at night.

Archangels

These are the higher angels, traditionally seven in number, who guard the throne of God, act as messengers for important events and may act as guardians of a city or nation. Some confusion arises because archangels appear in other religions apart from Judaism and Christianity. There are four in Islam and ten in the Kabbalah – the esoteric Jewish system of spirituality. In the Authorised Version of the Bible only three archangels are mentioned: Michael, Gabriel and Raphael, so they have tended to be credited with the functions of many non-biblical archangels. To them is added Uriel, who appeared in the apocryphal Book of Enoch, making the fourth traditional archangel who has passed into Western mystical traditions from the Middle Ages onwards. They have retained their importance in modern rituals (see pages 65–67).

Traditionally, seven archangels rule over the seven days of the week and correspond to the seven traditional planets, the five visible ones and the Sun and Moon.

I have found working with a different archangel each day to be very helpful in focusing on the different energies of the associated planet. I have taken one of the most popular archangel correspondence systems of the Western magical tradition, where each archangel also rules over a specific hour of the day and also night.

As with the planets, each archangel rules the first hour after sunrise of his own day. Although many people regard the archangels as male, others consider them to be androgynous, so I have called them 'he' merely for convenience. Dawn can be a particularly good time to contact an archangel to receive his special blessing and perhaps to receive messages in your mind.

Since even archangels are a very personal form of empowerment and protection, I have left their descriptions vague. There are angelic paintings from different periods that you can find in books, art galleries and through your Web browser.

Michael

He is archangel of the Sun and of Sunday. Michael, the initiator, brings illumination and inspiration in many spheres of life, through the efforts of our individual creative spirit. He appeared to Moses as the fire in the burning bush and saved Daniel from the lion's den.

According to the Koran, the cherubim were created from Michael's tears. He is the guardian of all who stand alone with their unique vision for bettering the world; all those who are not prepared to compromise their ideals in any way. This archangel can be invoked in ritual for all creative ventures, for original ideas and individuality, for combating fear, for contact with the Divinity and the higher self/spirit guides, for reviving barren land despoiled by industrialisation, and for cleansing air pollution (see also page 66).

Colour Gold.

Crystal Citrine or pure crystal quartz.

Incense or oil Frankincense or orange.

Gabriel

He is archangel of the Moon and of Monday. Gabriel, the integrator, brings increased spiritual awareness, mystical experiences, astral travel and significant dreams. These qualities will be found especially through prayer and meditation or in a beautiful natural place close to water. He brings deepening spirituality within the family and work environment. It was Gabriel who parted the waters of the Red Sea so that the Hebrews could escape from the Pharaoh's soldiers.

Gabriel can be invoked for protection against inclement weather, for travel across water, for taking away sorrow and for diminishing self-destructive tendencies, replacing them with the gentle growth of new hope. Gabriel also cleanses polluted seas, lakes and rivers (see also pages 66–67).

Colour Silver.

Crystal Moonstone or opal.

Incense Myrrh or jasmine.

Samael

He is the archangel who rules the planet Mars and Tuesday. Samael is sometimes called the 'Severity of God' and as such is an angel of cleansing and of righteous anger. One of the seven regents of the world, and said to be served by two million angels, Samael offers protection to the weak and vulnerable. He takes away doubts and weakness, replacing them with spiritual courage to stand against what is corrupt, especially by those who abuse power. He can be invoked for the aid of war-torn lands, oppressed minorities and endangered species.

Colour Red.

Crystals Garnet and bloodstone.

Incense Allspice and dragon's blood.

Raphael

He is the archangel of the planet Mercury and of Wednesday. Raphael, the harmoniser, offers healing of all kinds, and protection to children, bringing guidance and sustenance to all who are lost, whether emotionally or spiritually, and to all travellers on a physical journey. Raphael's name means 'God heals'.

Raphael can be invoked in all health matters, for spiritual knowledge and insight and for alleviating the worries of our daily lives that keep us bound to the earth. Most importantly he shows us how to teach others our spiritual insights. He heals technological and chemical pollution and the adverse effects of modern living (see page 66).

Colour Lemon yellow (some people visualise him as green).

Crystals Citrine and yellow jasper.

Incense Lavender and pine.

Sachiel

He is the archangel of the planet Jupiter and rules Thursday. Sachiel, the divine benefactor, is the angel of charity who says that only by giving freely to others will our own needs be met. He works constantly to help others and to improve the lives of humankind. He can therefore be invoked for good harvests, physical and emotional problems, and for increasing abundance and prosperity, not just for a minority but for the good of all. He helps lands where there is famine or disease and restores run down areas or cities where employment has been lost, blending new skills with traditional knowledge.

Colour Blue.

Crystals Lapis lazuli and turquoise.

Incense Sandalwood and sage.

Anael

He is the archangel who rules over Venus and Friday. Anael, the regenerator, is one of the seven angels of creation. He is prince of archangels and controls kings and kingdoms. Anael is pure altruistic love – love of one's fellow beings and of all creatures in the universe. He brings harmony to places and people and the restoration of natural balance, healing rainforests, bringing wildlife habitats to the city and greenery everywhere and helping animals who are cruelly treated, and endangered species.

Anael can be invoked for all matters of forgiveness both to ourselves for what is past and to others that we may be free from their influence.

Colour Green.

Crystals Jade and rose quartz.

Incense Valerian and rose.

Cassiel

He is the archangel of Saturn and rules over Saturday. Cassiel, the conservator, is called the angel of solitude and of temperance, bringing moderation in actions and dealings and development of inner stillness and contemplation.

Cassiel can be invoked for the reversal of undeserved bad fortune. He also works ecologically, conserving resources and keeping places in their natural state, and encouraging natural forms of energy. Cassiel also strengthens attempts at conserving history and tradition and reviving lost wisdom, especially among indigenous peoples, as a legacy for future generations.

Colour Purple.

Crystals Obsidian and jet.

Incense Cypress and thyme.

Ascended Masters

Spiritual leaders who have been described as particularly wise are known as Ascended Masters. After their earthly lives they have continued to help and advise humankind from the higher spiritual planes. The concept of Ascended Masters filtered from the Far East into the West via Theosophy. Indeed, Madame Blavatsky said that the true teachers of theosophical wisdom were the Mahatmas, the Old Souls or Masters of Wisdom as they were known in India who, though they had completed their own cycles of earthly incarnations, returned to teach those who might understand and disseminate their message. Most of the Mahatmas lived in remote regions of Tibet, Mongolia, or India, forming the Brotherhood of Adepts.

A number of sages and adepts has been identified as Ascended Masters by many people following a spiritual path who believe they have communicated with these higher beings. Among the religious and spiritual leaders who have continued to guide humankind, the most frequently identified are Jesus, the Virgin Mary, Gautama Buddha, the Hindu Krishna, an avatar or earthly form of the God Vishnu, the preserver of the universe, the Chinese sage, Confucius, and St Germain. You will also find icons who guide from the spirit planes in Native American spirituality and the Oriental world. There are countless others who have spoken through dreams, meditation and art forms, such as music or painting.

Ascended Masters are sometimes called the Great White Brotherhood, because of the white aura that is said to surround them. They include the Ascended Masters of all cultures, religions and ages.

Channelling Wisdom from a Higher Source

If there is a particular saint, Ascended Master deity figure or archangel to whom you feel affinity, you can work with him or her. Before you begin, collect images and statues and read about the life and any recorded channellings that have been experienced by others. One useful source is the Internet, where people are increasingly publishing their experiences. Use a crystal sphere or a blue beryl ball for channelling.

✦ Have a ritual bath and sit near your altar or outdoors in the early morning or evening light, so that light falls on your crystal sphere or ball.

✦ As you look into the sphere, create a pillar of light in your mind. You may continue to see brilliance or you may see a face or a person begin to form.

✦ Touch the hairline or crown of your head with your power hand, saying: 'Above me the sky.'

✦ Touch next the brow, saying: 'Within me the light.'

✦ Touch next the throat, saying: 'To receive wisdom true.'

✦ Finally, touch your heart and say: 'To kindle the flame within.'

✦ Next, ask that only goodness and light may enter.

✦ Then wait.

◆ You may feel as though your mind is filled with radiance and be aware of a vibrating or humming and perhaps flashes of different rays of colour.

◆ It may be that you hear a voice or are aware of music, or poetry or an overwhelming sense of being in the presence of Divinity, a sense of rightness as though you had been waiting all your life for this moment. You may hear words from the Bible, the I Ching, or religious teachings from a faith other than your own.

◆ You can ask who is speaking and you can ask questions, although channelling tends to be more effective if you listen and allow the wise spirit to direct the dialogue. Often the words are secondary to the feeling of being blessed and connected to the source of light, so you should not proscribe the moment by expectations or a specific agenda.

◆ The words may come through your own voice, in which case you can record them or you may choose to write them down afterwards or paint an image.

◆ Gradually the brilliance will fade from your mind and the voice will also recede as though through a tunnel.

◆ Thank the essence and sit quietly holding the crystal. Allow the vibrations to quieten down. You may feel a sense of loss, as though a beloved friend has gone away, in which case repeat the higher chakra incantation stated above and reconnect with the sense of completeness.

Channel no more than once a week, if possible at the same time and in the same place. If you are patient, you will learn more about the higher energy that pours down.

Gods and Goddesses

Another powerful source of higher energy is found in mythology and has been revived within the neo-pagan faith through god and goddess forms. They represent different qualities of the Great Goddess or the Supreme God, or personified aspects of a more abstract form, depending on how you conceptualise the undifferentiated Divinity. As with the archangels, there are many excellent sites on the Internet showing paintings and statues of the deities and where you can also read their myths. Below are a number of god/dess forms I have found helpful both for meditation and magic:

Agni, the Hindu god of fire, is said to be manifest as the vital spark in mankind, birds, animals, plants and life itself. He is manifested in lightning, in celestial Sun flares, in the sacred blaze rising from the altar and in household fires. Agni is the divine priest and acts as messenger to the gods, interceding with them on behalf of humankind.

Apollo, the Greek Sun god, was twin brother of Artemis, the Moon goddess. As god of the solar light, Apollo made the fruits of the earth ripen, and rode across the sky in his golden chariot seen as beams of pure light. He is said to be the most glorious of all the Classical gods and was patron of the arts, especially music, beauty and harmony.

Brighid or Brigid was the Celtic triple goddess whose worship was transferred to the Celtic Christian saint, St Bridget (St Bride in Wales). She was once a Sun Goddess and her special festival is Imbolc, the early spring pagan festival of light. On 1 February, now St Bridget's day, the maiden Goddess brought fertility to the land and the people, melting the snows with her white wand and was the goddess of poetic inspiration for the Bards. As mother she represented the goddess of midwifery and healing, while as crone she was patroness of the hearth fire, smiths and craftworkers. In her Christianised mother aspect she was called Mary of the Gael, the Irish Mary who was in legend midwife and foster mother of Christ.

The holy fire at the saints' shrine in Kildare, dedicated originally to the Goddess and then to St Bridget in the Christian tradition, is believed to have burned unquenched for more than a thousand years. It was tended first by 19 virgin priestesses called the Daughters of the Sacred Flame and later by the nuns of the Abbey at Kildare. Each nun tended the fire on a particular day, making 19 days in an ongoing cycle of devotion to the flame. The goddess and later the saint were said to care for the fire on the twentieth day of the cycle.

Cernunnos was a generic term, meaning 'horned one', for the various horned gods of the Celtic tradition. Cernunnos was the Celtic lord of winter, the hunt, animals, death, male fertility and the underworld, and was son and consort of the great goddess. Cernunnos' importance has been in his continuing presence as the horned god, the male principal in witchcraft through the ages, in modern witchcraft and other neo-pagan faiths.

Demeter, the Greek earth and corn goddess or barley mother, was the archetypal symbol of the fertility of the land. Demeter is often pictured as rosy cheeked, carrying a hoe or sickle and surrounded by baskets of apples, sheaves of corn, garlands of flowers and grapes. She refused to make the grain grow after her daughter Kore (also known as Prosperpine or Persephone) was carried off to the Underworld by Hades, and so brought winter into the world.

Grandmother Spider was the Native North American female creative principal who wove the web of the world, taught wisdom and various crafts to her people and protected them from bad dreams with her dreamcatchers. In Hopi myth, Grandmother Spider fashioned animals, birds, man and woman from clay. Grandmother Spider has returned many times in many guises to teach and guide.

Horus was the ancient Egyptian sky god, represented as a falcon or a falcon-headed man. His eyes were the Sun and Moon and his wings could extend across the entire heavens. He was frequently associated with the morning aspect of Ra the Sun god and worshipped as Re-Harakhty.

Isis, the Egyptian goddess, has been the one goddess of the ancient world whose worship as the great mother rivalled that of the Virgin Mary. She has been honoured in many forms, as goddess of the Moon, as Stella Maris – goddess of the sea – as Holy Virgin, sacred bride, mother of nature and, perhaps most importantly, in the Westernised ceremonial magical system as the mistress of enchantment. However, her widespread appeal over the millennia perhaps resides in the fact that she was a wife and mother as well as a great goddess. Like her consort, Osiris, she was regarded as mortal as well as a deity, dwelling on earth as well as queen of heaven; she also promised ordinary people, not just great pharaohs and kings, the hope of immortality.

Lug/Lugh, the willing sacrifice, the Celtic 'shining one', gives his name to Lughnasadh, Celtic festival of the first harvest (1 August). He is the Sun king who allowed himself to be cut down as a harvest offering and who was reborn each year according to different legends either at the midwinter solstice or the spring equinox.

Nut, the ancient Egyptian sky goddess, was called the mother of the gods and of all living things. Nut was invoked in life and death by humans for protection. Nut's body, covered in stars, arched over the Earth protecting it, as she touched it with her fingertips and toes and lay over her husband, Seb. Nut was mother of Ra, the Sun god, and early myths tell how he returned to her womb every night to be reborn at dawn.

Parvati, wife of Shiva, the father God in Hinduism, is the beautiful young goddess of the mountains. She is the catalyst and power source without which Shiva would be impotent. The marriage of Shiva and Parvati is still a model for humans, the great god and his shakti, or female essence, as the sacred marriage between earth and sky. They demonstrate the heights to be strived for by every married couple, momentarily experienced in tantric or sacred sexuality.

Thoth was the ancient Egyptian lunar god of the Moon, wisdom and learning. He was also god of time, languages, law and mathematical calculations who invented the calendar and hieroglyphic writing. He is often depicted with the head of an ibis or of a baboon. He was believed to be the father of healing wisdom, of magic and divination and his wisdom spread into the Western world through one of his descendants, the semi-legendary 1st-century magician, Hermes Trismegistos (Hermes was Thoth's Greek form, called Mercury in Rome).

Warramurrungundjui was the Australian Aboriginal creatrix, who emerged from the sea and gave birth to the first people. She carried a digging stick and a bag of food plants, medicinal plants and flowers. Having planted them, she went on to dig the very necessary water holes, and then, leaving her children to enjoy the fruits of her work, she turned herself into a rock.

Yemaya-Olokun, of the Yoruba peoples in West Africa, was an elemental force who not only lived in but also is the sea. Yemaya, also called Iemanja and the womb of creation, is the bringer of dreams and prosperity. In Brazil, where she is worshipped by followers of Santeria, altars are created on the shore with candles and food on New Year's Eve. These gifts are accepted by Yemaya on the morning tide.

Ancient Wisdom – Connecting with Archetypal Golden Ages

Atlantis and Lemuria are both legendary lost civilisations whose wisdom is said to have spread throughout the world after their demise. You may find that you visit them during your psychic travels or in dreams. But their major importance is that they act as the homelands for those following a psychic path. They also represent the symbolic, if not actual, source of much magical knowledge and healing in a number of later cultures. For example, Atlanteans are often credited with passing on their knowledge to early peoples enabling the great stone circles to be created as accurate planetary observatories.

Atlantis

We know about Atlantis from two books, *Timaeus* and *Critias*, written by the ancient Greek philosopher, Plato, around 360 BC. In the *Critias,* Plato described the lost Atlantis as a paradise on earth, peopled by demigods before it was engulfed by a tidal wave in a single day and night more than 11,000 years ago. He described a land of flowing fountains, exotic fruits, canals that enabled a second harvest to be reaped each year and animals of all kinds, including elephants.

Edgar Cayce had visions of Atlantis that showed it as so advanced in learning that much of modern-day science and technology is only now rediscovering what perished beneath the waves thousands of years ago. There are many theories and accounts of Atlantis, both in books and on the Internet, and I would suggest you read about its wonders and the theories of its location and demise, especially the Cayce material.

Lemuria

Believed to have existed even before Atlantis, Lemuria is considered the source of the wisdom of indigenous peoples, for example the cultures of Native North America and of the Australian Aborigines. Lemuria is also sometimes referred to as Mu, the Motherland of Mu, the Earth Mother.

It was believed that Lemuria was situated in the Southern Pacific, between North America and Asia/Australia. Legend tells that the holy people or the prophets of the Lemurian culture had foreknowledge of the great flood that historically and mythologically appears in almost every culture. They began to store information in crystals. These crystals were taken deep within the Earth when the Lemurian Wise Ones made their own exodus there – all crystals are thus said to be a powerful focus of channelled Lemurian wisdom.

A year before the flood, the Wise Ones began going underground and created communities there. The people living beneath the earth were safe from the flood and when the waters receded, the people emerged once more in many different places to impart their wisdom in lands now separated from each other by water. Creation myths of the first humans emerging from holes in the earth appear in a number of indigenous cultures.

Working with the wisdom of the lost lands

There is much you can read about both Atlantis and Lemuria, but with both civilisations you can work entirely through visions and you may be surprised how similar your own images are to those of other writers. This is because you are accessing the same cosmic memory.

✦ If possible, sit by the sea with your eyes closed or play a CD of ocean sounds.

✦ For Atlantis, hold an amethyst and visualise yourself within a huge purple crystal pyramid. This has been described in a number of Atlantean channellings. Alternatively, you can create one with a basic wooden frame and a purple transparent throw or from Perspex.

✦ Focus on the sound of the sea, and as you walk out of your pyramid, stand seaward observing the activities of the busy port, the statues and other crystalline pyramids. See if you can find one of the many wise teachers in their purple robes to whose wisdom you can listen.

✦ For Lemuria, visualise huge tropical trees or work with your own tall pot plants – the best Lemurian vision I had was in a tropical house in a botanical garden close to the sea.

✦ Hold a crystal quartz – transmitter of Lemurian wisdom – and as you push through the undergrowth in your vision, join a group sitting around a sage who is holding a huge rainbow crystal sphere, and listen to the sage's words. Seek visions in his magical crystal, then walk around the settlement and watch rituals being made to earth, sea and sky.

✦ When you feel yourself returning to the daily world you may be surprised how much time has passed.

Each time you visualise the ancient places, use the same entry point but move rapidly to the place where you ended your last visit. Note down in pictures and words the teachings. This method can work especially well if you find channelling a more abstract source less fruitful.

Mystical Experiences

Mysticism can be defined as an overwhelming sense of being in complete unity or oneness with a deity or the cosmos. Mystical experiences occur in all times and religions, usually within the framework of the existing belief system of the mystic.

I do believe it is possible for us all to have these moments of illumination when we are at one with the pure god/dess. As you develop spiritually, you may be rewarded by such moments of pure bliss when you are one with the light. Since such experiences are inevitably spontaneous, you cannot create one; however, there are situations in which these moments out of time do occur, whether within a conventionally religious setting or within the framework of the natural world.

Communicating with Divinity

If you have a specific faith, whether one of the conventional religions or as a neo-pagan, make time for regular sessions of prayer, either in a church or temple or under the temple of the stars. Some of the lovely old cathedrals can inspire believers of many faiths or those who hold no specific one to make the Divine connection. Marian shrines and altars and Hindu mother goddess statues can be especially helpful in focusing on the Great Mother.

Unlike channelling, you do the talking, either aloud or in your head. This should not be a cosmic shopping list, but about yourself as you truly are and how you would like to be. This truthfulness and humility can be quite difficult because we have to temporarily lay aside all we have learned, even the knowledge acquired in channellings from archangels or masters. We become as a child again. At the end we have to go back to the beginning and cannot learn how to pray except by praying. Before beginning your prayers you may find it helpful to read short passages from the writings of one of the mystics or a sacred book.

When you have finished praying, leave a flower, or if in a church or cathedral, light a candle for someone who needs healing. You may be rewarded by an unexpected shaft of sunlight or a feeling of deep peace that was last experienced when you went to sleep as a child after a particularly happy day.

Achieving Peak Experiences

The United States psychologist Abraham Maslow defined mysticism in terms of peak experiences that encompass the whole spectrum of mystical states of consciousness, secular as well as religious. The following are ways in which you can reach moments when you are at one not only with nature, but also with the source of Divinity. These may occur for seconds only but they are invariably life enhancing. Therefore, if you experience yourself in the presence of the sacred, which may be a multi-sensory experience, those few moments may change your whole life.

Continue praying, increase your reading of sacred works from any tradition, and experiment with some of the following. These experiences are special in themselves, but also serve to move you ever closer to that moment when we can hold the key to the universe, and if we are lucky, can retain just a kernel of that perfection and never feel alone or afraid of death again.

✦ Sit on a sunny shore or by a fountain in sunlight looking at the rippling water and allowing the sound to fill your mind.

✦ Make love at an ancient site or on the seashore under a full Moon or in newly mown grass with someone with whom you share spiritual as well as physical love and merge as one flesh and spirit.

✦ Listen to a choir, especially Gregorian chants, in a cathedral as sunset filters through the windows.

✦ Watch the dawn rise over a standing stone at midsummer (there are many that are accessible to the public and rarely visited), knowing you are one with those who have also witnessed the dance of the Sun over the millennia.

✦ Go into a museum in the early morning, one where you are allowed to hold Roman pottery or touch the statues. Again, allow yourself to become one with the ancient world.

✦ Lie on the grass or a sunbed in the darkness and look up at the stars, focusing on one point and letting the others merge and dance so that the Milky Way flows like a river of star milk.

✦ Run downhill in a fierce wind, ride a horse at full speed along sand or through the desert, roll in snow, swim underwater among shoals of fish or even through the illuminations of the pool lights at your local swimming baths.

✦ Splash through the path of moonlight or sunlight in the sea, covering yourself with the radiance and singing at the top of your voice.

✦ Soothe a crying baby or infant, whether your own or one you are caring for who belongs to a friend or relative. Watch joy break through or hear the soft contented sigh as the child drifts into sleep.

✦ Do something really nice for someone who is cantankerous, or offer to help someone who is struggling even if you are busy or preoccupied, and be rewarded by a smile or even a grunt of thanks.

✦ Say something kind to a rival or a person who gossips about you to boost their self-esteem.

✦ Blow bubbles from a children's bubble set from the top of a hill, or fly a beautiful kite and let it go to be found by a child to whom it will give pleasure.

Spirituality and Your Life – Where to Next?

It will take a lifetime, or maybe more than just one, to make the journey towards spirituality. You may decide to develop some of the topics I have described in this book through further reading, training courses or personal explorations, and you may take up psychic counselling or healing whether professionally or for those you meet.

Certain aspects of psychic work will seem more natural to you than others and you may choose to concentrate on three or four core areas. However, you will find over the months that whether you continue to develop different aspects of work started in this book or whether you follow your own unique path while building on some of the ideas, the ripples will spread in your everyday life.

Whatever your age, you will become the tribal wise man or woman at work, home and socially. Your aura will have expanded and become more radiant as a result of opening yourself to so many spiritual energies and possibilities. Others, even strangers, will be drawn to ask your advice and healing. This is the responsibility that comes with increased awareness, but it is a good one because you have the opportunity to be of service to others and to act as caretaker of your particular corner of the universe.

Mastering the ten steps is the easy part. Following the spiritual path in the daily world is the real challenge. However, through our channellings, meditations and visualisations, we can regain the optimism of a child, and have the ability to take delight in every new day and to see beauty in every place, however mundane.

If we can achieve this and take pride and pleasure in our work, however routine, demanding or stressful, and see good or God/the Goddess in everyone and every situation, no matter how apparently unpromising, then we can walk with angels, ride the Milky Way and still have time to feed the cat and dance through puddles on the rainiest day. Life will hurt more because you will be more sensitive to pain and sorrow, not only in people, but also in animals, plants and nature generally – but you will also be able to send healing and to increase the positivity in the world.

Go out into the garden or the countryside, pick a dandelion clock, a flower or a feather and make two wishes, one for yourself and one for humanity. Send it by water or air into the cosmos and know that you are the beloved child of a very special and very beautiful universe.

Further Reading

Amulets and Talismans

Gonzalez-Wipler, Migene, *Complete Guide to Amulets and Talismans,* Llewellyn, St Paul, Mn., 1991

Thomas, William and Pavitt, Kate, *The Book of Talismans, Amulets and Zodiacal Gems,* Kessinger, New York, 1998

Ancient Wisdom

Eason, Cassandra, *The Encyclopedia of Magic and Ancient Wisdom,* Piatkus, 2000

Lemesurier, Peter, *Gods of the Dawn: The Message of the Pyramids and the true Stargate Mystery,* Thorsons, 1998

Angels, Archangels, Nature Spirits and Devas

Bloom, William, *Working with Angels, Fairies and Nature Spirits,* Piatkus, 1998

Burnham, Sophie, *A Book of Angels,* Ballantine, New York, 1990

Davidson, Gustave, *A Dictionary of Angels,* Free Press, New York, 1971

Eason, Cassandra, *A Complete Guide to Fairies and Magical Beings,* Piatkus, 2001

Aromatherapy

Price, Shirley, *Practical Aromatherapy,* Thorsons, 1996

Tisserand, Maggie, *Aromatherapy for Women,* Thorsons, 1995

Worwood, Valerie Ann, *The Fragrant Pharmacy,* Bantam, 1996

Auras, Chakras and Energy Work

Andea, Judith, *Wheels of Light,* Bantam Books, New York, 1993
Arewa, Shola Caroline, *Opening to Spirit,* Thorsons, 1999
Brennan, Barbara Anne, *Hands of Light,* Bantam Books, New York, 1987
Davies, Brenda, *The Seven Healing Chakras,* Ulysses Press, California, 2000
Eason, Cassandra, *Aura Reading,* Piatkus, 2000

Candles

Buckland, Ray, *Advanced Candle Magic,* Llewellyn, St Paul, Mn.,1996
Eason, Cassandra, *Candle Power,* Blandford, 1999

Channelling, Higher Energies and Spirituality

Bechert, H. and Gombrich, R., *The World of Buddhism,* Thames and Hudson, 1991
Blavatsky, Helena, *The Key to Theosophy,* Theosophical University Press Handbook, 1991
Bowes, Pratima, *The Hindu Religious Tradition,* Routledge and Kegan Paul, 1978
Dalai Lama and Cutler, Harvey, *The Art of Happiness,* Coronet Books, 1999
Linn, Denise, *Altars,* Rider, 1999
Neale, Tony, *Channelling for Everyone,* Crossing Press, 2000
White, Ruth, *Karma and Reincarnation,* Piatkus, 2000

Crystals and Crystal Healing

Bravo, Brett, *Crystal Healing Secrets,* Warner Books Inc., New York, 1988
Eason, Cassandra, *Crystal Healing,* Quantum, 2001
Galde, Phyllis, *Crystal Healing, The Next Step,* Llewellyn Books, St Paul, Mn., 1991

Dowsing

Bailey, Arthur, *Anyone can Dowse for Better Health,* Quantum,1999
Eason, Cassandra, *Pendulum Dowsing,* Piatkus, 2000
Lonegren, Sig, *Spiritual Dowsing,* Gothic Images, 1986

Dreams

Fornari, Hannah, *The Dreamers' Dictionary,* Hamlyn, 1989
Parker, Russ, *Healing Dreams,* SPCK, 1988

Earth Energies, Ley Lines and Labyrinths

Begg, Ean, *The Cult of the Black Madonna,* Arkana, 1995
Martineau, John, *Mazes and Labyrinths,* Wooden Books, 1996
Molyneaux, Brian Leigh, *The Sacred Earth,* Macmillan, 1991
Sullivan, Danny, *Ley Lines,* Piatkus, 1999

Ghosts

Eason, Cassandra, *Ghost Encounters,* Blandford, 1997
Spencer, John and Anne, *Encyclopedia of Ghosts and Spirits,* Headline, 1992

Gods, Goddesses and Mythology

Gimbutas, Marija, *The Gods and Goddesses of Old Europe,* Thames and Hudson, 1986
Jones, Alison, *Dictionary of World Folklore,* Larousse, 1995
Walker, Barbara, *The Encyclopedia of Women's Myths and Secrets,* Pandora, 1983

Healing

Eden, Donna, *Energy Medicine,* 1999, Piatkus.
Roden, Shirley, *Sound Healing,* Piatkus, 1999
Verschure, Yasmin, *Way to the Light,* Samuel Weiser, Maine, 1996

Herbs and Incenses

Culpeper, Nicholas, *Complete Herbal,* Foulsham, 1994
Cunningham, Scott, *Complete Book of Oils, Incenses and Brews,* Llewellyn,
    St Paul, Mn., 1991
Vickery, Roy, *A Dictionary of Plant Lore,* Oxford University Press, 1995

I Ching

Sherrill, W. A. and Chu, W. K., *The Anthology of the I Ching,* Arkana, 1989
Wilhelm, Richard and Baynes, Cary, *I Ching,* Arkana, 1992

Magic and Ritual

Eason, Cassandra, *Complete Guide to Magic and Ritual,* Piatkus, 1999
—— *Practical Guide to Witchcraft and Magical Spells,* Quantum, 2001

Matthews, Caitlin and John, *The Western Way. A Practical Guide to the Western Mystical Tradition,* Arkana, 1986

Starhawk, *Dreaming the Dark,* Beacon Press, Boston, 1997

Maternal Intuition

Eason, Cassandra, *Psychic Families,* Foulsham, 1995

—— *Mother Love,* Robinson, 1998

—— *The Mother Link,* Ulysses Press, California, 1999

Mediumship and Spiritualism

Berube, Raymond G. and North, Nancy, *You, the Medium,* Northray Publishing, 1995

Williamson, Linda, *Contacting the Spirit World,* 1998, Piatkus

Mysticism

Maxwell, Meg and Tschudin, Verena, *Seeing the Invisible,* Arkana, 1990

Willis, Roy, *The Complete Guide to World Mysticism,* Piatkus, 1999

Psychic Powers

Druhan, Marlene, Marie, *Naked Soul,* Llewellyn, 1998

Eason, Cassandra, *Psychic Power of Children,* Foulsham, 1994

Evans Hilary, *Frontiers of Reality: where Science meets the Paranormal,* Thorsons, 1989

Eysenck, Hans and Sargnt, Carl, *Explained the Unexplained,* Weidenfeld and Nicolson, 1982

Flora, Mary Ellen, *Clairvoyance: Key to Spiritual Perspective,* CDM Publications, 1993

Rhine, Joseph, *The Reach of the Mind,* William Morrow, New York, 1947

Shamanism

Johnson, Kenneth, *North Star Road,* Llewellyn, Mn., 1986

Telasco, Patricia, *Shaman in a 9 to 5 World,* Crossing Press, California, 2000

Wahoo, Dhyani, *Voices of our Ancestors,* Shambhala, 1987

Smudging

Eason, Cassandra, *Smudging and Incense Burning,* Quantum, 2001

Wakpski, Diane, *Smudging,* Black Sparrow Press, US, 1996

Symbols/Divination

Biedermann, Hans, *Dictionary of Symbolism,* Facts on File, New York, 1992
Eason, Cassandra, *Complete Guide to Divination,* Piatkus, 1998

Tarot

Eason, Cassandra, *Complete Guide to the Tarot,* Piatkus, 1999
Nichols, Sallie, *Jung and the Tarot,* Samuel Weiser, Maine 1988

Resources

Chakra and Energy Work

UK

Caroline Shola Arewa,
Inner Visions,
PO Box 22032,
London SW2 2WJ

US

The Barbara Brennan School of Healing,
PO Box 2005,
East Hampton,
New York 11937

Australia

The Sabian Centre,
PO Box 527,
Kew,
Victoria,
Australia 3101

Dowsing

UK

The British Society of Dowsers,
Sycamore Barn,
Hastingleigh,
Ashford,
Kent TN25

US

The American Society of Dowsers,
Dowsers Hall,
Danville,
Vermont 05828-0024

Australia

Dowsers' Society of New South Wales,
c/o Mrs. E. Miksevicius,
126 Fiddens Wharf Road,
Killara, NSW,
Australia 2031

Southern Tasmania Dowsing
Association,
PO Box 101,
Moonah,
Tasmania,
Australia 7009

Canada

The Canadian Society of Dowsers,
Bernard Urben,
21 Oberon Street,
Nepean,
Ontario K2H 7X6

New Zealand

New Zealand Society of Dowsers,
PO Box 41-095,
St. Luke's Sq.,
Mt. Albert,
Auckland 3

Earth Energies

UK

Caerdroia,
(Journal of Caerdroia, the mazes and
labyrinths research group.)
53 Thundersley Grove,
Thundersley,
Benfleet,
Essex SS7 3EB

Gatekeeper Trust,
(Earth energies and sacred sites.)
The Secretary,
Roses Farmhouse,
Epwell Road,
Upper Tysoe,
Warwickshire CV35 0TN

The Ley Hunter Journal,
PO Box 92,
Penzance,
Cornwall TR18 2BX

US

NEARA,
(New England Antiquities Research
Association: study and preservation
of New England's stone sites in their
cultural context; pre-Columbian
contact, dowsing, epigraphy; journal and
groups.)

NEARA Membership,
Priscilla Ross,
Whalley Rd.,
Charlotte,
Vermont 05445

USA Stonewatch,
(Earth Energies)
334 Brook Street,
Noank,
CT 06340

**Psychic Research Study
Societies and Journals**

UK

ASSAP
(Association for the Scientific Study of
Anomalous Phenomena.)
Dr. Hugh Pincott,
St. Aldhelm,
20 Paul Street,
Frome,
Somerset BA11 1DX

The Churches Fellowship for Spiritual
and Psychic Studies,
The Rural Workshop,
South Road,
North Somercotes, Nr Louth,
Lincolnshire LN11 7BT

The Ghost Club,
Tom Perrott,
93, The Avenue,
Muswell Hill,
London N10 2QG

The Scottish Society for Psychical
Research,
John and Daphne Plowman,
131 Stirling Drive,
Bishopbriggs,
Glasgow G64 3AX.

US

American Society for Psychical Research,
5 West 73rd Street,
New York, NY 10023.

Shamanism

UK

Faculty of Shamanics,
Kenneth and Beryl Meadows,
PO Box 300,
Potters Bar,
Hertfordshire EN6 4LE

Shamanka,
(A women's shamanic empowerment
organisation.)
Middle Piccadilly,
Hotwell,
Dorset DT9 5LW

US

Dance of the Deer Foundation,
Center for Shamanic Studies,
PO Box 699,
Soquel CA 95073

Foundation of Shamanic Studies,
PO Box 1939,
Mill Valley CA 94942.

Smudging equipment, smudge sticks, smudge herbs and incense

UK

Dreamcatcher Trading,
47 Bruce Road,
Sheffield,
South Yorkshire S11 8QD

US

Arizona Gateway Trading Post,
Mail-HC 37,
Box 919-UPS 14265,
N. Hiway 93,
Golden Valley AZ 86413

Australia

Earth Aromas Earthcraft,
Magpie Flats Herb Farm,
273/295 Boyle Road,
Kenilworth,
Qld 4574

Spiritual Healing

UK

British Alliance of Healing Associations,
Mrs Jo Wallace,
3 Sandy Lane,
Gisleham,
Lowestoft,
Suffolk NR 33 8EQ

National Federation of Spiritual Healers
Old Manor Farm Studio,
Church Street,
Sunbury on Thames,
Middlesex TW16 6RG

US

World of Light has a list of healers:
PO Box 425,
Wappingers Falls,
NY 12590

Australia

Australian Spiritualist Association,
PO Box 248,
Canterbury,
New South Wales 2193

Canada

Spiritualist Church of Canada,
1835 Lawrence Ave East,
Scarborough,
Ontario M1R 2Y3

Other titles by Cassandra Eason

0 7499 2304 0 **£7.99 PB**

0 7499 2162 5 **£9.99 PB**

0 7499 2311 3 **£7.99 PB**

0 7499 2240 0 **£12.99 PB**

0 7499 2323 7 **£7.99 PB**

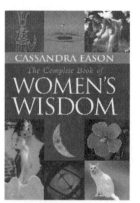

0 7499 2209 5 **£17.99 HB**